Language, Meaning and God

Language, Meaning and God

Essays in honour of Herbert McCabe OP

edited by
Brian Davies OP

Geoffrey Chapman
London

A Geoffrey Chapman book published by
Cassell Publishers Limited
Artillery House, Artillery Row, London SW1P 1RT

© Geoffrey Chapman, a division of Cassell Publishers Limited, 1987

First published 1987

ISBN 0 225 66495 X

British Library Cataloguing in Publication Data

Language, meaning and God: essays in honour of Herbert McCabe.
  1. Christianity – Philosophy
  I. McCabe, Herbert   II. Davies, Brian, *1951*–
  201   BR100

Printed and bound in Great Britain by
Biddles Ltd, Guildford and King's Lynn

CONTENTS

PREFACE   vii

BIOGRAPHICAL NOTE   ix

BIBLIOGRAPHY OF WORKS BY HERBERT McCABE OP   x

NOTES ON CONTRIBUTORS   xi

 1   CHARITY AS FRIENDSHIP   1
     Fergus Kerr OP

 2   PRAYER, HUMPTY DUMPTY AND THOMAS AQUINAS   24
     Simon Tugwell OP

 3   CLASSICAL THEISM AND THE DOCTRINE OF DIVINE
     SIMPLICITY   51
     Brian Davies OP

 4   DISTINGUISHING GOD FROM THE WORLD   75
     David B. Burrell CSC

 5   FEUERBACH, MARX AND REDUCTIVISM   92
     Denys Turner

 6   AQUINAS ON KNOWLEDGE OF SELF   104
     Anthony Kenny

 7   SOME SEVENTEENTH-CENTURY DISAGREEMENTS
     AND TRANSUBSTANTIATION   120
     P. J. FitzPatrick

 8   FAITH, OBJECTIVITY, AND HISTORICAL
     FALSIFIABILITY   145
     Hugo A. Meynell

 9   THE GENRE OF THE FIRST GOSPEL   162
     Margaret Davies

10   'THE COMING OF THE SON OF MAN': Mark's gospel
     and the subversion of 'the apocalyptic imagination'   176
     Timothy Radcliffe OP

Contents

11   TAKING AWAY THE SIN OF THE WORLD   190
     Brian Wicker

12   THE THEORY AND PRACTICE OF AUTOBIOGRAPHY   209
     J. M. Cameron

13   PRAYER, POETRY AND POLITICS   228
     Enda McDonagh

PREFACE

The essays in this volume have been written and brought together to celebrate the sixtieth birthday of Herbert McCabe OP in 1986. Their appearance testifies to the respect due to him and to the affection in which he is held.

Contributors were asked to write on issues of particular concern to Fr McCabe. So the result is a collection of more than specialist interest. As well as containing studies in the thought of St Thomas Aquinas (with whom friends and students of Fr McCabe will always associate him), it deals with topics such as the philosophy of God, the nature and importance of biblical texts, and matters of primary social and moral importance.

I am grateful to all the contributors for their interest and co-operation in the production of this book, and to Anne Boyd of Geoffrey Chapman for her encouragement and help in seeing it to publication.

Brian Davies OP
Blackfriars, Oxford
August 1986

BIOGRAPHICAL NOTE

Herbert McCabe (baptized John Ignatius) was born on 2 August 1926 in Middlesbrough, England, where he attended St Mary's College before going to Manchester University to study chemistry. Here, however, he changed course and took a degree in philosophy. He joined the Dominican Order (the Order of Preachers) in 1949. After completing his studies he worked for three years in an inner city parish in Newcastle upon Tyne and was then sent to Manchester to find a suitable house near the university to replace the Dominican parish house in Salford. From the new house he travelled to lecture and give talks to student societies in most of the universities of Britain and worked for the extra-mural departments of Manchester, Oxford and Keele as well as the Workers' Educational Association, lecturing in theology and philosophy.

In 1964 he was sent to Cambridge to take over the editorship of *New Blackfriars* from Illtud Evans OP, who had fallen ill. Eighteen months later his editorial on the departure of Charles Davis from the Church (in which he argued that the manifest corruption of the Church was no good reason for leaving her) led to his dismissal at the behest of the Roman authorities and even to his suspension from the priesthood (a move that was rescinded after five days). In 1970 he was re-appointed as editor by the Provincial Chapter and remained until he resigned in 1979, when he went to teach for a period in Ireland.

His main theological interests have been in sacramental theology and the theology of God, in which he is much influenced by his teacher Victor White OP. He has also written on moral philosophy and on social and political matters. He has been concerned with the Christian–Marxist dialogue and with the Irish–British lack of dialogue (he claimed his citizenship of the Irish Republic in 1974).

At present, Herbert McCabe is Novice Master for the English Province of the Dominicans. He also lectures in theology and philosophy at Blackfriars, Oxford and in the Department of Theology and Religious Studies in the University of Bristol.

PUBLISHED BOOKS AND ARTICLES

The New Creation (London, 1964) (Dutch edition: *De Nieuwe Schepping*, 1966; Brazilian edition: *Sacramentos – Uma Nova Criação*, 1968).

Law, Love and Language (London, 1968) (US edition: *What Is Ethics All About?*, New York, 1969).

Knowing and Naming God (Blackfriars *Summa Theologiae*, vol. III, London and New York, 1964).

The Teaching of the Catholic Church (London, 1985).

There were monthly Editorial Comments on theological topics and current events in *New Blackfriars* November 1965–February 1967 and October 1970–October 1979.

The following articles appeared in *New Blackfriars* unless otherwise stated:
'Dr Robinson's Book', July 1963.
'Transubstantiation and Real Presence' (*The Ampleforth Journal*, 1969).
'Morals and Authority' (*Doctrine and Life*, December 1969).
'Prayer' (*Doctrine and Life*, August 1970).
'Eucharistic Presence', August 1972.
'Transubstantiation: A Reply to G. Egner', December 1972.
'The World Will Hate You' (*Doctrine and Life*, August 1972).
'The Immaculate Conception' (*Doctrine and Life*, December 1975).
'Sacramental Language' (*Irish Theological Quarterly*, 1976).
'The Myth of God Incarnate', August 1977.
'God: Creation', October 1980.
'God: Freedom', November 1980.
'God: Evil', January 1981.
'The Class Struggle and Christian Love' (in *Agenda for Prophets*, a symposium edited by Rex Ambler and David Haslam, London, 1980).
'Thoughts on Hunger Strikes', July 1981.
'Obedience', June 1984.
'The Involvement of God', November 1985.
'A Long Sermon for Holy Week', February, March, April 1986.

Most of these papers together with some sermons appear in *God Matters* (London, 1987).

NOTES ON CONTRIBUTORS

Fergus Kerr OP is a graduate of the University of Aberdeen. He entered the Order of Preachers in 1956 and taught philosophy and theology at Blackfriars, Oxford, from 1966 to 1986. He is the author of *Theology after Wittgenstein* (Blackwell, 1986).

Simon Tugwell OP is Regent of Studies at Blackfriars, Oxford. He teaches theology at the University of Oxford and at the Angelicum (Rome). His many publications include *Did You Receive the Spirit?* (1972), *Prayer* (2 vols, 1974), *The Way of the Preacher* (1979), *Reflections on the Beatitudes* (1980) and *Ways of Imperfection* (1984).

Brian Davies OP is Vice-Regent of Studies at Blackfriars, Oxford. He is tutor in theology at St Benet's Hall, Oxford and Reviews Editor of *New Blackfriars*. His publications include *An Introduction to the Philosophy of Religion* (Oxford University Press, 1982) and *Thinking About God* (Geoffrey Chapman, 1985).

David B. Burrell CSC is Professor of philosophy and theology at the University of Notre Dame. His publications include *Analogy and Philosophical Language* (Yale University Press, 1973), *Exercises in Religious Understanding* (University of Notre Dame Press, 1973), *Aquinas: God and Action* (Routledge and Kegan Paul, 1979) and *Knowing the Unknowable God: Ibn-Sina, Maimonides, Aquinas* (University of Notre Dame Press, 1986).

Denys Turner is Head of Department and lecturer in theology at the University of Bristol. He is the author of *Marxism and Christianity* (Basil Blackwell, 1983).

Anthony Kenny is Master of Balliol College, Oxford. His many publications include *The Five Ways* (Routledge and Kegan Paul, 1969), *Wittgenstein* (The Penguin Press, 1973), *Will, Freedom and Power* (Blackwell, 1975) and *Aquinas* (Oxford University Press, 1980).

P. J. FitzPatrick is Reader in philosophy at Durham University. He has written on various topics, including contraception (for), Newman (against), and transubstantiation (in *New Blackfriars*).

His philosophical interests include imagery in Plato, belief and truth, and the views of Leibniz on the Eucharist. He lives in Sunderland, where he is chaplain to an old people's home.

Hugo Meynell taught in the departments of philosophy and of theology and religious studies at the University of Leeds for eighteen years. Since 1981 he has taught at the University of Calgary in the department of religious studies. He has published ten books, mainly on philosophical and theological topics. These include *Sense, Nonsense and Christianity* (Sheed and Ward, 1964), *God and the World* (SPCK, 1971), *An Introduction to the Philosophy of Bernard Lonergan* (Macmillan, 1976) and *The Intelligible Universe* (Macmillan, 1982).

Margaret Davies is lecturer in biblical studies at the University of Bristol. She has specialized in the theological, literary and rhetorical functions of the gospels, with publications in particular on the gospels according to Matthew and John.

Timothy Radcliffe OP is Prior of Blackfriars, Oxford, where he is also a lecturer in doctrine and biblical studies.

Brian Wicker was chairman of Pax Christi for thirteen years from the early 1970s. In 1980 he was appointed Principal of Fircroft College, Birmingham, where one of his innovations has been the establishment of a course in peace studies. His publications include *Culture and Liturgy* (1963), *Culture and Theology* (1966), *First the Political Kingdom* (1967), *The Story-Shaped World* (1975) and *Nuclear Deterrence: What Does the Church Teach?* (1985).

J. M. Cameron was Professor of philosophy at the University of Leeds from 1960 to 1967. He was Master of Rutherford College and Professor of philosophy at the University of Kent, Canterbury, from 1967 to 1971. From 1971 until his retirement he was University Professor at St Michael's College, University of Toronto. He has published many articles, some of which were collected in his book *The Night Battle* (1962).

Enda McDonagh is Professor of moral theology at St Patrick's College, Maynooth, Co. Kildare, Ireland. His publications include *Invitation and Response* (Gill and Macmillan, 1972) and *Social Ethics and the Christian* (Manchester University Press, 1979).

1

CHARITY AS FRIENDSHIP

Fergus Kerr OP

'What is one to make of a man who, at sixty years of age, conscious though he was of declining powers of memory, took up the study of Greek and established an atelier for the production of translations, and who was learning Hebrew in his eighties? Late development is generally reckoned, after all, to have its limits.'[1] Robert Grosseteste, the man in question, having taught theology at Oxford for many years, was elected Bishop of Lincoln in 1235. As the largest diocese in England at the time it demanded a great deal of attention, and the record amply shows how energetically he fulfilled his responsibilities. He was, for all that, able to continue, and even to extend, his already manifold scholarly activities. He presided over a team which produced revisions and fresh versions of Latin translations of much Greek Christian literature, including the Dionysian corpus. About 1240 they turned to Aristotle. Fragments of an earlier translation survive, but, as Herman the German noted at the time, Grosseteste's version of Aristotle's *Nicomachean Ethics*, available by 1246–47, was the first complete edition.[2] Its appearance was certainly one of the great intellectual events of the century. It survives in almost 300 manuscripts. It has been published by the Dominican scholar R. A. Gauthier, using a good late thirteenth-century text discovered in 1972 in Trinity College, Dublin.[3]

Albert the Great was among the first to make use of Grosseteste's translation of the *Ethics*. He moved from Paris to Cologne in the summer of 1248 in order to set up the first Dominican study-house in Germany. It is possible that Thomas Aquinas, then about twenty-four years of age, accompanied him. There is no doubt that Thomas attended Albert's course on the *Ethics*, sometime between 1248 and 1252, because a copy of the notes that he took has survived.[4]

1

The date of Thomas's own study of the *Ethics*[5] remains obscure, largely because its purpose is disputable. The traditional story, following the memorandum of Tolomeo of Lucca, his *socius*, ascribes the work to the early 1260s, when Thomas was probably conventual lector in the Dominican priory in Orvieto. This smallish Umbrian town, splendidly sited on an isolated rock, had just become an important administrative and intellectual centre because the newly elected Pope Urban IV was to spend his short pontificate there. Albert the Great, for instance, having just rid himself of episcopal office, came for the winter of 1262–63. Urban certainly commissioned Thomas to produce his *Expositio* of the four gospels – the *Catena aurea* as it has been called since the fourteenth century: an immediate success and one of his most widely diffused works in the Middle Ages. Containing not one word by himself, it is an anthology of passages from Latin and Greek patristic texts. At Urban's request Thomas also wrote his *Contra errores Graecorum* at this time, without apparently ever trying to learn any Greek, though still only in his late thirties.

His principal duty in Orvieto, as conventual lector, would have been to expound the Scriptures to the Dominican community. It was up to the lector to choose the text and Thomas expounded the Book of Job. The result, no doubt considerably written up, contains many references to Aristotle's *De partibus animalium*, a translation of which was completed on 23 December 1260 by the Flemish Dominican William of Moerbeke, later to become Archbishop of Thebes.

Thomas's exposition of the *Ethics* is little more than a paraphrase, so elementary and pedestrian that it seems likely enough that he undertook it at this period as part of the internal course of studies for the less bright young friars in the community in Orvieto who were not going to be sent to any university.

R. A. Gauthier, however, a formidable authority in these matters, ascribes Thomas's *Sententia libri Ethicorum* to 1271–72, when he was back teaching in Paris: Weisheipl concurs.[6] The argument is that the *secunda secundae* of the *Summa Theologiae*, begun early in 1271, shows signs of fresh study of certain sections of the *Ethics*. The famous Socratic thesis that one cannot knowingly do wrong (*Ethics*, VII) appears, however, in the *prima secundae* (Ia IIae, 77, 3), and is first discussed in a set of disputations (*De Malo*, q.3) which Gauthier dates to the winter of 1266–67, when Thomas was in Rome, setting up the study-house of his own province. The relevant passage in Thomas's commentary on the *Ethics* certainly reads more like a preparation for that disputation than anything written after the discussion of the Socratic paradox in the *prima secundae*. It is also difficult to believe, as V. J. Bourke notes,[7] that, back in Paris, with Grosseteste's notes and Albert's commentary readily accessible, Thomas needed to embark on his own paraphrase of the *Ethics*.

It does not matter very much. According to Harry Jaffa, Aristotle's ideas are more lucidly expressed in Thomas's commentary than they are in the original.[8] Gauthier is surely on stronger ground when he judges that Thomas's commentary on the *Ethics* is of little help to the student of Aristotle. It is greatly excelled, as Bourke says,[9] 'except in humility', by the work of Gauthier and Jolif, the standard modern commentary.[10]

What matters, of course, is what happened to Aristotle's *Ethics* in the *secunda pars* of the *Summa Theologiae*. Over a million words long, it must have been composed at the rate of a thousand words a day if it was completed in the twenty-seven months that the bio-bibliographers allow. It has been described as 'Thomas's most original contribution to theology'[11] and as 'Aquinas's greatest work'.[12] It may, with more precision, also be described as one of the great texts in the history of moral philosophy as well as of Catholic theology – and, in both respects, still largely unexplored territory. It advances on Aristotle in many ways, not counting questions affected by Thomas's theological interests (where improvements may not always be obvious to non-Christian readers). But I want to concentrate here on a central topic in Christian theology which is interestingly and decisively illuminated by an idea Thomas took from the *Ethics*: namely, his well-known thesis that charity is a kind of friendship – on analogy with Aristotle's conception of friendship.

_____ II _____

Considering how often he covers the same ground in one work after another, with little or no substantial change in the argumentation, it is surprising to find that Thomas discussed the nature of charity only twice in his career, and interesting that his approach changed dramatically. Something happened between the discussion in his *Scriptum* on the *Sentences* of Peter Lombard, dated about 1256, and the discussion in the *secunda pars* of the *Summa* and the closely associated disputed question *De Caritate*, both dated to 1269–72. What happened, clearly, was that Thomas re-read Aristotle's *Ethics*.

In the *Scriptum*,[13] for a start, Thomas deals with the nature of charity in the context of Christology: 'Did Christ have faith, hope and charity?'. In the *Summa*, of course, Christology is held over to the *tertia pars*, and the discussion of the theological virtue of charity becomes the centre piece (almost literally) of the newly independent *secunda pars*. The consideration of Christian love is no longer embedded in questions about the human nature of Christ; the placing of charity becomes a decisive move in a radically theocentric description of human beings as moral agents. Focused by happiness and virtue, Aristotle's *eudaimonia* and *aretē* (human flourishing and human excellence), the *secunda pars* inaugurates a style of Christian ethics which has not yet borne fruit in many people's lives.

Thomas introduces Aristotle's theory of friendship so incisively when he comes to consider charity in the *Summa* that one cannot help sharing his relief at being able to leave behind the ruminant account in the *Scriptum*.

In the *Scriptum* the discussion naturally starts from Peter Lombard's definition of charity as a certain *dilectio*: 'a love in which God is loved for his own sake and one's neighbour for or in God'. Thomas first lists seven other terms which might seem to offer a better clue than *dilectio* to the place of charity: it might be envisaged with Augustine as *concupiscentia*, desire (for God); with Dionysius as *amor* (*erōs* in Greek); as *benevolentia*, wishing eternal life for oneself and for others; as *concordia*, unifying the church; as *beneficentia*, doing good; as *pax*, the bond that unites souls; and as *amicitia*, friendship, since, as Aristotle says, 'Friendship resembles an overflowing of love'. (This text will not reappear in the *Summa*, presumably because Thomas checked the original and found that Aristotle is saying something quite different.)

Thomas is going to plump for friendship, but he now has to list five serious objections to doing so: friendship is between people who love one another, charity extends to one's enemies; friendship involves being together, charity brings us into contact with transcendent beings like angels; friendship is public, charity is absolutely hidden; friends try to see one another as much as possible, Jerome says that this is not true in regard to charity; and, fifthly and finally, friendship is possible only with a few people and they have to be of good character, while charity extends to everybody, including wicked people.

Thus Thomas places himself between seven plausible glosses on the nature of charity, incidentally showing that thirteenth-century Catholics had a much richer range of associations than most people have today, and a set of five objections to seeing it as a kind of friendship, all of them suggested no doubt by Aristotle's *Ethics* although only two are referred explicitly to that source.

Thomas's *responsio*, his solution of the problem, unfolds in four steps. Taking up the immediately preceding discussion of the nature of *amor* in terms of some fulfilment of desire, 'quieting of appetite', he isolates the desire which rational beings have: since it includes an element of rational choice, *electio*, it is appropriately called *dilectio*: a love that selects one person out of a crowd. Thus Peter Lombard's definition is vindicated, if on what seems to be merely etymological or even assonantal grounds.

Next, Thomas argues very schematically that charity thus understood as *dilectio* includes elements of desire for God, wishing well to one's neighbour, concord, doing good, and peace, while *amor* adds that extra something: namely, desire's coming to rest in possession of the beloved.

Thirdly, the hitherto unmentioned notion of *amatio* comes into the story, adding to *amor* a certain *intensio* and *fervor* (straining and burning). The concept of friendship adds two further elements to the picture: this love has to be reciprocated, friends know that they love one another: and secondly, neatly rounding the discussion off, friendship is rooted 'not only in feeling (*passio*)', but also in choice, *electio*.

Thus, in the fourth step, Thomas can conclude: 'Friendship is the most perfect among the kinds of love, since it includes all that we have mentioned; charity is obviously to be placed in the category of the most perfect kind of love; it is therefore the friendship between man and God in which man loves (*diligit*) God and God man, and thus an association exists between them: If we walk in the light, as he is in the light, then we have fellowship (*koinōnia*) with one another' – QED.

The terms with which Thomas started are thus all included, in one way or another, in the notion of friendship. Thomas now adds that 'charity, *caritas*, supplements friendship by specifying that the friend is God, thus more precious and more dear, *carior*'.

The five difficulties in the way of seeing charity as a kind of friendship are dealt with in the following way. As to the problem of being friends with your enemies, it may be suggested that a friend loves his friend's sons, brothers and the like, even though they may not return this love: it is God whom we love by charity, men only to the extent that they belong to God. Secondly, we rise to having conversation with God and the angels because by charity we become *deiformes*. Thirdly, friendship is said to be visible and public but your friend's love is known *per signa probabilia*, not *per certitudinem*, which goes for charity also: there are signs from which one can judge that a person is charitable. Fourthly, as to Jerome's objection, Thomas replies that Jerome wants only to cut out the idea that the friendship which is charity is principally

Fergus Kerr

for one's fellow human beings whereas it is 'joined by Christ's glue, *Christi glutino copulata'* – a striking phrase from a letter to Paulinus which has nothing whatever about charity in the context, although Jerome elsewhere speaks of *glutino caritatis haerens*. The fifth difficulty goes with the solution to the first one.

In contrast with all that, the discussion of charity in the *Summa* is remarkably sure-footed, elegant and condensed. Notions like *amor, concupiscentia*, etc., have been, or are to be, redistributed to other places in the *secunda pars*, thus lightening the argument. The atmosphere is also cleared of the imagery of longing and yearning, of being hot and sticky. It is as if the mutual absorption of two lovers in one another had been abandoned in favour of the model of colleagues engaged in a common adventure. The etymological considerations have been replaced by an argument, and the source of that argument is plainly Aristotle's *Ethics*.

The text goes as follows, in R. J. Batten's translation:[14]

> According to Aristotle not all love has the character of friendship, but only that which goes with well-wishing [*benevolentia*], namely when we so love another as to will what is good for him. For if what we will is our own good, as when we love wine or a horse or the like, it is a love not of friendship [*amicitia*] but of desire [*concupiscentia*]. It makes no sense to talk of somebody being friends with wine or a horse. Yet goodwill alone is not enough for friendship for this requires a mutual loving [*mutua amatio*]; it is only with a friend that a friend is friendly. But such reciprocal good will is based on something in common [*communicatio*].
> Now there is a sharing [*communicatio*] of man with God by his sharing his happiness with us, and it is on this that a friendship is based. St Paul refers to it, *God is faithful by whom you were called into the fellowship* [*koinō-nia*] *of his Son*. Now the love which is based on this sort of fellowship [*communicatio*] is charity. Accordingly it is clear that charity is a friendship of man and God (IIa IIae, 23, 1).

In other words: for friendship to exist we have (1) to wish our friend well for his own sake; (2) the well-wishing has to be reciprocated; and (3) it has to be rooted in a certain community of life. The object of friendship-love has to be a being with his or her own separate and intrinsic value. It cannot be a chattel or any extension of the one who is loving, as a bottle of wine or a horse

6

would be. One wishes the other well, that is to say, beginning from acknowledgement of his or her independence and otherness. You cannot be friends, in the appropriate sense, with somebody who is your slave, infatuated with you, or onesidedly dependent upon you in some other way. Friendship is a kind of loving that respects and fosters the independent worth of the other person. Secondly, for there to be friendship of the relevant kind, the parties have to have this attitude to one another: each has to be able to let the other *be*, so to speak. Thirdly, they have to have something in common which gives rise to and sustains this relationship. On Aristotle's view, friendship of this kind exists only between persons who resemble each other in being virtuous. The relationship is grounded on shared goodness of character.

This is a daring model for charity. It has had little success in Catholic theology and spirituality. But to begin to measure its audacity we have to recreate Aristotle's picture of friendship in some more detail. That will help to explain why this model attracted Thomas, and perhaps also why his account of charity has never been widely accepted. First, then, we have to look briefly at the idea of love which Aristotle's picture is designed to correct.

—— III ——

In 367 B.C., when he was seventeen, Aristotle joined Plato's circle in Athens. Plato was then about sixty, with twenty years ahead of him. It could not have been long before the young philosopher read the *Symposium*, the dialogue about love and friendship which Plato had composed some years earlier, perhaps even about the time that Aristotle was born.

The climax of the *Symposium* no doubt comes in the lengthy speech in which Socrates recounts the theory of love that he learned from Diotima of Mantinea, his 'instructress in the art of love'. In the dialogue, then, we have Diotima's lesson in *ta erōtika* retailed by Socrates – which already shows how far Plato himself is from endorsing her doctrine. What has happened, for historical reasons we have no space to examine here, and for psychological reasons that will become evident in due course, is that Diotima's programme has come to be regarded as 'the Platonic theory of love'. It certainly voices a deeply and understandably attractive view. It has had fateful effects in the development of Christian spirituality and asceticism. In the *Symposium* itself, however, by the device of having Diotima's doctrine quoted by Socrates, who

7

admittedly makes it his own, Plato distances himself from it. Then, by bringing on the drunken Alcibiades, in what is often disregarded as a ribald anti-climax, Plato exposes Socrates to raw but searching criticism. (For that matter, the entire conversation is supposedly being repeated by a certain Apollodorus who had in turn heard an account of it many years before from one of the original participants.)

The dramatic date of the banquet is January 416 B.C. Agathon, the host, a tragic poet (of whose work less than forty lines survive), is celebrating his success in the Dionysiac festival: he is in his late twenties. Socrates is fifty-three. Alcibiades, the legendarily handsome, able and doomed military leader, is thirty-four. He is passionately in love with Socrates, who, by now bald, pot-bellied and twice married, has loved Alcibiades for about twenty years. By the time Plato composed the *Symposium* it was at least fifteen years since Socrates had drunk the hemlock, and twenty years since the murder of Alcibiades. In a complete interpretation of the dialogue we should have to reconstruct a good deal of the political and intellectual background as well as flesh out the personal relationships among the participants. The dialogue is not just a string of set speeches: on the contrary, one line of thought is extended or undercut by another, and it is important to know who is speaking and with what interests. But we shall have to be content with a brief account of the two final speeches.[15]

Pausanias, one of the earlier speakers, has defended '*paiderastia* and the practice of philosophy and virtue in general'. Aristophanes, the future comic poet, in a riotously funny fantasy, traces the pain of erotic desire to our each being half of an original globular androgyne. Agathon praises the god of love, the youngest and tenderest of the gods, 'of flexile form' (Jowett), dwelling in a place of flowers and scents, etc., and 'the cause of what is fairest and best in all other things'. Thus the way is prepared for Socrates' speech.

'Human beings love the good', Diotima eventually tells him. What are people doing, then, who show 'all this eagerness and heat which is called love'? It turns out that, to enter the greater and more hidden mysteries of love, one must begin young to seek the company of corporeal beauty – 'to love one beautiful body only'. The beautiful thoughts that this experience will generate soon make you realize that the beauty of one body is the same as that of another – which abates your violent love of the first individual (which you will now 'despise and deem a small thing'). You will now become a steadfast lover of *all* beautiful bodies. At the next stage beautiful *souls* will come to seem more precious to you than beautiful *bodies*. Then you will be 'compelled to contemplate and see the beauty in institutions and laws, and to understand that the beauty of them all is of one family, and that personal beauty is a trifle'. By this time you are well away, so that you 'cease to be like a servant in love with one beauty only, that of a particular youth or man or institution'. Thus, 'using these as steps only', you at last come to see 'the divine beauty, pure and clear and unalloyed, not infected with the pollutions of the flesh and all the colours and vanities of mortal life'.

That is where Diotima's lesson concludes. *People*, or rather *young men*, already reduced to the status of 'beauties', as though they might not rather be interestingly and attractively intelligent, humorous, kind, loyal, kooky, and a thousand other things, are finally treated as the lowest rungs on the individual's climb to the secure vision of that which is absolutely and immutably beautiful. The very idea of loving a man for himself, never mind a woman for herself, has no place in this programme. To let flesh-and-blood men and women be such objects of affection would be to stop on the bottom step of the ascent to the vision of the beautiful. We are to love one another as place-holders for absolute beauty. What we love in another human being is the (necessarily very partial and flawed) presence of the transcendental form of the beautiful in him or her. All along it is his beauty, not the man himself, that is loved; and his beauty is homogeneous with the beauty of poetry-writings, legislation and suchlike. If a man had eyes to see the divine beauty, Diotima tells Socrates, he would then be immune to the attractions of gold, and garments, and fair boys.

Desire thus becomes so exclusively and absorbingly focused on the Form of the Beautiful that the erotic attractions of human beings disappear. By concentrating one's desire solely on the Idea of Beauty one becomes invulnerable to the beauty of any particular human being. Since their beauty is all the same, other people become inter-substitutable; they lose their refractory particularity. Diotima's programme trades on an understandable inclination in any passionate man or woman to transcend the risks of love. You can never be let down or betrayed or rejected by the Idea of the Beautiful. Diotima's course in erotics would secure immunity against all the pain and the uncertain pleasures of being in love with human beings.

Just as Socrates finishes his 'encomium of love' a great knocking at the door announces the late arrival of Alcibiades, very drunk, roaring and shouting, supported by a flute-girl and some companions, with his head garlanded with ivy and violets. Socrates, as soon as Alcibiades recognizes him, appeals to Agathon for protection: 'Since I became his admirer I have never been allowed to speak to any other beauty. . . . If I do, he goes wild with envy and jealousy, and not only abuses me but can hardly keep his hands off me', etc. Alcibiades, invited by the company to make a speech in praise of love, insists that he will 'speak the truth'. He makes an embarrassing confession of his passionate desire for Socrates, which he offers as praise of the older man's magnificent self-control. At great length he describes how he once tried to seduce Socrates but ended lying the whole night long, 'having this truly superhuman wonder in my arms' – and 'nothing more happened'. He goes on to tell of Socrates' extraordinary powers of endurance: he can go without food, he can drink wine endlessly without ever getting drunk, he can walk bare-foot on ice, he has been seen standing motionless in thought for twenty-four hours on end, and so on.

When Alcibiades finishes the company laugh – 'for he seemed to be still in love with Socrates'. Socrates now asserts that the whole speech was got up to make the handsome young Agathon transfer his affections from him (Socrates) to Alcibiades. Agathon moves closer to Socrates: 'I must move instantly, that I may be praised by Socrates'. 'The usual way', Alcibiades comments wryly: 'how readily he has invented a specious reason for attracting Agathon to himself.'

The discussion now ends, a large party of revellers breaks in, everybody drinks enormous quantities of wine, Socrates keeps on arguing and compels Agathon, the tragic poet, and Aristophanes, the comic poet, to agree that there is no difference between tragedy and comedy – but they are too sleepy to argue and eventually, at dawn, Socrates puts them to bed and goes off to have a bath.

The comic and the tragic poets are put to bed by the philosopher whom neither drink nor drowsiness nor the warmth of a man's naked body can touch. Alcibiades, laughed at and rejected, leaves the room without anyone's noticing. Diotima's formula for dealing with the risks of passion has, in various transformations, shaped the European imagination from Plotinus to Dante. Socrates is portrayed in the *Symposium* as a successful practitioner of the ascent to divine Beauty – or so readers commonly think. With the appearance of Alcibiades the dialogue is thought to drift into frivolity – his speech seems like a comic turn, which lowers the metaphysical tone. Philosophers, of course, usually regard the *Symposium* as 'literature', as if it did not contain enough philosophical content for them to explore. But there is another way of reading the text. The dialogue as a whole, and certainly the final confrontation between Socrates and Alcibiades, surely touches on ethical issues of great importance. Plato leaves us to decide whether Alcibiades's embarrassingly naked vulnerability is satisfactorily treated by the icy control that Socrates displays – which, in any case, does not stop him from getting Agathon to sit beside him. If equating tragedy and comedy is as profound a thought as many commentators on this passage seem to think, then no doubt the wisdom of Socrates is the last word. But surely Plato is leaving us free to regard it as an absurd thesis, sprung from the mind of a philosopher who understands neither comedy nor tragedy. The 'success' of Diotima's system is perhaps to be measured by the sight of the hurt and rejected Alcibiades. Plato himself, after all, is the author of the *whole* dialogue.

—— IV ——

What Aristotle made of the *Symposium* when he first encountered it we cannot determine. The student of the *Nicomachean Ethics* learns much more from the text if it is seen as a deliberate and critically informed response to certain Platonic doctrines. But the discussion of friendship in the *Ethics* must be dated to 334–322 B.C., when Aristotle had reached his maturity as a thinker. We cannot reconstruct what he thought at earlier stages. His apparently numerous dialogues have not survived, except for some fragments. They were famous in antiquity for their style: Cicero, in the first century B.C., admired them, while David the Invincible, the fifth-century Armenian Christian writer, speaks of them as 'overflowing with controlled eroticism'.[16] One would not say so much of the works that have come down to us.

Interestingly enough, however, Aristotle's dialogues included his own *Symposium*, though our sources speak of it more often as his 'book on drunkenness' (*Peri Methēs*).[17] The surviving fragments mostly appear in the amazing writings of Athenaeus of Naucratis (*fl. c.* A.D. 200). They do not add up to anything very significant. They do not even inspire much confidence that Aristotle wrote them. Consider, for example, the following fragment: 'The liquor made from barley called beer has a certain peculiarity; people who are intoxicated by other liquors fall in all sorts of directions – to the left, to the right, on their faces, on their backs; only those who are intoxicated with beer always fall backwards and lie on their backs'. Plutarch, in another fragment, says that, in his *Peri Methēs*, Aristotle noted that 'old men are over-taken most easily, and women least easily, by drunkenness': Plutarch expresses his surprise that Aristotle did not work out the reason for this circumstance – 'a thing he was not wont to fail to do'.

Aristotle wrote another dialogue called the *Eroticus*: it might have had more bearing on our subject here but, perhaps fortunately, very little of it survives.[18] Athenaeus makes the following claim: 'Aristotle says that lovers look at no other part of the body of their beloved than the eyes, in which modesty dwells'. Sixth-century vase-paintings of men wooing boys perhaps lend some support to this unlikely thesis, but such remarks do not remind us of Aristotle at his best. Athenaeus has an incomparable nose for trivia, but the evidence does not allow us to decide whether the fragments that survive show the crassness of his readers or the fatuity of Aristotle's dialogues.

— V —

Two of the ten books of the *Nicomachean Ethics* are devoted to discussing friendship. Aristotle is, among other things, out to show how a man who loves the good nevertheless loves his friends – and not just as stand-ins for the Idea of the Good but for their own sake.

Attempting to deal with one's desire for others by concentrating on something higher results in treating them as counters. Friendship, on Aristotle's view, is absolutely indispensable for life: 'For no one would choose to live without friends, but possessing all other good things' (NE, VIII, 1155a). The rich need friends on whom to practise beneficence, the poor turn to friends for succour, the young need friends to protect them, the elderly to tend them. 'Even when travelling abroad', Aristotle notes, 'one can observe that a natural affinity and friendship exist between human beings everywhere.' Friendship is the bond of the community. Indeed, justice seems to involve friendship at a certain point. But above all, Aristotle says, 'friendship is not just a necessity, it is also beautiful' (1155a).

It is a much debated question, so Aristotle tells us, whether friends are necessary for one's happiness: 'People say that the supremely happy are self-sufficing, autarkic, and so have no need of friends: for they have the goods of life already, and therefore, being complete in themselves, require nothing further' (NE, IX, 1169b). They have reached that radical independence of other people which Diotima's programme of erotic exercises is intended to secure. Such a man becomes so self-sufficient that he becomes indifferent to the presence of other people. There is nothing for them to do for him – but the deeper motivation of this ideal of an autarkic condition surely lies more in the absence of other people's threatening and exciting qualities than in the re- dundance of their practical skills. The good man cannot be harmed, so Socrates argued: what is of supreme value, that is to say, is an internal condition that can no longer be affected by the outside world. The lesson of Diotima is the only way to escape the torments of erotic passion, and all the other wounding and be- wildering elements in the surrounding world.

This interest in cultivating self-sufficiency shows how intense and often violent people's emotional life was: the whole point is to get one's feelings under the management of *reason*. It is no coincidence that Socrates sought to get people to agree that a man cannot do wrong *knowingly* – that one can do wrong only through lack of knowledge. Nor is it a coincidence that, in Book VII of the *Ethics*, Aristotle goes to great lengths to make room, between virtuous and vicious conduct, for the moral phenomenon of weakness of will. Socrates simply denied even the possibility of such behaviour, on the grounds that, once a man had the truth about the situation, it would be monstrous to suppose that any- thing could distract him from doing the right thing. 'This theory', Aristotle comments, 'is manifestly at variance with plain facts; and we need to investigate the state of mind in question more closely' (NE, VII, 1145b). There is no use in wielding mere theory to deny the existence of inner moral conflict; it is more reasonable to attend to the facts ('Don't think, but look', as one might say). Aristotle's reaction to Socrates' theory reveals its depth and au- dacity only if we allow ourselves to appreciate the latter's horror at the presence in ourselves of something that eludes rational control. He has had to work so hard to differentiate rational behaviour from emotional reaction that he simply cannot enter- tain the possibility that a man of reason might nevertheless act against his better judgement. Aristotle, however, feels relaxed enough about the claims of reason to look calmly at the existence of moral dilemmas.

In a similar way, in the next two books of the *Ethics*, Aristotle feels free to investigate the nature of friendship, attending patiently to the complexity of the phenomenon rather than subjugating it to the yoke of theory. He gestures briefly in the direction of Hesiod, Euripides, Heracleitus, Empedocles and proverbial wisdom in general on the cosmic dimensions of love, before inviting us, characteristically, to 'look at the human side of the question' – to attend, that is to say, to 'character and emotions' (NE, VIII, 1155b). For example: is everyone capable of friendship, or does the very possibility rest on one's having a certain *character*? Again: is there only one form of friendship? Is *philia* as uniform and homogeneous, and therefore as potentially impersonal and inter-substitutable, as Diotima's *erōs*? Here Aristotle makes his first criticism of Platonist doctrine: 'Those who hold that all friendship is of the same kind because friendship admits of degree, are relying on an insufficient proof, for things of different kinds can also differ in degree'. In effect, that is to say, he resorts once again to that perception of the analogical behaviour of certain concepts which is perhaps his most decisive contribution to philosophy.

When you listen to what we say, so Aristotle goes on, you find that *philia* is not mentioned in connection with inanimate objects. The concept always involves a return of affection and wishing the other's good. Bottles of wine may head ineluctably in a certain man's direction, but this is not because they have the feelings towards him that he has for them. In the second place, 'it would be ridiculous to wish well to a bottle of wine: at the most one wishes that it may keep well in order that one may have it oneself'.

Thus the crucial insight is introduced: 'in the case of a friend we necessarily say that we wish the good to him for his sake, *ekeinou heneka*' (1155b). That final phrase runs like a refrain throughout Aristotle's discussion. It marks the world of difference between loving a man for the sake of the good and wishing the good for a man *for his sake*. Aristotle must have known what he was doing. The phrase embodies a polemic against any theory of personal relationships which effectively empties the other person of intrinsic worth and particularity. Aristotle has begun his long campaign to remind his readers that friends are considered to be 'the greatest of external goods' (1169b). Far from being self-sufficient, the moral agent honours the essential value of external attachments. What comes 'from outside' is the greatest of his goods. *Philia*, that is to say, is necessarily a relationship with somebody else – who is allowed to retain his separate existence. Friendship, then, includes an other-relatedness which is inevitably also a source of great vulnerability. Friends die. The very possibility that Diotima's erotic ascent seeks to exclude from the life of the happy man is thus recognized as indispensable to it.

To do justice to our humanity Aristotle rehabilitates our vulnerability. He cannot admire men who have trained themselves to be indifferent to any particular mundane joys: 'such *anaisthēsia* is simply not human' (NE, III, 1119a). Indeed, he goes on to say, every animal prefers to eat one thing rather than another: 'if there is a creature to which one thing feels just like another, it must be very far removed from humanity'. His respect for humanity comes out again and again. It would be eccentric, he says, to picture the happy man as a singular and solitary figure: 'Nobody would choose to have all possible good things on the condition that he must enjoy them alone, for human beings are social beings and naturally live together' (NE, IX, 1169b). Whatever the problems of living with other people, Aristotle cannot conceive of a kind of human life that would transcend them. He certainly does not want us to become radically different: 'No one would choose to possess every good in the world on condition of becoming somebody else, but only while remaining himself, whatever he may be' (1166a).

You might be tempted to think it desirable for your friend to have what would surely be the greatest gift of all – to become divine; but if a friend in the proper sense wishes his friend's good for that friend's own sake, *ekeinou heneka*, then that friend would have to remain *himself*, in his separate otherness – 'so that [one] will really wish him only the greatest goods compatible with his remaining a human being' (1159a). Finally, in a palpable hit at Plato, 'you could not endure even the Absolute Good itself for ever, if it bored you' (1158a).

It may seem a noble prospect to cultivate self-sufficiency by radically exclusive attachment to the Idea of the Good: one might become impervious to the vicissitudes and vulnerabilities of life. Independence of the beauties around one, with their overwhelming and ever-changing attractions, may seem the higher way to happiness. For Aristotle, however, friendship itself is 'the beautiful thing' (1155a).

Philia is not uniform and homogeneous, like Platonic *erōs*: Aristotle has an analogical vision of the world. We may leave aside purely exploitative relationships, in which the parties each aim at using, or having enjoyment out of, the other, one treating the other as a horse or a bottle of wine. Such relationships do not count as friendship at all. But we may genuinely want the best for one another in some relatively limited enterprise – for instance as business partners or as theologians. One might lose by doing so: the other may make the faster buck or find the way, with humiliating ease, to refute one's pet theory. The other man's good is what one wishes, his separate independence is respected; but he is wearing a certain hat: our acquaintance with each other is as business partners or as theologians. Look around you, Aristotle seems to say: friendship occurs on that kind of basis.

Such friendships, according to Aristotle, 'seem to occur most frequently between the old, as in old age men do not pursue pleasure but profit. . . . Friends of this kind do not indeed frequent each other's company much, for in some cases they are not even pleasing to each other' (1156a). With these friendships he somewhat curiously classes 'family ties of hospitality with foreigners' – but *xenia*, guest-friendship, counted as one of the deepest and most essential expressions of our humanity. To place it here only shows how highly Aristotle regards the mutuality of genuine well-wishing for the other person's sake when both parties meet on relatively limited ground.

Friendships may also arise on the basis of enjoying one another's jokes: we find one another's company pleasant. Each wants the best for the other if the singing and the crack are to be memorable. Here, among friendships that are founded on people's pleasure-giving qualities and qualifications, Aristotle locates the mutual well-wishing of lovers *qua* lovers. In one paragraph he notes the problems of fickleness and jealousy that dominate the discussion in Plato's *Symposium* – 'the young are prone to fall in love', etc., but nothing is said or even hinted about the fevered eroticism among the middle-aged intellectuals at Agathon's party.

Friendship in the richest sense, however, is grounded, not on people's supportive or pleasure-giving qualities, but on their *goodness*: 'Such friends are both good in themselves and, so far as they are good, wish the good of one another. But it is those who wish the good of their friends for their friends' sake, *ekeinōn heneka*, who are friends in the fullest sense, since each loves the other for what the other is in himself and not for something he has about him which he need not have' (1156b). Each loves the other, not on the basis of any inessential personal quality such as some relevant expertise or delightful skill, but for what the other person most deeply is as a moral agent. Such friends are of course a help to one another; they also delight in one another's presence. But the relationship rests on something more radical than these relatively transient and incidental qualities. One may, after all, lose the relevant competence or become distressingly wasted by disease. The stability in love that Aristotle envisages is open only to those who are, in a tricky Greek phrase, *kat' aretēn homoion*: 'alike, or at one, at the level of goodness, moral excellence, or *humanity*' (1156b). Long before Aristotle's time the key word *aretē*, etymologically connected with Ares (Mars), god of war, had ceased to mean prowess, valour, 'being a man', bravery and the like, and come simply to mean human excellence as such. It is thus in their humanness at its finest that friends in the richest sense ground their relationship. 'Hence their friendship lasts', Aristotle observes, 'as long as they continue to be good; and *aretē* is durable.'

Virtue endures – we may have the stability in love that people who are at one on this level of radical humanity can achieve: no less, but also no more. It is quite astonishing, and surely very moving, to watch Aristotle describing a kind of loving that no voice in Plato's *Symposium* could name. For there, particularly in Socrates' great speech but also elsewhere in the dialogue, it is assumed that the desire to possess and control is characteristic of all love – which, in any case, is of only one kind. Jealousy, anger at one's vulnerability, fear of instability, and so on, could be defeated only by submitting to the discipline of training one's love exclusively upon objects less fickle, unreliable, and imperfect, than human beings. Over against all that, Aristotle reminds us that there is a kind of human love that really respects and enhances the separate good of the other person. It is a love which includes other kinds of love, which arise on more limited and unstable grounds. The open-endedness and stability of this kind of love cannot compete with that ascent to secure vision of 'the divine beauty, pure and clear and unalloyed, not infected with the pollutions of the flesh and all the colours and vanities of mortal life', like the Platonic *erōs*; but in its acceptance of the human condition Aristotle's *philia* certainly has its own beauty.

—— VI ——

Now for the speculation.[19] We do not know why Aristotle's account of love appealed so much to Thomas Aquinas that he went back to study the *Ethics* much more carefully, at some indeterminable point between 1256 and 1272, with the result that he radically revised his approach to the nature of charity. We certainly know that he never read Plato's *Symposium*. He clearly knew that Aristotle was often polemicizing against Platonic doctrines. When he gave such prominence to Aristotle's model of friendship in the first question about charity in the *Summa*, did he realize that he was taking sides in a debate that was already sixteen hundred years old? If that is unlikely, did he turn to Aristotle by a kind of instinct to disengage himself from a certain neo-Platonic mysticism of love?

As we saw, the discussion in the *Scriptum*, if it does not exactly reek of sublimated eroticism, nevertheless has a certain neo-

Platonic redolence. It is a good deal more interesting, however, to find a completely new question in the *Summa*, paralleled only in exactly contemporary writings: namely, whether it is God alone who is loved in the case of charity (IIa IIae, 25, 1). That is to say: Do we love our neighbour, in charity, or is it God alone whom we love? Why did Thomas set himself this hitherto undiscussed question? Who ever doubted that 'he who loves God should love his brother also'? Why should Thomas want to discuss whether charity's love does or does not have any other object than God – unless he suspected that we might be tempted to think that love of God and love of neighbour were radically different in kind? Or perhaps that the object of charity's love for our neighbour was not the neighbour himself but really only God in the form of our neighbour? Are we merely 'channels' for the circulation of divine love, such that God in me would love God in you and we should both disappear from the scene? After all, it seemed to Peter Lombard, a great authority in Thomas's day, that charity was the Holy Spirit in the believer's soul, and not something *human* (IIa IIae, 23, 2). The difficulties in the way of practising Christian love may well give rise to the idea that it must be something in which human beings have no part. Charity, thus envisaged, perhaps begins to remind us of that vision of an invulnerable and imper-sonal love such as Socrates describes in the *Symposium*.

Again, did Thomas detect, in a certain spirituality, a deter-mination to love everyone so impartially that one actually loved no one in particular? Why does he go into such detail about the *ordo caritatis* (IIa IIae, 26), arguing that we are bound to love certain neighbours more than others (art. 6), that our charity should be directed to those who are nearer to us more than to those who are better (art. 7), that we ought to love our kindred more than other people (art. 8), and so on? Who needed to be persuaded of such banalities? Whose problems was Thomas attempting to resolve with these arguments? Whose distress at finding charity towards some people much easier than towards others required to be thus assuaged? What theory of spirituality needed the therapy of these considerations?

Spiritual success has often seemed to require detachment from particular circumstances and people, including even oneself. Our neighbour becomes an 'occasion' for the exercise of charity – very much as the first beautiful boy in Diotima's system is a place-holder for the Idea of the Beautiful. Charity can be understood as, ideally, making people inter-substitutable. Charity reduced to doing good, to well-meaning 'do-goodism', is evidently common enough to have become proverbial. Worse still, however, and much more likely to be in Thomas's sights, is a whole style of Christian spirituality, no doubt afflicting clergy and religious most of all, in which something very like Diotima's ascetical exercises, suitably transformed, has flourished like blight. It is surely significant, for example, that, discussing the priorities to be observed in loving objects out of charity, Thomas resists the thesis that our own body has either a low or indeed no place in the *ordo caritatis*: 'Our bodily nature, far from issuing from an evil principle, as the Manichees imagine, is from God' (IIa IIae, 25, 5). Manes, a Gnostic Christian who lived in Persia in the third century, produced a system that struck people at the time as a 'Pauline heresy'. How much connection it had historically with the doctrines and practices associated with the Cathari and the Albigenses that posed by far the greatest internal threat to the Catholic Church in the thirteenth century need not be discussed here. Indeed, if there was no direct influence at all, that would only confirm the case for the perennial vitality of a spirituality that seeks to cope with the vulnerabilities and vicissitudes of human life by practising a detachment which denies the intrinsic value of anything but whatever lies outside the world.

As so often, it is a recurrent temptation in Christian doctrine and piety that Thomas wants to expose and eradicate – and, again as so often, it is to Aristotle that he instinctively turns to help him to articulate the sane alternative. It should not be concluded that he thus bypasses the traditional Christian sources. On the contrary: in the very years that he was transforming the *Nicomachean Ethics* into the *secunda pars* of the *Summa* he was also lecturing on the fourth gospel, which resulted in the finest of his scripture commentaries. In his last years he seems to have become more and more passionately committed to the works of Aristotle and St John the Evangelist. It is not just that Aristotelian emphases enabled Thomas to detect Christian deviations; they also allowed him to make breathtakingly audacious theological assertions.

Perhaps I should note at this point that Thomas does not always have everything well worked out. He was not out to produce a mathematically consistent system, whatever some readers fear and others would like to think. He sometimes betrays his best insights. Like any great thinker – starting with Plato and Aristotle – his creative advances occasionally leave pools of earlier ideas overgrown or undrained. To my mind at least, when he argues that the companionship of other human beings is not *de necessitate* in heaven – 'Were there but one single soul enjoying God it would be happy though without a neighbour to love' – he would have done better to think a little harder about what

Aristotle is saying in the text that he cites (Ia IIae, 4, 8). 'The reader may well feel', as Thomas Gilby remarks at this point in his translation, 'that this article marks a relapse into a primness of the *Nicomachean Ethics.*' While the question – one of the few that Thomas never discussed elsewhere but apparently invented as he worked on the *secunda pars* – would have been quite unintelligible to Aristotle or anyone else in the fourth century B.C., is it so clear that this lamentable 'primness' is fairly attributed to the *Ethics*?

The syndrome in theology and piety that attracted Thomas's criticism over the years, as everyone knows, was a certain supernaturalism that effectively devalued our humanity and our world. Christology, for example, is for Thomas predominantly a confrontation with docetic temptations. Indeed, in one of the extremely rare first-person remarks in all his millions of words, he corrects his earlier docetic understanding of how Jesus acquired knowledge (IIIa, 9, 4). It is no surprise to find that it was reflecting on Aristotle's philosophy of mind that enabled Thomas to catch himself out. We have already noted that the Catholic Church in his day had scarcely recovered from the deep internal trauma of Albigensianism. The great external challenge in the thirteenth century came from Islam: how much Thomas owed, and knew that he owed, to that source need not be detailed here – it was, for a start, the main conduit of the works of Aristotle. But he also feared that some Islamic theologians spoke of the power of God in such a way as to deprive human beings of their intrinsic reality: 'To make the creature almost nothing in the sight of the Holy One, far from respecting the divine majesty, only reduces it' *(Summa contra Gentiles*, III, 69, freely translated). Since God is an omnipotent agent and so responsible for everything in the world, how can we understand the human act as something for which we are responsible? It was to elucidate this question that Thomas turned to Aristotle's account of causality.

It is not surprising, then, that, when at last he had to reconsider the topography of charity, Thomas instinctively appropriated Aristotle's criticism of the Platonic theory of love that is voiced in Socrates's speech in the *Symposium*. He did not, of course, know what he was doing: having no access to the relevant Platonic texts he could not have made the comparison or located the radically different approaches to love in the *Symposium* and the *Ethics* respectively. Indeed, given his customary reverential exposition of texts which he is often correcting and even rewriting, it might be asked whether he had enough idea of the modern way of taking up a critical stance to a text to be able to see how different the two approaches are. His *intuition*, at any rate, drew him to the Aristotelian side in the profound conflict that I have tried to identify.

One way, for emotionally fragile creatures such as we human beings are, to cope with the wonderful but bewildering and often wounding realities of the world, is to immunize ourselves against them all by uniting ourselves with the one totally reliable and stable reality which will by definition never desert or betray us, or in some other way get out of control. In the end, paradoxically enough, one becomes rather like Aristotle's notion of god: *chōristheis*, separate, uninvolved, apart in oneself (NE, VIII, 1159a).

But if one's conception of God runs rather in a direction that is illuminated by the doctrine of the Incarnation, including of course a proper doctrine of the Church, after the fashion which Thomas adumbrates in the *tertia pars* of the *Summa*, an entirely different perspective opens out. If God has shared his own goodness with human beings, so that this love is reciprocal, then they have become *good*: lovable, desirable, beautiful, intrinsically valuable. Each partner in the relationship loves the other for his or her *character* – for what the other most deeply and radically *is* in himself or herself. In such love neither partner is lost in or enslaved by the other. On the contrary: each loves the other precisely for the sake of his or her *otherness*. In such mutual respect for the separateness of each partner it is therefore at last possible for us to let God be *God* in the knowledge that God lets us be *us*. But this means, of course, that we have to live with each other – and God is no more securely in our control than we are in his, at least if by that we desire to be his favourite doll.

As so often, however, since Thomas's theology is certainly 'systematic' in the sense that the very nature of the investigation compelled him to travel criss-cross over the ground in every direction, memories of many other tractates or 'treatments', in the *Summa* and elsewhere, crowd in. What he ventures about charity as friendship illuminates, and is in turn illuminated by, things that he says on a string of other matters. But such explorations must be left for another occasion.

To sum up, then, we may say this: when Thomas re-read Aristotle's *Ethics* he found a new depth to the idea of charity as a kind of friendship. In charity we are friends with God. There can be no friendship, in the fullest sense, except between equals – but God has made us his equals. This kind of friendship, according to Aristotle, is based on each partner's acknowledging the other's goodness. Secondly, they let one another *be*: each delights in the other's existence, and the freer the one allows the other to be the more fully and truly they are revealed to each other. What is crucial, I think, is that there is no question of one partner's losing his or her identity in the other. The lover is not infatuated with the beloved. There is no annihilation of self in submission to, or submersion in, the absolute other. The relationship is modelled on the kind of 'space' that friends accord one another: *koinōnia*, conversation, even a kind of 'symposium'. For Thomas, as for Aristotle and Plato, what is defining about human beings is that we find ourselves in language. Even in that divine way of loving which is charity we neither are nor want to be struck dumb. We are friends with God. We do not lose ourselves in that self-hating spirituality that has afflicted so many people's lives nor in some ascetical detachment that would save us from the vulnerabilities of love.

In thus rethinking the nature of charity in the light of Aristotle's analysis of love with the incisiveness and clarity that he shows in the *Summa* Thomas must surely have thought that he had opened up a new theological perspective that his followers would develop. In fact, however, as happened with nearly all his most original and characteristic insights, this proposal was soon distorted out of all recognition or simply consigned to oblivion.[20] It was explicitly rejected by Durand de Saint-Pourçain, the leading Dominican thinker in Paris by the second decade of the fourteenth century; but then he objected to all the essential Thomist insights and escaped being silenced by Dominican censorship only by becoming a bishop. Dominicans, alas, no doubt unwittingly, did more than anyone else to bury Thomas's idea. In Germany, again by the first years of the fourteenth century, in the teachings of such Dominican luminaries as Helwic the Teuton and Johannes Korngin von Sterngassen, the idea of friendship with God had become assimilated into those currents of piety that bloomed in the mystical writings of Tauler and others. The network of mystics in the Rhineland and Switzerland who took the name of 'friends of God', with their emphasis on the personal union of their souls with God, not to mention their tendency to attack certain aspects of ecclesiastical life for 'externality', had effectively diverted the idea of charity as friendship into the solitary merging of the individual with the absolute which, if I am right, Thomas was instinctively rejecting. As a result, such thoughts as Catholics have about the nature of charity would now be captured perfectly well by the account Thomas offered in the *Scriptum*. A moralistic notion of 'doing good' is the sole runner, except perhaps in the case of special cloistered souls, for whom ascetical loss of self in disinterested and impartial love may still be conceivable. What Thomas, and Aristotle before him, were out to free us from still seems to be the natural thing to think.

NOTES

1 James McEvoy, *The Philosophy of Robert Grosseteste* (Oxford, 1982), p. viii.
2 Daniel A. Callus, 'Robert Grosseteste as Scholar' in *Robert Grosseteste: Scholar and Bishop*, ed. D. A. Callus (Oxford, 1955), p. 62.
3 *Aristoteles Latinus*, XXVI, 1–3 (Brussels and Leiden, 1972–74)
4 A. Pelzer, 'Un cours inédit d'Albert le Grand sur la Morale à Nicomaque, recueilli et rédigé par saint Thomas d'Aquin', *Revue néoscolastique* 23 (1922).
5 *Sententia libri Ethicorum*, Leonine ed. (Rome, 1969).
6 James A. Weisheipl, *Friar Thomas d'Aquino* (Oxford, 1974), p. 380.
7 Vernon J. Bourke, 'The *Nicomachean Ethics* and Thomas Aquinas' in *St Thomas Aquinas 1274–1974 Commemorative Studies* (PIMS, Toronto, 1974), vol. 1, pp. 239–259, esp. p. 254.
8 Harry V. Jaffa, *Thomism and Aristotelianism. A Study of the Commentary by Thomas Aquinas on the Nicomachean Ethics* (Chicago, 1952), p. 6.
9 Bourke, p. 259.
10 *L'Ethique à Nicomaque, Introduction, traduction et commentaire*, by R. A. Gauthier and J. Y. Jolif (3 vols, Louvain and Paris, 1958–59).
11 Weisheipl, p. 256.
12 Anthony Kenny, *Aquinas* (Oxford, 1980), p. 24.
13 *Scriptum super libros Sententiarum*, critical ed. in progress, Book III, distinction 27, question 2, article 1.
14 *Summa Theologiae*, Blackfriars ed., vol. 34 (London and New York, 1975).
15 Discussion of the *Symposium* took a new turn with the splendid essay by Gregory Vlastos, 'The Individual as Object of Love in Plato' in his *Platonic Studies* (Princeton, 1973), chapter 1; but readers who know Martha Craven Nussbaum's marvellous book, *The Fragility of Goodness: Luck and Ethics in Greek Tragedy and Philosophy* (Cambridge, 1986), will easily see how deeply I am indebted to it in the rest of this essay.
16 Cited by Nussbaum, p. 503.
17 *The Works of Aristotle*, trans. ed. Sir David Ross, vol. XII, *Select Fragments* (Oxford, 1952), pp. 8–14.
18 *Ibid.*, pp. 25–26.
19 I am indebted here to lectures given at Le Saulchoir, Paris, in the winter of 1962–63, by Jacques Pohier.
20 R. Egenter, *Die Lehre von der Gottesfreundschaft in der Scholastik und Mystik des 12. and 13. Jahrhunderts* (Augsburg, 1928).

2

PRAYER, HUMPTY DUMPTY AND THOMAS AQUINAS

Simon Tugwell OP

The history of the word 'prayer' represents an outstanding triumph of the Humpty Dumpty school of philology, whose basic premiss as enunciated by its founder is 'When *I* use a word, it means just what I choose it to mean – neither more nor less'.

Originally there can be no doubt whatsoever that words for 'prayer' meant 'petition'. Latin-speaking Christians, for some reason, adopted the unclassical word *oratio* (whose classical meaning is 'speech'), but they used it in exactly the same way as the more classical *precatio*, and in fact both words survived side by side into the modern Latin languages. And this original meaning was still strongly felt, at least in some circles, in the middle of the twelfth century. Thus, rather to the distress of the Sources Chrétiennes editor, the Carthusian John of Portes could write a whole letter on how to pray (*de modo orandi*) which is all about saying prayers of petition.[1] And one of the problems addressed by Hugh of St Victor in his *De virtute orandi* is that some people are evidently quite disturbed by the fact that when we pray (and it seems to be the liturgy that is envisaged here) we say a lot of things to God in which we do not ask for anything: it is mockery rather than prayer to come before God as if to ask for something and then suddenly turn aside to other things which are quite irrelevant (PL 176, 981–982).

By the time we get to the seventeenth century not only has prayer, by and large, stopped *meaning* 'petition', at least in Catholic circles,[2] it has come to be possible to present a supposedly complete analysis of prayer without even mentioning petition. In the *Doctrine Spirituelle* of the Jesuit Louis Lallemant we read that 'there are three sorts of prayer: meditation, or discursive prayer, which is suitable for beginners who are in the purgative way; affective prayer, which is suitable for people making progress who are in the illuminative way; and contemplation or prayer of union, for the perfect who are in the unitive way'.[3]

The tendency of pious words to lose their meanings is already apparent in the thirteenth century. In IV *Sent.* d.15, q.1, a.4, q.3 St Thomas remarks that 'according to some people there are two kinds of prayer: there is the prayer of contemplatives ... and there is another kind which groans over our sins'. One of the people who wanted to treat 'prayer' (*oratio*) as polysemous like this was Alexander of Hales, who announces that 'prayer is taken in many ways: sometimes as meaning an external act, sometimes as meaning any good deed, sometimes as meaning an interior act, when the soul is caught up into God by contemplation' (IV *Sent.* d.31, 10d). St Bonaventure followed a similar path, though he made a modest attempt to tidy things up a bit: 'Properly speaking prayer is an ascent to God in order to enjoy something or to obtain something or to pay some debt, but in a broader sense "prayer" is used to include any contemplative act related to God; in its broadest sense it includes every good deed' (IV *Sent.* d.15, p.2, a.1, q.4). Since 'contemplation' was similarly losing its grip on any precise meaning, the reduction of prayer to 'any contemplative act' was not calculated to shed much light on the matter. As St Thomas says, '"Contemplation" is sometimes taken in a strict sense to mean the act of the intellect thinking about the things of God ... but in another sense it is taken more generally to mean any act in which people separate themselves from worldly affairs to attend to God alone' (IV *Sent.* d.15, q.4, a.1, q.2, ad 1).

As various Humpty Dumpties worked their linguistic miracles, the word 'prayer' was pushed and pulled in a variety of directions. Its most expansive territorial claim is clearly Bonaventure's 'broadest sense', in which 'prayer' is taken to include 'every good deed'. This totally vague account of prayer, which is the first interpretation of the word proposed by Peraldus in his very influential *Summa de Virtutibus*, in the first chapter of the treatise on prayer,[4] grows out of a long tradition of trying to cope with the precept in I Thess 5:17, 'Pray without ceasing'. St Augustine interpreted this precept with reference to that desire for beatitude which should motivate our whole lives (*Ep.* 130, 9, 18) and suggested that 'your very desire is your prayer and if your desire is continuous, so is your prayer. . . . If charity always persists, you are always crying out' (*Enarr. in Ps.* 37, 14). A somewhat muted version of the same doctrine was propounded by Haimo of Auxerre in his comment on the Pauline precept: after suggesting that it could mean no more than fidelity to the canonical Hours, he says, 'Or it refers to someone who is always thinking about God and desiring to please God. As long as you are thinking well and desiring good, you are always praying, for whatever good is done by the righteous is to be reckoned as prayer and you will never cease to pray if you never cease to be righteous' (PL 117, 775D). A potted version of this comment was included in the standard Marginal Gloss: 'The righteous never stop praying unless they stop being righteous. Anyone who always acts well is always praying'.

As an exegetical ploy this extension of the word 'prayer' does not, perhaps, cause any great confusion, but when 'any good deed' comes to be seen as just one meaning, and the most comprehensive meaning at that, of the word 'prayer', without any reference to any exegetical context, then trouble will not be far off, and trouble of at least two kinds.

First of all, once it has become possible to say that I am praying simply by acting well, the question cannot be avoided why I should also be expected to pray in any other sense. The process which led to the expanded interpretation of prayer goes into reverse: instead of starting with the specific notion of prayer as a fairly easily recognized activity in its own right and then wondering how that activity can be carried over into the rest of my life to satisfy the Pauline precept, I can now start with my life as a whole and wonder where prayer as a specific activity fits in.

And the second kind of trouble makes it quite difficult to find any answer to this question: a redefinition of prayer in terms of virtuous Christian living is ideally suited to the requirements of people who are thoroughly embarrassed at the whole idea of asking God for things. As early as Origen we hear of some Christians who were maintaining that by 'prayer' the Bible must really mean something else (*De Oratione*, 5, 1) and it is fairly clear that Clement of Alexandria himself cannot really see any use for prayer in its original sense, so he happily uses Maximus of Tyre's formula[5] that prayer is a *'homilia* with God' (which is nicely ambiguous, as *homilia* can mean either 'talking' or 'communing') to gloss over the specific nature of prayer as petition, and this then permits him to conclude that 'the whole life' of the real Christian, the Christian 'gnostic', 'is prayer and *homilia* with God'. And it is noticeable that on his view it is only people who are not virtuous who 'pray to obtain what they have not got', and such people are ill-advised to pray anyway, because as likely as not they will ask for things they would be better without (*Strom.* VII, 39, 6; 73, 1; 44, 1–4).

If prayer is to avoid simply disintegrating into a congeries of unrelated 'meanings' and if prayer, in its original sense, is to be rescued from becoming a pointless, if not actually undesirable and demeaning, activity, then obviously some way must be found of showing how prayer, in its original sense of petition, is an intelligible and religiously significant activity and how it is possible for prayer, in some such specific sense, to permeate a whole life.

By a rather more restrained bit of encroachment 'prayer' also managed to annex thanksgiving. Again the most sinister implication of this development is that it lets people off the hook who are embarrassed by petition, giving them free rein to emulate the Pharisee in the parable in Luke 18:11–14 who, as Augustine points out, is not at fault because of his thanksgiving but because he does not ask for anything more (PL 38, 656–657). Thanksgiving originally became part of prayer only in the very precise sense that words for prayer could be used to cover the whole of 'a prayer' considered as a kind of rhetorical artefact, and so Origen was probably only interpreting an age-old tradition in including thanksgiving as one of the *topoi* of prayer (*De Oratione*, 33). But it is interesting that in his interpretation of I Tim 2:1, with its famous list of 'entreaties, prayers, pleas and thanksgivings', Origen cautiously says no more than that these four items 'border on' the discussion of prayer (*De Oratione*, 14). St Bernard uses the same list in a much more dramatic way to suggest that thanksgiving is not only a kind of prayer, it is the highest kind of prayer to which most of us should hardly dare to aspire in this life (*De diversis*, 25). But at any rate some people retained the sense that thanksgiving, however closely related to prayer, is a distinct activity. The Carthusian writer already mentioned, John of Portes, treats prayer and thanksgiving as parallel but distinct practices,[6] and Peraldus devotes a separate chapter to thanksgiving, at the beginning of which he notes that thanksgiving is often 'mingled with prayers' (*De Virt.* III, 5, 8).

Far more portentous for the later history of Christian piety is the tendency for prayer and contemplation to converge, both of them becoming decidedly vague terms in the process, so that almost any religious practice can count as either prayer or contemplation, though contemplation often has a rather snootier ring about it.

One incentive to blur the outlines of prayer came precisely from the list in I Tim 2:1, on which there was from quite early on a double tradition. Ambrose has a text in which *oratio* comes before *obsecratio* and he interprets the list as indicating the proper sequence of moves which we ought to make when we pray, on the analogy of secular 'orators' who are trying to win the favour of some judge (*Sacr*. VI, 22–25). *Oratio* (which comes first in Ambrose's list) is taken to mean praise (which, in a secular context, is a conventional way of softening someone up for a touch and so is a sensible preliminary to petition). *Obsecratio* is not very clearly defined, but it is identified as 'supplication' and is a gradual manoeuvring into place for presenting one's petition by saying something to get the 'judge' to listen patiently. It does not seem to be significantly different from praise and is omitted altogether in Ambrose's analysis of the Lord's Prayer. Then comes the actual 'plea', followed by renewed praise and thanksgiving. The programme is illustrated by the Lord's Prayer with the prayer that followed it in the local rite of the Mass and also by a not very convincing analysis of Psalm 8. Although it seems not to be strictly necessary to have all the 'parts' of prayer in every prayer, there is no doubt that every prayer should essentially conform to the suggested pattern. The four items, then, are regarded as four elements in a single act of petition, and this is not problematic; but the artificiality of Ambrose's analysis of Psalm 8 reveals the difficulties inherent in taking the list as indicating a sequence, and there seems to be little reason why *oratio* should be required to mean 'praise'. Even if praising someone is a recognized form of 'speech' (*oratio*) it is not the only or even the typical form of speech; and there seems even less reason to interpret *oratio* as 'praise' in the context of *oratio* meaning 'asking' ('prayer').

Cassian opted for a totally different way of reading I Tim 2:1 (*Conf.* 9, 11–17): he takes the four items as indicating not parts but kinds (*species*) of prayer, and he allocates the different kinds of prayer to Christians at different levels of progress, so here we have an early version of the doctrine of 'grades of prayer' which has so obsessed more recent spiritual writers. He takes the four terms in the standard order and interprets *obsecratio* as a petition for mercy on one's sins, *oratio* as meaning 'vow' (like the Greek *euchē*), *postulatio* as intercession made for other people, and thanksgiving as meaning an ecstatic appreciation of all God's gifts, past, present or to come. Although any of us may practise any of these kinds of prayer at any time, and there is a particularly intense sort of prayer which packs them all into one inarticulate and fire-like prayer, nevertheless the normal procedure is for people to progress from one kind of prayer to the next. The implication is that petition (apart from intercession) is beginners' prayer and ought to be left behind in due course.

Later on, both ways of exploiting I Tim 2:1 continue to be

found. The Marginal Gloss follows, more or less, in Ambrose's footsteps, applying the four terms listed to the sequence of parts in the Mass (and Hugh of St Cher generalizes the point to make it apply to all public prayers). It also suggests another sequence, applying the four terms to the different things that are prayed for: first and most difficult is the conversion of sinners (*obsecratio*), then there are things that converts need in order to lead a Christian life in this world (*oratio*), then there is prayer for their eternal reward (*postulatio*) and then thanksgiving crowns the whole process.

The application of I Tim 2:1 to the Mass goes back to Haimo and appears to be no more than a quite arbitrary deployment of terminology to fit a quite arbitrary analysis of the structure of the Mass. No explanation is given why *oratio* should apply particularly to the consecration, nor is there any comment on the relationship between prayer and thanksgiving.

The Gloss's alternative interpretation is clearly related to the ascetic doctrine found in the letter of John of Portes (though John does not refer to I Tim 2:1). John suggests that we progress, typically, from praying chiefly about our sins to praying chiefly for guidance in this life and then finally to praying chiefly for heaven. Again no reason is given why *oratio* should apply particularly to prayer for what we need in this life.

The Gloss, with its choice of interpretations, wavers between seeing in the Pauline list a catalogue of 'parts' of prayer and taking it as designating different 'kinds' of prayer (the 'kinds' being identified by different objects of petition – with 'thanksgiving' tagging along behind as a rather odd kind of prayer since it is not any kind of petition).

St Bernard plumps squarely for kinds of prayer, in the sermon already referred to. And he, like Cassian, suggests that we progress from one kind to another. In his account *obsecratio* is proper to people still constantly teetering on the brink of sin, who do not dare approach God in their own right, so they call upon the saints and appeal to Christ's Passion and so on. *Oratio* is for people who have definitely left sin behind them and now dare to approach God and talk to him themselves (Bernard here makes use of Cassiodorus' etymology of *oratio* as *oris ratio*).[7] When we have gained confidence in addressing God we can proceed to ask him for things, and this is *postulatio*. The final stage is when we are almost in heaven and so, like the citizens of heaven, we praise God and thank him, rather than pestering him with requests.

William of St Thierry follows Bernard in identifying petition with *postulatio* and he regards it as the prayer of the beginner, 'animal' prayer, even if it is occasionally practised even by mature Christians (*Golden Ep.* 177; *Expos. Cant.* 15). It is essentially the prayer of the person who does not know how to pray, who desires something other than God and seeks 'neither feeling nor affection towards God' (*Expos. Cant.* 14). Prayer proper, *oratio*, is a much more exalted business: it is 'the affection of someone cleaving to God and an intimate and pious conversation with him, the stability of an enlightened mind enjoying God for as long as it may' (*Golden Ep.* 179). Thanksgiving is 'the unfailing direction of a good will towards God' and so there is, in William's view, no real difference between ceaseless prayer and ceaseless thanksgiving (*ibid.*, 180–181).

Among the Dominicans, Hugh of St Cher basically follows the Gloss and then throws in St Bernard for good measure, and Peraldus has a thoroughly muddled chapter on the 'kinds of prayer' in which all sorts of different ways of distinguishing between different kinds of prayer are lumped together, including a distinction between 'fruitful and unfruitful prayer', a distinction between prayer for oneself and prayer for other people and the distinctions suggested by William of St Thierry on the basis of I Tim 2:1.

St Thomas discusses I Tim 2:1 several times in the course of his writings: in his early commentary on the Sentences (IV, d.15, q.4, a.3), in the only slightly later lectures on I Timothy and then in the *Summa Theologiae*, IIa IIae, q.83, a.17. In the Sentences commentary he seems unable to make up his mind whether he is discussing parts of prayer or kinds of prayer, and indeed he says that the Pauline list involves both kinds of analysis. The parts of prayer, in the sense of the elements needed to make up a complete prayer, and the kinds of prayer seem to get thoroughly mixed up, in fact. *Obsecratio* is both a kind of prayer in that it is a prayer for a particular kind of object (something difficult), but it is also a part of prayer in that the commemoration of holy things is the basis for our appeal to God. Thanksgiving does not appear to be a kind of prayer, but then it is not clear that it is really a part of prayer either: if we conclude a prayer with thanksgiving it is in order to 'leave the door open for a later prayer'. And *oratio*, following the Gloss, is taken to mean specifically prayer for things needed in this life and, as such, it is the 'lowest' kind of prayer; if it seems odd to give the generic name 'prayer' to what is actually the lowest form of prayer, Thomas points out that it is the same with the word 'angel'. In response to Ambrose's 'rhetorical' analysis of prayer (which Thomas probably knew only indirectly) Thomas has to deal with the objection that praise as a form of *captatio benevolentiae* is superfluous when we are addressing God, whose *benevolentia* is already certain; he retorts that in the case of prayer the *captatio* is meant to have an effect on us, not on God, and praising God can arouse a feeling of devotion in us.

In the lectures on I Timothy Thomas abandons the relegation of *oratio* to the lowest rank in the hierarchy of 'prayer' and, so far as I know, he never again says anything to suggest that there is any hierarchy of prayer. He now makes rather more of the possibility of treating the Pauline text as a rhetorical analysis of prayer, which he then applies to the typical pattern of the church's collects. But the rhetorical analysis is not entirely convincing, since in fact collects do not generally have the four elements in the order suggested by the Pauline list! It is clear that it is not really rhetorical analysis which interests Thomas now, but rather an analysis of what is involved in asking people for something. First we have to be able to suggest some reason why our intended benefactor should give us anything, then we have to show that our case is a reasonable one, then we actually make our request. So, applying this model to prayer, we must first reflect on why God can be expected to give us anything, and the answer has to be sought with reference to his own mercy rather than our merits, and this gives quite a plausible use for *obsecratio*. Then comes *oratio*, which Thomas now identifies according to Damascene's definition, adopted by Bonaventure, as 'an ascent of the mind to God'. This corresponds, not very felicitously, to persuading our intended benefactor that our case is reasonable! In prayer we are not trying to persuade God, instead we are trying to ensure that our own hearts are raised to God. To this end, having thought about the grounds we have for expecting God to give us something, we need to 'meditate' on the fact that the holy thing adduced in *obsecratio* is the cause of our salvation. Then comes the actual petition (*postulatio*), followed by thanksgiving. No attempt is made to explain how thanksgiving is involved in prayer.

Thomas then comments on the Gloss's application of the Pauline list to the Mass. Before the consecration we are commemorating holy things; at the consecration there is *oratio* 'because there is a *meditatio* of the things Christ did'. If *meditatio* is being used in its archaic sense (a 'rehearsal' of what Christ did) then it is hard to see how this phase differs from the preceding one of *obsecratio*; but since Thomas has used *meditari* in a more modern sense ('think about') in connection with *oratio* only a few lines earlier, it is probable that he means that the consecration is *oratio* because it is specially a time for us to meditate on what Christ did.

31

Finally Thomas refers to the Gloss's alternative exposition, in terms of the different objects of petition.

We notice that there is still no real attempt to show why thanksgiving is to be considered as a 'part of prayer', and it is striking to see how readily *meditatio* is worked into the account of prayer. William of St Thierry had used the words so that 'prayer' and 'meditation' became almost indistinguishable and Hugh of St Victor had set in motion (though he cannot be held responsible for it) the idea that meditation and prayer are both parts of contemplation and, in the Sentences commentary, Thomas had interpreted this in such a way as effectively to let meditation become almost a part of prayer.

In the *Summa* Thomas has got his act together in a much more cogent way. Although he announces an article on the 'kinds of prayer', when he actually gets there he formulates his question simply in terms of 'parts of prayer', and, as in the commentary on I Timothy, but without the reference to rhetorical practice, he analyses the things that are needed in the make-up of a prayer. Now, at last, he manages to show how all the ingredients listed are precisely parts of petition. If we want to ask God for something then first of all we must approach him, so there has to be an 'ascent of the intellect to God'. Then we have to make our petition, and this is where 'kinds' of prayer come in, because there are several different ways of making a petition (we may ask vaguely for help, or we may ask specifically for some particular kind of boon, or we may content ourselves with explaining what the matter is without explicitly making any petition at all). Finally there has to be some basis for the petition to be granted, and on our side this means gratitude for favours received before (because ingratitude for past favours makes it unlikely we shall receive any more) and on God's side it means his own holiness, since in the last analysis God gives gifts to us just because he is what he is, though the appeal to him can be made in terms of specific 'holy things', such as the nativity of Christ.

As in the commentary on I Timothy *oratio* is identified as the mind's ascent to God, but it is now given a new and more straightforward role in prayer. There is no further talk of 'meditation' in connection with it, it is simply the 'ascent' that is needed if we are to succeed in talking to God at all. And, though Thomas does not develop this point, it is now much easier to see how 'prayer' can be said to be a 'part of prayer'. Already in the commentary on the Sentences Thomas had defined prayer, following William of Auvergne maybe,[8] as a kind of petition whose specific characteristic is that it is made to God. Thomas shows no

32

signs whatsoever of following Bonaventure in wanting 'ascent of the mind to God' to cover a whole range of options, of which petition is only one. He is talking quite straightforwardly about prayer as petition, prayer in its old-fashioned and well-defined sense. But what makes a petition *prayer* is that it is addressed to God. It is therefore not unreasonable to suggest that if 'prayer' also has to be the name of one ingredient within 'prayer', that ingredient should be the one which specifies what prayer is, namely the address to God. One might suggest an analogy. If the word 'lobbying' had been kept strictly to the lobbying of Members of Parliament, it would not be unreasonable to say that what makes lobbying *lobbying* is the fact that it is (unlike other ways of badgering people) aimed specifically at MPs. So if, for some reason, we had to analyse the component parts of 'lobbying' and name one of them 'lobbying', we might be tempted to say that the part which had the best claim to the name would be our actual going to the Houses of Parliament.

In the *Summa* it is noticeable that there is no further reference to different objects of prayer as specifying different kinds of prayer. St Thomas apparently no longer considers it useful to make this kind of distinction, and he is surely right. Whatever we are praying for, the actual praying is the same.

It is also quite clear in the *Summa* that Thomas has completely lost interest in discovering sequences in I Tim 2:1. Almost all the traditional interpretations agreed in treating the order of the words in the Pauline list as significant, but in the course of what is quite a short article Thomas manages to suggest four different arrangements of the ingredients! He would hardly have done this if he thought that the order mattered.

One thing which is notably absent throughout all Thomas' discussions of I Tim 2:1 is the Cassian-type suggestion of a succession of different kinds of prayer through which we pass as we make spiritual progress. Nor does he ever seem to be seriously tempted by any definition of prayer which would exclude petition. In the *Catena Aurea* on Luke 11:1 he cites a text from pseudo-Basil which says that there are 'two modes of prayer: one consisting of praise, with humility, the other consisting of petition, and this is lower' (PG 31, 1328D), but the only point he seems interested in in this text is its animadversion against rushing straight into petition without a preliminary word of praise. In the *Summa*, where several of the texts originally culled for the *Catena Aurea* re-appear, there is no further mention of these two 'modes of prayer'. Nor, apart from the single reference in the commentary on the Sentences, do we hear any more about the distinction Thomas says 'some people' make between the prayer of 'contemplatives' and the prayer of the rest of us. From start to finish what St Thomas is interested in in IIa IIae, q.83 is prayer in its original sense of petition.[9]

One of the most remarkable developments of piety in the twelfth century was the increasing emphasis on affective intensity, and this was certainly one factor in the convergence of 'prayer' and 'contemplation', since both terms were tending more and more to mean essentially a fervent desire for God. It is in this context that a definition of prayer emerged which was to enjoy a considerable success: 'Prayer is a devout (*pius*) affection of the mind turned to God' ('mind' here not having any particularly intellectual connotations and perhaps better translated by the use of some phrase like 'devout inner affection').[10] So firmly was prayer associated with affectivity that St Albert can simply assert that 'prayer is the perfection of our affectivity and knowledge is the perfection of our intellect' (*De Div. Nom.* 3, 6, Cologne ed., XXXVII, p. 104, 62–63). This claim is made, it is true, in an objection and Albert himself explains the role of prayer in the theological endeavour in terms of petition, but he does not deny the suggestion that prayer is linked essentially with affection. Slightly earlier Alan of Lille, in his commentary on the Lord's Prayer, argued for a typically rigorous dissociation between the secular use of *oratio* (meaning 'speech') and the theological use of the same word: in theology, he says, *oratio* means 'an affection of the soul'.[11] This is the background to the very first question raised in St Thomas' treatise on prayer in the commentary on the Sentences (IV, d.15, q.4, a.1), whether prayer is not 'an act of our affectivity', and the batting is opened immediately by the all-pervasive *pius affectus* definition of prayer.

Closely associated with this kind of definition of prayer is the tendency to connect prayer intimately with 'devotion', as for instance in the writings of St Francis.[12] And what was meant by 'devotion' can be seen from two definitions proposed as current by Peraldus: 'Devotion is a tenderness of the heart, which makes people easily dissolve in tears' and 'Devotion is the fervour of a good will such that the mind cannot contain it and shows it outwardly by certain manifestations'.[13]

The implications of this devotional view of prayer can be seen very clearly in Peraldus. Although on the whole Peraldus retains a fairly clear sense that prayer is essentially petition, so that the 'obstacles' to prayer are all in fact obstacles to impetration, he nevertheless includes a long quotation from William of St Thierry which makes out that the 'labour' of *obsecratio* is fulfilled in obtaining only one thing: 'the consolations and sweetnesses of prayer'.[14] That is to say, the point of praying is not to obtain anything that one is praying for, but to obtain a more enjoyable, emotionally more intense and more satisfying, prayer! And this seems to be the view of Bonaventure, who says that prayer should culminate in 'a wonderful exultation and jubilation' and that we should not stop praying until we have reached this point (*De triplici via*, 2, 3).

It was this notion of prayer that forced 'some people' to postulate the distinction between the prayer of 'contemplatives' and other prayer. Although the discussion of prayer in academic circles had no fixed abode in the theological agenda, the main context provided by the Lombard for such a discussion was *satisfactio* (penance). And since a penance was, by definition, meant to be something painful, prayer (as a penance) had to be seen as a form of mortification. So Raymund of Peñafort, for instance, lists prayer as a form of 'maceration of the body'.[15] What lies behind this idea is not in the slightest bit obscure. I am sure that all Dominicans above a certain age remember what a relief it was to have Matins cut down from nine psalms to three during the Easter season, and our reaction surely attested the *poenalitas* of the normal régime of nine psalms. But in a different context the whole idea of prayer as a penance could look very peculiar. As William of Auxerre argues, 'Any penance is painful, but prayer is not painful; on the contrary, it is sweet and delightful and enjoyable' (*Summa Aurea*, III, 27, 2). It is in this context that he introduces the distinction between the 'prayer of the contemplative' and other prayer: 'Some prayer is entirely delightful, such as the prayer of the contemplative . . . this kind of prayer is not painful and so it does not count as a penance' (*ibid.*, IV, 11, 2).

In his commentary on the Sentences Thomas takes up the subject of prayer in the course of his treatise on *satisfactio*, so he cannot evade the issues raised by people like William of Auxerre. In IV, d.15, q.1, a.4 he intimates that he is not happy with the proposed distinction between the prayer of contemplatives and other prayer, preferring to say that all prayer involves 'affliction of the flesh' even if the spirit does enjoy it, precisely because the intensity of interior love necessarily weakens the flesh. In d.15, q.4, a.7, q.1 he attempts a rather more ambitious solution, but it is not terribly convincing. In the body of the article he contents himself with saying that any penance involves a 'recompense' for past sin and a prophylactic against future sin, and he is on strong ground in suggesting that prayer meets these criteria without difficulty: the root of sin is pride and by humbly subjecting oneself to God in prayer one is making recompense for past sin and cutting off the root of future sin. But in the ad 1, where he tackles the objection that prayer is not painful enough to be a penance, he is much less sure of himself. Vocal prayer, he suggests, is 'painful' because it involves an 'external labour'. Mental prayer is enjoyable, but still with an admixture of pain, because (on the authority of Gregory) it involves groans of compunction, which Thomas suggests may be caused either by the thought of our sins or by longing for heaven. And in any case the raising of the mind is an affliction of the flesh, and any affliction of the flesh affects the mind too. As a parting shot Thomas comments that 'prayer cannot be humble without pain', which seems rather cynical!

Unfortunately Thomas did not complete the treatment of penance in the *Summa Theologiae* and so we do not know how he would have dealt with the problem of prayer as penance there. In IIa IIae, q.83 he entirely abandons the whole problematic, since he now follows William of Auxerre and Peraldus in locating the discussion of prayer in the context of the virtue of justice and, in that context, apparently sees no need at all even to allude to the discussion of whether prayer is painful or not and drops only the merest hint that vocal prayer has a particular relevance to prayer as penance (a.12). There is a very brief note, however, in the *Summa contra Gentiles* (IV, 72), which suggests that Thomas was now happy to accept prayer as a form of penance simply because it involves a subjection of our spirit to God, without the cumbersome discussion of how it can count as 'painful'.

The other aspect of the discussion, the relationship between prayer and consolations, comes into Thomas' thinking in a different context, beginning with his commentary on I Cor 14:14, 'If I pray with a tongue, my spirit prays, but my mind is without fruit'. He implies, at the beginning of his comment, that if the spirit alone prays we are 'refreshed in our affection', whereas if we understand what we are praying then we are 'refreshed in our affection and in our intellect', which is clearly better. But he then moves on to a more penetrating analysis: there are two kinds of 'fruit' in prayer, the merit which prayer wins and 'spiritual consolation and devotion conceived as a result of prayer'. The former is not lost even if our attention wanders while we pray, but the latter is lost. And, Thomas goes on, if merit were lost because of inattention, 'many prayers would be without merit, because it is hardly possible to say one Our Father without one's mind wandering'.

This is clearly a preview of IIa IIae, q.83, a.13, and it is interesting to see how far Thomas has moved in the intervening time. In the *Summa* he identifies *three* effects of prayer. Merit and 'spiritual refreshment' are still listed, but it is the other effect which is said to be 'proper to prayer', and that is impetration (which is no more undermined by distractions than merit is).[16] It is clear that Thomas is now far more seriously concerned with the precise specificity of prayer as asking God for something, so that of course the essential result being looked for is the granting of one's petition. Merit and consolation are incidental benefits.

In the ad 2 Thomas responds to the suggestion that attentiveness is necessary, because otherwise there will be no ascent of the mind to God, and here he drops what is, I think, the only hint in the treatise in the *Summa* that contemplation may be involved in prayer: because of human frailty 'it happens that when the mind of someone praying is ascending to God by contemplation, it suddenly wanders because of some weakness'. If this is to work as an answer to the objection, it has to be taken as implying that the ascent of the mind to God is not necessary to prayer, if 'ascent' had to mean a sustained contemplative concentration on God. And a.17 certainly makes it clear that what Thomas means by the famous phrase is something much more mundane: the mind must ascend to God if we are to ask him for anything in the same sense that we have to approach anyone we want to ask a favour of. It would seem to be rather fanciful to call such a minimal ascent 'contemplation' and it is clear that Thomas thinks far more readily of prayer as a part of the contemplative life (in the sense that the intellect can only ascend to the knowledge of God by God's gift, which must therefore be asked for in prayer) than he does of contemplation as a feature of prayer.

What, then, is prayer exactly? As we have seen, there was a powerful, even if not very ancient, tradition identifying prayer as a state of affectivity. There was also a much longer tradition making desire the essential element in prayer, and Peraldus tried to combine the two by identifying the *pius affectus* of the 'affective' definition as being 'desire'.[17] It is interesting that Thomas' view of the problem seems to have shifted: in the commentary on the Sentences it is against the 'affective' definition that he tries to define his own position, whereas in the *Summa* he sees the main threat as coming from the identification of prayer as desire and apparently sees no need any longer even to mention the 'affective' view of prayer.

Several Parisian theologians reacted against the 'affective' doc-

trine. William of Auvergne allowed that the *pius affectus* formula
might be accepted as a commendation of prayer and as a comment on it, but not as a definition, and the same is true of any
apparent identification of prayer as meaning desire, groaning,
ascent of the mind to God or whatever. In William of Auvergne's
view there has been a great deal of quite fruitless dispute in the
schools on the basis of such formulae. Strictly speaking prayer
has to be defined as a species of petition, and its specific characteristic is that it is addressed to God or to the saints and angels
because of God; it is therefore petition with a specific nuance of
reverence towards the author of all things (*De Rhetorica Divina*, 1).

William of Auxerre similarly points out, like his namesake, that
there is a difference between desiring something and asking for
something, and argues that prayer is properly 'pleading'; as such
it is to be considered as an act of reason. 'So prayer can be
described like this: prayer is properly a movement of the mind
(*animi*) to impetrate some desired good by way of mercy and
bounty or generosity' – the last phrase being added to make it
clear that asking for something is a different way of getting it
from earning it (*Summa Aurea*, III, 17, 1).

The two Williams attained a fair degree of clarity, but the
general state of muddle is vividly illustrated by the extraordinary
treatise on prayer in the commentary on the Sentences by Roland
of Cremona (who was much influenced by William of Auxerre).[18]
In his first article he tries to define what prayer is and argues
himself into the position of saying that the word is not strictly
being used in the same sense in 'vocal prayer' and in 'mental
prayer' and that it can be defined as 'a quality of the rational being
which is adapted to the impetration of grace or glory or something related to the attainment of grace or glory'. Asking for
anything else he refuses to call 'prayer' (against which St Thomas,
in his commentary on the Sentences, IV, d.15, q.4, a.1, q.2,
quite properly retorts that even someone asking God for quite
inappropriate things is still praying). By the time he reaches his
fourth article (on whether prayer is a virtue) Roland wants to say
that prayer is an 'act' (he seems to have forgotten about its being a
'quality') and he takes it for granted that it is an act of the virtue of
religion and therefore a part of justice, though he incidentally
reveals how many widely different positions were being argued
for in the schools, identifying prayer with humility, with temperance, with one or all of the theological virtues or even taking it as a
non-specific virtue. His own view is that 'inner prayer is in all our
powers: sometimes it is in our reason, as when we direct the
mind's eye to God alone and this kind of prayer is in the intellect;

sometimes it is in our concupiscible power, as when we enjoy the pleasure of sweetness and relate it to God, the joy crying out to him; sometimes when we pray we get angry with our sins and rise up against them and direct that to God, and such a rising up is prayer. But properly inner prayer is only the prayer which is in the intellect. . . . But there are certain affections attached to prayer and they can be called prayers. Similarly prayer can refer to an intellect "fat" with affection, so that the two together are taken as a full, fat prayer'.[19] One is left wondering whether Roland has the foggiest idea what he is talking about.

St Thomas takes up the question 'What is prayer?' at the beginning of his treatise in both the commentary on the Sentences and the *Summa*. In both he is firmly committed to the idea that prayer is an act of reason, precisely because it is petition. But he gets sidetracked once or twice in the earlier treatise. First of all he gets sidetracked by the word *oratio* and embarks on a thoroughly unconvincing attempt to get from *oratio* meaning philosophical argument, via *oratio* meaning a forensic speech, to *oratio* meaning prayer, in the process showing how prayer can be an act of speculative reason. In the *Summa* he goes straight to the point: prayer is an act of practical reason, because asking for something is, quite straightforwardly, one way of trying to get something done. And by this time he seems also to be convinced (rightly) that the analogy with forensic speeches does not really help the discussion of prayer.

Also, in the earlier treatise, he cannot quite escape from the lesser consequences of the 'affective' doctrine of prayer. The *pius affectus* definition he takes to be a 'material definition': what we turn to God in prayer is our *affectus*, in the sense that it is from God that we look for the fulfilment of our feeling of desire. In the *Summa* he simply drops the *pius affectus* from the discussion.

He also offers, in the earlier treatise, a rather dramatic explanation of where groaning comes into prayer: it is a kind of 'basis' for prayer, because petition is superfluous where there is no need for anything, so prayer comes out of the recognition of our own wretchedness and helplessness, which makes us groan. In the *Summa* groaning is reduced to a quotation from Augustine in a.14, ad 1, showing how we can go on praying for a long time without any of the 'much-speaking' forbidden by Christ; it is not given any role in prayer as such, and this is surely right. After all one of the things we are supposed to pray for is our daily bread, and most of the time our need of daily bread is not so intense that it makes us groan, nor (mercifully) are most of us helpless in the face of such a need.

One element which is strikingly missing from both Thomas' treatises is the Augustinian doctrine, quoted by Peraldus, that the effectiveness of prayer is proportionate to the fervour of one's feelings.[20] Nor does one find any of the high drama suggested by Peraldus about our needing to pray constantly because we are always on the verge of disaster,[21] or even the idea that we can learn how to pray from the importunate and degrading behaviour of beggars.[22]

Thomas' increasing clarity about prayer precisely as petition, and about petition as an act of practical reason, allows him increasingly to deal clearly with some of the problems which tended to befog discussions of prayer.

As we can see from William of Auxerre and Roland of Cremona there was considerable debate over whether prayer was a virtuous act, and if so to what virtue it belonged. In his commentary on the Sentences Thomas, clearly helped by William of Auvergne, identifies prayer as petition qualified by reverence, and since it is the virtue of worship (*latria*) which offers reverence to God, prayer must be an act of worship. And it is the element of worship, Thomas says (and he implies that this is commonly accepted), which makes prayer effective in impetrating. So what makes prayer an act of this particular virtue is not the petition, as such, but the reverential quality of the petition (IV, d.15, q.4, a.1, q.2).

In the *Summa* (IIa IIae, q.83, a.3) Thomas offers a much tighter exposition of how prayer counts as an act of worship (though here he discusses it in terms of the virtue of religion). He is clearly concerned to show how asking God for things, as such, can be seen as an act of religion, and he raises the crucial question far more clearly than he had before: it is the business of religion to offer worship to God, but prayer asks for something rather than offering anything, so how can it be an act of religion? The idea of prayer as offering something was highly acceptable to William of St Thierry (e.g. *Golden Ep.* 173), but then he was not enthusiastic about petition. William of Auvergne comments on various aspects of the 'sacrifice of prayer' (*Rhet. Div.* 40–42), but seems unable to get beyond a devotionalist interpretation, so that what we offer to God in prayer is our fervour, enthusiasm, contrition and so on. St Thomas seems to have been the only one to distinguish clearly between prayer as such and various incidental (and maybe desirable) qualities that prayer might (or might not) have and to show that prayer as such is a genuine act of worship. By asking God for something we are, intrinsically, subjecting ourselves to him, because asking (by definition) is what we do when we are not in a position to command, when the matter is not subject to our control. So what we are doing, just by praying, by expressing our petition, can be seen as a sacrifice and the most valuable sacrifice we could offer: we are sacrificing our own mind to God. We are also confessing our need of God, as the author of all our good. On this basis Thomas can do full justice to what an ordinary prayer actually is, even the child's simple prayer for a new bicycle, while showing that precisely that act of prayer is a highly significant act of worship. Of course we pray because we want something, but this simple fact is far from being devoid of religious significance, because all our wanting is ultimately subject to the commandment of charity and our interpreting our wants practically in the form of petitions is an integral part of the virtue of religion. Once the discussion of prayer is focused sharply like this on petition, its status as a virtuous act becomes transparent.

Another very vexed topic was the so-called 'conditions of impetration'. A tradition of uncertain provenance had pieced together bits of earlier tradition to identify four basic conditions for impetration, and these had caused no end of trouble because of a confusion between two different claims: the claim (which is no doubt what was originally intended) that when these conditions are met impetration is guaranteed, and the claim that if any of these conditions are not met impetration will not result. And the whole discussion was further confused by a general tendency to regard impetration as a form of meriting.[23]

In the commentary on the Sentences (IV, d.15, q.4, a.7, q.3) Thomas formally discusses the 'conditions of impetration' and points out clearly enough that merit and impetration are two different matters, so that a prayer may be meritorious without necessarily impetrating anything, and he also explains why the four conditions are necessary to guarantee impetration. Before he gets to the discussion of prayer in the *Summa* he had already made an important and emphatic comment on the subject in the treatise on grace (Ia IIae, q.114, a.7, ad 2): 'Prayer's impetration rests on mercy, whereas strict merit rests on justice, and so people impetrate by praying many things which they do not merit in strict justice'. So in IIa IIae, q.83 the discussion of the 'conditions of impetration' is resolved into two much more appropriate questions: Is prayer meritorious? and do sinners impetrate anything by their prayers? (articles 15–16). In article 15 Thomas shows what is involved in a good, Christian prayer, and any prayer of this sort will be meritorious; but however excellent the prayer, it cannot twist God's arm: it is simply God's grace which makes prayer effective in impetrating. This, of course, follows directly from taking petition seriously as what it is; petition by definition involves a situation in which the petitioner cannot *oblige* anyone to do anything. The re-orientation of the question usefully averts the implication of the conventional discussion that in some circumstances God is bound to give us what we are asking for. And in the actual interpretation of the four 'conditions' there is a significant change. The requirement of 'perseverance' was interpreted in the earlier treatise as the antidote to the risk that some obstacle on our part might arise between our making the prayer and the fulfilment of our petition. In the *Summa* the point Thomas stresses is that if we are praying for ourselves, devoutly, and asking for something which is really needed for our salvation, then we shall certainly receive it, but we shall receive it at the right time (of which, of course, God is the judge), and if we stop praying for it that might (though Thomas does not say it necessarily will) interfere with the granting of it. The later treatise thus makes it much clearer that in praying we really are entrusting our concerns to God and he must do whatever he sees fit about them.

If a prayer can be meritorious without impetrating, what about the converse? It was quite traditional to issue warnings that if we do not obey God, he will not listen to our prayers. Peraldus returns to this point several times.[24] But Thomas, in the *Summa*, insists that the prayers of sinners can be heard and that they can impetrate, even though obviously a sinner (that is to say a real sinner, someone who is not in a state of grace) cannot merit anything. Quoting Augustine (*Tr. in Ioann. Ev.* 44, 13), Thomas says, 'If sinners are not heard by God, it was a waste of time the publican saying, "Lord, be merciful to me a sinner"'.

In the *Summa* (a.7) Thomas also tidies up the discussion by explicitly connecting the discussion of prayer for other people with the 'conditions of impetration' (which he had failed to do, really, in his earlier treatise). And he states bluntly that the 'conditions' are necessary only for infallible impetration, they are not therefore necessary for impetration as such.

Another vexed problem was whether or not it was proper to ask for temporal things in prayer. There was a long ascetic tradition against praying for temporal things, and the Interlinear Gloss on Matthew 6:33 implied that one should not ask for such things at all. On the other hand the Lombard's Gloss on II Cor 12:9 says, 'When you ask for temporal things ask in a nuanced way and, with fear, commit them to God so that he will give them if they will be beneficial, but not if he knows that they will get in your way' (PL 192, 85D). The question asked by William of Auxerre and Roland of Cremona is, accordingly, whether one should pray unconditionally for temporal things.[25]

Thomas, from the outset, realized that there are really two distinct questions: should we ask God specifically for anything at all, rather than just leaving it to him to decide what will be best? And should we ask God at all for temporal things?

The case against praying for specific things is an obvious one, but in the commentary on the Sentences Thomas is unable to deal with it very happily. He proposes three difficulties: it is danger-ous to ask for anything we ought not to ask for, and we do not know what we ought to ask for (cf. Rom 8:26); we ought to cast our cares upon God, and if we tell him what ought to be done we appear not to be doing that; the only reason for specifying our desires is to let someone know what we want, and God already knows our desires. In response Thomas can apparently only suggest more or less 'ascetic' reasons for praying specifically: praying for something specific helps us to concentrate our atten-tion (which, he says, is very necessary in prayer – something he would not have said so emphatically later on, I think). It also reveals the state of our own desire to us (not to God, who already knows it), so that we can tell what progress we are making. And thirdly it will make our petition more fervent. All of this seems rather peripheral to what we are actually doing when we ask God for something specific. In response to the first objection Thomas signally fails to notice the obvious response: it cannot be danger-ous to ask for the wrong things, if we presume that God will not give us anything that is going to be bad for us; the objection only works if we treat prayer as a kind of magic, effecting its own answer independently of God. If prayer is taken seriously as petition, then clearly it is intrinsic to it that we are referring some matter to God and formally not taking it upon ourselves to deter-mine the outcome. Instead, Thomas says that it is not always true that we do not know what we ought to pray for, and the apostle's words have to be interpreted as having a limited application. In some cases we know quite well what to pray for (the implication being that in such cases there is no danger in praying). This is a rather cavalier way of dealing with St Paul and it implies a con-siderable reduction of the scope of petition. The answer to the second objection, however, makes a point which would have been much better used in dealing with the first objection: in doubtful cases we cast our cares upon God by leaving it to him to decide what happens; in undoubtful cases we cast our cares upon him by making it clear that we are looking for his help. This implies that in undoubtful cases we are not leaving it to God to decide what happens! The third objection is already disposed of by the assertion that it is to ourselves, not to God, that we are revealing our desires (which seems difficult to accept as an interpretation of what we do when we pray – surely asking God for something is not a form of self-examination) (IV *Sent.* d.15, q.4, a.4, q.1).

In the *Summa* and in the commentary on Romans Thomas offers a far more profound solution to the question. There has been some controversy about the date of the Romans commentary, but it seems likely that it is later than the treatise in the *Summa*.[26] In IIa IIae, q.83, a.5, in the body of the article, Thomas still relies on his earlier distinction between doubtful and undoubtful cases; in the latter the saints pray unconditionally (presumably they pray conditionally in the first case, or perhaps Thomas means us to take his quotation from Valerius Maximus seriously enough to infer that in doubtful cases we should confine ourselves to vague petitions). The new element comes in the ad 1: although of ourselves we cannot know what we ought to pray for, the Holy Spirit helps us by forming holy desires in us, which make us plead rightly.

It is in the Romans commentary that we get Thomas' fully mature view. Here he no longer suggests that St Paul's principle has only a limited application. In general, of course, we do know what to pray for, but the difficulty is in applying the general considerations to particulars. In specific instances there is always a certain residual ambiguity. We want to practise the virtues, but can we ever be sure that, here and now, it is right to practise precisely this virtue in precisely this way? It is in dealing with this problem that we need the help of the Holy Spirit. If he forms right desires in us it is clear that Thomas means us to believe that he forms quite specific right desires (otherwise he is not helping us where we need help). Even with faith, hope and charity, we still need the gifts of the Holy Spirit to free us from foolishness and ignorance (Ia IIae, q.68, a.2, ad 3). The particularity of prayer, therefore, is a consequence of the way in which grace works in us, not merely giving us a general capacity to live in a new way, but activating this capacity in quite specific ways. And since grace does not work against our freedom, the specific acts produced by the inspiration of the Holy Spirit must always appear in us as willed by us, and therefore as specific desires which can and should be turned into specific prayers.

On the problem of praying for temporal things there is little development between Thomas' two treatises. In both he formulates the essential and useful principle that we can lawfully pray for anything we can lawfully desire, and we can lawfully desire temporal things, provided such desire is always controlled by the over-all context of our movement towards final beatitude. The only new feature appears both in the commentary on John 16:23 and in IIa IIae, q.83, a.6 (assuming that the Leonine text in the latter is correct, against the Piana reading adopted in the Blackfriars edition): against the anxiety that praying for temporal things might drag us down, Thomas claims that praying for temporal things (in the context of our whole Christian aspiration towards God) elevates and gives value to temporal things.

The suggestion that it might be dangerous to pray for particular things re-appears only in a very muted form in the *Summa*, and Thomas deals with it briskly: simply by virtue of asking for temporal things in view of our ultimate beatitude we are implicitly asking God only to grant them in so far as they will be helpful towards salvation (a.6, ad 4).

By taking prayer very precisely and insistently in its old-fashioned sense of 'petition', Thomas has been able to make sense of what we actually do when we pray for things (and, for that matter, of what the church does in her official prayers). But there still remains one enormous question: is not the whole idea of asking God for things essentially incoherent? God knows what is needed better than we do, so what is the point of our asking him for things? And he has made up his mind from all eternity what he is going to do, so again what is the point of us coming along now and asking him to do certain things? If what we are asking for is something he has already decided to do, then our prayer is otiose; if it is something he has not decided to do, he is not going to change his mind now, because he is changeless. These fundamental questions were already tackled by Origen (*De Oratione*, 5–6), but they seem not to have been taken up in subsequent discussions of prayer. There is no hint of them in the earlier scholastic treatises that I have looked at, or in Thomas' own treatise in the commentary on the Sentences. The main area in which the problem of the relationship between prayer and God's will was discussed was the very confined question of whether predestination is helped by the prayers of the saints.[27] It is in his discussion of this topic in *De Veritate*, q.6, a.6 that Thomas first goes into the whole question thoroughly, including a review of the various philosophical doctrines which make nonsense of prayer (a review which is probably based on Albert's account of various ancient debates about determinism in *Physica*, 2, 2, 19 – a work almost certainly composed while Thomas was a student of Albert's in Cologne). Thomas evidently saw the importance of this whole discussion for the interpretation of prayer in general, and in his lectures on Matthew he incorporated an outline of it in his comments on the Lord's Prayer.[28] In the *Summa* this process reaches its culmination in the crucial article 2 of IIa IIae, q.83, where Thomas discusses whether prayer is *conveniens* (which could almost be translated 'coherent' and should certainly not be translated as 'useful', as in the Blackfriars edition). The vital point, learned from the traditional discussion of the relationship between prayer and predestination, is that our prayers are a form of secondary causality, planned from all eternity and deployed, like any other causes, by divine providence. That prayer is a genuine form of causality is affirmed in Ia, q.23, a.8 in so many words. This means that prayer, precisely as petition, can be seen as playing a fully authentic role in the working out of events in the world; it does make a difference to what happens. It is as true to say that X happens because I prayed (and would not have happened if I had not prayed) as it is to say that the kettle boils because I put it on the fire (and it would not have boiled if I had not put it on the fire). But this does not mean that I have caused God to change his mind or anything. It can be said, in one sense, that God does X because I asked him to (just as it would be true to say that God boils the kettle because I have placed it on the fire); but the whole story is that I asked him to do X because he caused me to ask him to do X as part of the whole process of his doing X. As Thomas explains in the splendid chapters 95–96 of *Summa contra Gentiles*, III, God moves our desire, which prompts our prayer, and God carries the whole process through to the fulfilment of our desire. And, as the same chapters bring out, this is an admirable expression of the friendship that there is between God and us.

Prayer, then, is one of the ways in which God fulfils his own purpose and one of the ways in which he involves us, as his friends, in the working out of his purpose. If we are in a state of grace, of friendship with him, then our prayers are readily seen as genuine acts of charity, produced by the essential gift of the Holy Spirit, charity itself, and the gifts of the Holy Spirit which attune us in detail to the will of God, and they do not in any way have to be interpreted as anything other than what they appear to be, namely petitions asking God for things. If we are not in a state of grace, our prayers can be seen as manifestations of some kind of preliminary grace leading us towards the establishment or renewal of a state of friendship with God.

But we may still have a residual worry that this is all rather pointless. Why should God want to work in this way? Why should he want to use the rather odd secondary cause which is our prayer? Thomas does not tackle this question directly, but he drops periodic hints as to how it might be answered. It is, of course, silly to imagine that God needs our prayers for his own sake; it is for our benefit that he has set things up in such a way that our prayers play a part. In a.1, ad 3 Thomas suggests that the reason (or one reason) why God wants to give us some gifts in response to our petitions (rather than just giving them to us unasked) is to foster in us 'a certain confidence in having recourse' to him, and in this connection Thomas cites an unidentified text from Chrysostom which comes from the Greek catena he had had translated for the purposes of the *Catena Aurea*: 'Consider what a joy is granted you, what a glory is given you, to talk with God in your prayers, to converse with Christ, asking for whatever you want, whatever you desire'. Prayer is a way, then, of maintaining and developing a certain attitude in us of confidence in God, so that we will turn to him readily and talk happily with him about everything that is on our minds – which is, arguably, no small part of friendship. In the very Augustinian a.14 a rather different line is suggested (which is itself derived from Augustine): prayer is a way of keeping alive and intensifying our desire. In as much as charity involves a desire for God and a shaping of all other desires in the light of our desire for God, it is quite plausible to suggest that a periodic explicitation of our desires will help us to keep an eye on ourselves to make sure we do not settle down either into a state of emotional torpor or into a state of disorderly desires.

But it is perhaps a good thing that Thomas did not devote an article specifically to this kind of question, because prayer is, after all, a matter of talking to God, not a matter of self-cultivation or self-monitoring; it becomes the latter, to some extent, chiefly because of a loss of nerve about prayer as petition. The real service rendered to theology by Thomas is his demonstration that petition does make sense as such, and that it is a very dignified occupation (as he says in Ia, q.23, a.8, it gives us the 'dignity of causality'), and that it is a thoroughly respectable act of religion, of worship. In effect Thomas has vindicated the theological and religious seriousness of the ordinary prayers of ordinary Christians, and the value of this became particularly clear in the sixteenth century, when the Dominicans were the chief proponents of the pious practices of ordinary Christians against the encroaching tyranny of the new interioristic understanding of

spirituality.[29] It was no doubt because of the authority of St
Thomas that Luis of Granada begins his book on prayer (in which
he shows almost no interest in petition) with the declaration that
prayer, properly speaking, means petition. It was the authority of
St Thomas which gave the Dominican Juan de la Cruz the theological strength to come to the defence of the ordinary business of
'saying your prayers'. And it was, surely, St Thomas who was,
indirectly, responsible for the fact that the Roman Catechism
(which was largely the work of Dominican theologians) treats of
prayer entirely in the sense of petition, in sublime disregard of
what both Jesuits and Carmelites were by now meaning by the
word.[30]

NOTES

1 *Lettres des premiers Chartreux*, II, SC 274 (Paris, 1980), pp. 150–170. The
editor feels obliged to point out that the letter is not a 'treatise on
prayer', it deals only with one specific facet of prayer, and he is clearly
happy to be able to suggest that at the end of the letter the author
(John of Portes) 'adds a word to suggest that there are many other
forms of prayer beside petition, for example thanksgiving' (pp. 38–
40). Actually John of Portes makes no such suggestion; all he does is
point out that thanksgiving is necessary as well as prayer!
2 The Protestants, by and large, reverted to the original usage and
generally mean 'petition' when they say 'prayer'; in due course they
too lost their nerve.
3 *La Doctrine Spirituelle du P. Louis Lallemant*, VII, 1, 9 (Montreal and
Paris, 1959), p. 338.
4 *Summa de Virtutibus*, part III, tractate V, part 7, chapter 1. Already in
1250 Peraldus' *Summa* seems to have been a standard textbook in
Dominican circles, and Leonard Boyle OP is probably right to see it as
one of St Thomas' chief targets in his criticism of the intellectually
inadequate ways in which theology was being taught, including
moral theology: L. Boyle, *The Setting of the* Summa Theologiae *of Saint
Thomas* (Toronto, 1982), pp. 20–23.
5 Maximus of Tyre 5, 8, where Maximus tries to cope with Socrates'
praying by suggesting that he was not really asking for anything, he
was 'communing with the gods'.
6 He composed a separate letter on thanksgiving: *loc. cit.*, pp. 170–186.
7 Cassiodorus, *Expos. in Psalt.* 39, 14 and 85, tit. (PL 70, 285C, 610C).
8 *De Rhetorica Divina* 1: *Opera Omnia* (Paris, 1674), I, p. 337.
9 The translation of q.83, a.1 in the Blackfriars edition is extremely
misleading, suggesting as it does that Thomas is interested in different meanings of 'prayer'; in fact, as the parallel text in the commentary on the Sentences proves beyond doubt, Thomas is interested in
different meanings of *oratio* ('speech', 'petition') and what he is

saying is simply that he is not here talking about *oratio* in the sense of 'speech'.

10 This definition is sometimes attributed to Augustine and is presumably derived from the late twelfth-century Cistercian work *De spiritu et anima* 50 (PL 40, 816), which was sometimes ascribed to Augustine. But the rather more compact formula which was extracted and compressed from *De spiritu et anima* travelled around widely on its own and Peraldus, for instance, clearly does not recognize it as coming from *De spiritu et anima* since he cites it anonymously and then proceeds to quote, as a distinct text, the original words of *De spiritu et anima* (*Summa de Virt.*, *loc. cit.*, chapter 2).

11 Ed. N. Häring, *Analecta Cisterciensia* 31 (1975), pp. 149–177; for the text referred to here, see para. 4.

12 Cf. *Letter to Antony* 2, *Regula Bullata*, 5, 2.

13 *Summa de Virt.* III, 5, 7, 10. This text manifestly underlies what is said about St Dominic in the prologue to *The Nine Ways of Prayer of St Dominic*: ed. S. Tugwell, *Mediaeval Studies* 47 (1985), p. 82. In IIa IIae, q.82 St Thomas pioneers a much less emotional interpretation of *devotio*.

14 Peraldus, *op. cit.* chapter 10; William of St Thierry, *Golden Epistle*, 184–185.

15 *Summa de Poenitentia et Matrimonio* (Rome, 1603), p. 468.

16 It is fascinating to see how the doctrine that the specific and proper results of prayer is impetration gets lost in Savonarola's otherwise very faithful reproduction of IIa IIae, q.83, a.13 in his *Orazione Mentale*, 2, 2: *Operette Spirituali*, I (Rome, 1976), p. 166. Savonarola is clearly much more interested in immediate spiritual consolation than he is in impetration.

17 *Op. cit.*, chapter 2.

18 It comes in book III of Roland's commentary on the Sentences, which was edited by A. Cortesi (Bergamo, 1962); the treatise on prayer comes on pp. 765–810.

19 *Op. cit.*, pp. 790–791. I'm afraid it is not my fault if Roland makes prayer sound like an advertisement for cheese.

20 Augustine, *Ep.* 130, 9, 18 (PL 33, 501); Peraldus, *op. cit.*, chapter 4.

21 *Ibid.*, chapters 3 and 6.

22 *Ibid.*, chapter 4, and also in his sermon translated in S. Tugwell, *Early Dominicans* (New York, 1982), p. 172.

23 The confusion between meriting and impetrating is particularly evident in Roland of Cremona, *op. cit.*, pp. 773–782, and in the convoluted debate over St Paul's prayer in II Cor 12:8 in William of Auxerre, *Summa Aurea*, III, 27, 4: ed. J. Ribaillier (Grottaferrata, 1986), pp. 526–534, and Roland of Cremona, *op. cit.*, pp. 785–795.

24 *Op. cit.*, chapters 4 and 5.

25 William, *op. cit.*, III, 27, 5; Roland, *op. cit.*, pp. 796–801.

26 J. A. Weisheipl (*Friar Thomas d'Aquino*, Oxford, 1974, pp. 247–249) argues that it was during his second regency in Paris that Thomas lectured on Romans and I Corinthians; if this is correct, the comments

on Romans 8 would be close in time to IIa IIae, q.83 (the *secunda secundae* was completed at an amazing speed between the end of 1270 and the spring of 1272, which implies an average of nearly twelve questions a month, putting q.83 round about May-June 1271; the Romans lectures would presumably have to be dated to the academic year 1271–72). But there is strong evidence that in fact Thomas lectured on Paul in Naples after he left Paris in 1272 (Tolomeo of Lucca, *Historia Eccles.* XXIII, 9), so I think it is almost certain that the Romans commentary should be dated to 1272–73.

27 Various traditional authorities indicated that predestination is helped by the prayers of holy people, so the matter had to be discussed: cf. for example Alexander of Hales, I *Sent.* d.41, 11: Quaracchi ed., pp. 418–419; William of Auxerre, *Summa Aurea*, I, 9, 3, 4, III: Grottaferrata ed., pp. 192–193; Bonaventure, I *Sent.* d.41, a.1, q.1: Quaracchi ed., pp. 728–729. The essential patristic text, which provided the key to the solution, is Augustine, *De dono perseverantiae*, 22, 60: 'Perhaps they are predestined in such a way as to be granted to our prayers'.

28 For the complete text see H. V. Shooner, 'La *Lectura in Matthaeum* de S. Thomas', *Angelicum* 33 (1956), pp. 131–132.

29 Cf. the remarks of M. Andrés in *Los Recogidos* (Madrid, 1976), p. 394.

30 On this 'Dominican tradition', cf. S. Tugwell, 'A Dominican Theology of Prayer', *Dominican Ashram* 1 (1982), pp. 128–144.

3

CLASSICAL THEISM AND THE DOCTRINE OF DIVINE SIMPLICITY

Brian Davies OP

____ I ____

People often suppose that theology is grounded in an understanding of the nature and attributes of God considered as a particular individual. It is, for example, pretty axiomatic among modern philosophers of religion that God is a person, where 'person' means something like a consciousness or mind with beliefs and thoughts.[1]

Yet this line of thinking would have seemed strange to earlier generations of thinkers. Here I am referring to what is sometimes called the tradition of classical theism, by which I mean the doctrine of God which you can find in writers like Augustine, Anselm and Thomas Aquinas.[2] For it is characteristic of classical theism to say that God is incomparable and incomprehensible. *De Deo non possumus scire quid sit* – 'It is impossible to know of God what he is'.[3] *De Deo scire non possumus quid sit, sed quid non sit* – 'We cannot know what God is, but only what he is not'.[4] These are assertions which classical theists ask us to accept in all seriousness, and in doing so they do not just mean that God is a mysterious sort of thing which we cannot understand because we are not quite clever enough or because our researches are still in their infancy. They mean that God belongs to no class at all and that he defies the conceptual equipment by means of which we identify things and single them out as members of a world.

Thus it is that in the writings of classical theists we come across the doctrine of divine simplicity. God has no nature in any intelligible sense. He is divinity through and through without parts or aspects. On this account, everything that God is *is* God. Or, as some classical theists express it, God *has* no attributes but *is* his attributes. And these are nothing less than God himself. As St Anselm puts it:

You are therefore the very life by which You live, the wisdom by which You are wise, the very goodness by which You are good to both good men and wicked. . . . You are truth, You are goodness, You are blessedness, You are eternity, and You are every true good. . . . There are no parts in You, Lord; neither are You many, but You are so much one and the same with Yourself that in nothing are You dissimilar with Yourself. Indeed You are unity itself not divisible by any mind. Life and wisdom and the other (attributes), then, are not parts of You, but all are one and each one of them is wholly what You are and what all the others are.[5]

Writing in the same vein, Aquinas argues that we can speak of God either by means of concrete terms (as if 'God' were the name of an individual in the world) or by means of abstract terms (as if it were the name for a non-individuated nature). In his view, 'God is Wisdom' or 'God is Goodness' are just as true as 'God is wise' or 'God is good'. Or, as Aquinas himself says:

God is both simple, like the form, and subsistent, like the concrete thing, and so we sometimes refer to him by abstract nouns to indicate his simplicity and sometimes by concrete nouns to indicate his subsistence and completeness; though neither way of speaking measures up to his way of being, for in this life we do not know him as he is in himself.[5a]

By 'form' here Aquinas is alluding to what, for example, is shared by all people when it is truly said that each of them is human. We might call it their common humanity. Aquinas's point then is that though we cannot call particular people 'Humanity' (we cannot say that Mary is Humanity or that Fred is Humanity), we can refer to God by the name signifying his nature. Mary and Fred are not Humanity, but God is Divinity.

Yet is this teaching at all believable? And is it of any theological significance? Edmund Hill has recently called it 'profound theology . . . a mature metaphysics of divine being' which sets us on the road to a proper account of the Trinity.[6] That is a minority view, however. Much more typical of the contemporary verdict is the conclusion of Ronald H. Nash. 'It would appear', says Nash, 'that Christian theologians have no good reason to affirm the doctrine of divine simplicity. It seems doubtful that the doctrine adds anything significant to our understanding of God. . . .

Perhaps, like Emil Brunner, we should conclude that the doctrine has no practical value; it is pure speculation "which has nothing at all to do with the God of the Christian Faith".[7]

—— II(a) ——

What is wrong with the doctrine of divine simplicity? Here we might mention two lines of criticism.

(a) First, so it might be said, the doctrine leads to absurdity. This is Alvin Plantinga's chief objection to it.[8] 'If God is identical with each of his properties', says Plantinga, 'then each of his properties is identical with each of his properties, so that God has but one property.'[9] The conclusion here is false, says Plantinga, because God has several properties. It is, he adds, also false because 'if God is identical with each of his properties, then, since each of his properties is a property, he is a property',[10] while 'if God is a property, then he isn't a person but a mere abstract object; he has no knowledge, awareness, power, love or life'.[11]

Part of Plantinga's worry here is that the doctrine of divine simplicity is incompatible with theism. And others have felt the same. One way of affirming the doctrine is to hold that God is not an individual. Sometimes it is said that God is not a thing or a being.[12] And yet, so it has been asked, how can God exist if he is not an individual? And what is the difference between 'God is not a thing or a being' and 'Nothing whatsoever is God'?

The suggestion that God is not a thing or a being will strike some people as simple atheism.[13] 'God is not an individual' strikes many as nonsense. According to Robin Attfield, for instance, if God is not an individual, he can have no understanding or purposes and there is nothing he can do. If God is not a comprehensible individual, 'no reference to God is possible and no talk about God is coherent. For we have no idea what kind of individual we are picking out or discussing'.[14] To be, says Attfield, entails being of a sort, as Aristotle maintained. Conversely, to be of no sort is to be inconceivable. It follows, therefore, that God is indeed an individual, and he belongs to the sort 'members of which are necessarily timeless, placeless and omnipotent'.[15]

(b) A second possible criticism turns on the notion of existence. Defenders of the doctrine of divine simplicity speak as though they identify God's nature with the fact that God exists. Take, for example, Aquinas. As his treatment of God's simplicity draws to a close, he denies that in God there is a mixture (*compositio*) of *essentia* (essence) and *esse* (existence). According to Aquinas, God

53

is existence. He is *suum esse* (his own being) or *ipsum esse subsistens* (subsistent existence itself).[16] But some would now deny this on the ground that it misconstrues the logic of assertions concerning existence.

Why? The likely answer would be that there is no such thing as existence *simpliciter*, and there is nothing which can be it or have it as a property. On this account, existence is what is expressed when it is asserted that a concept has instances. It is a property of concepts or predicates rather than a property of objects or subjects. To say that something exists is not to describe it or to tell us something about it. It is to say of some description or account that it truly applies to something or other.[17] In terms of this position the conclusion would seem to be that, in its Thomist form at any rate, the doctrine of divine simplicity is a piece of nonsense. It tries to tell us what God is by using expressions which could never tell what anything is.

Some would add that it implicitly endorses the so-called Ontological Argument, which Aquinas officially rejects.[18] According to the Ontological Argument, which is mostly associated with Anselm and Descartes, God must exist since the notion of God is the notion of something with existence as an essential property.[19] Critics of the argument have urged that, since existence is not a property of objects, one cannot deduce the existence of God from the concept of God. Some have then gone on to say that, by the same token, Aquinas on divine simplicity is misguided. As Terence Penelhum puts it:

> The distinctive character of the concept of existence precludes our saying that there can be a being whose existence follows from his essence; and also precludes the even stronger logical move of *identifying* the existence of anything with its essence. These are the Anselmian errors all over again. . . . Since Aquinas differs from Anselm in holding that God's existence has to be inferred from his effects and not from the mere concept of God, he is traditionally credited with having seen what is wrong with the Ontological Proof. He did see it was wrong, but not *why* it was, for he commits the same error himself. He says that we do not have the requisite knowledge of the divine nature to deduce God's existence from it; but his own argument leads us from finite beings to a being whose existence does follow from his nature, and this entails that *if* we knew God's nature we could deduce his existence from it –

and *this* is the mistake. To say that although God's existence is self-evident in itself it is not to us, is to say that it *is* self-evident in itself, and the error lies here. It is not our ignorance that is the obstacle to explaining God's existence by his nature, but the logical character of the concept of existence.[20]

—— II(b) ——

Are these objections decisive, however? To start on a positive note, let us first consider what might be said in their defence.

To begin with, then, if A and B are identical, then A and B might be the same thing. So if the properties of God are identical with each other, they could be the same property, and God could be that property if God is his properties. Yet it seems odd to say that different properties can be the same property, and just as odd to say that God is a property. There must be some sense in which to say, for example, 'God is wise and powerful' is to say two different things about him, that he is wise *and* that he is powerful. It must also be somehow true that if we say 'God is wise and powerful' we say something *about* God and do not simply name him (as if 'is wise and powerful' were a synonym for 'God'). Fred may be bald, but his baldness is not him. Similarly, it would seem nonsense to hold that God and, say, his wisdom are the same (supposing, that is, that we ascribe wisdom to God, and supposing we say that it is an attribute or property of him).

Then again, is there any clear sense to assertions of the kind 'God is not an individual' or 'God is not a thing'? Neither 'individual' nor 'thing' serve by themselves to pick out one thing rather than another. In Wittgenstein's terms, they are 'formal' concepts as defined in *Tractatus* 4.126–4.12721. One might therefore conclude that being told that God is neither an individual nor a thing is not to be told anything of God at all. Alternatively, one might hold that if God is neither an individual nor a thing (or an object or a being, as is sometimes said), then God is nothing, which anyone can be forgiven for reading as 'God does not exist'.

So arguments like those of Plantinga and Attfield are clearly on to something. And the force of their drift can surely be appreciated if we remember what is typically said of God – that he acts, for example. To say that something acts is to say that it undergoes a process or that it brings one about. Acting is something that is done. It is ascribable to genuine subjects or agents. And what, one might ask, are subjects or agents if they are not things or individuals? Even Aquinas calls God a *res* (thing).[21] He also concedes that God is an individual in some sense. He ascribes to God the individuality proper to things whose nature is not material.[22]

The argument concerning existence seems likewise to be getting at something important. It is, for instance, hard to believe that if we ask whether God exists, and if we ask what God is, the answer to the second question could be the same as the answer to the first. 'There is a God' does not say what God is. As Aristotle observes, 'There is nothing whose essence it is that there is such a thing, for there is no such kind of thing as *things that there are*'.[23]

The reply might be that to say that something exists is indeed to say something about it and that existence is therefore a property which something can have or with which it can be identified. It might be held that '— exists' can be what is sometimes called a 'first-level predicate', that it can function like '— is hot' in 'John is hot'. But there is much to be said against this conclusion. We might define a first-level predicate as an expression which yields a proposition when attached to one or more proper names.[24] Such expressions will do the same if attached to a definite description like 'The Pope who succeeded John Paul I'. But while we get an intelligible proposition by, say, attaching 'The Pope who succeeded John Paul I' to the expression 'eats Polish sausage', we get a curious result by attaching to it 'exists'. What does 'The Pope who succeeded John Paul I exists' mean? And what, outside philosophy, would '— exists' mean if attached to a proper name? If you tell someone out of the blue 'Brian Davies exists', will he not presume that something peculiar is going on? And will he not be right?

Well, maybe not. Some people, at any rate, seem to have no problems with utterances like 'Brian Davies exists'. Yet now there is another point worth mentioning. This is that paradox seems entailed by the suggestion that existence is a property of objects or individuals. Are we to suppose that, for example, an existing cat is different from a non-existing one? And what if we deny that such and such exists on the assumption that to do so is to deny that it has a particular property? If we say, for example, 'Honest theologians do not exist', then we purport to be talking about honest theologians, we seem to presuppose that they are there to be talked about, but we also deny that they are real. It therefore seems that assertions like 'Honest theologians do not exist' are implicitly contradictory and that assertions like 'Honest theologians exist' are true of necessity. But that is just unbelievable. There must be an honest theologian somewhere, though no theologian is bound to be honest.

With reference to all this, a useful corrective comes in the work of Frege. According to him, 'the content of a statement of number is an assertion about a concept'.[25] This, says Frege, is perhaps clearest with the number 0.

> If I say 'Venus has 0 moons', there simply does not exist any moon or agglomeration of moons for anything to be asserted of; but what happens is that a property is assigned to the *concept* 'moon of Venus', namely that of including nothing under it. If I say 'the King's carriage is drawn by four horses', then I assign the number four to the concept 'horse that draws the King's carriage'.

There are difficulties here, but we can at least say that Frege looks to be right about one thing. For he goes on to say that 'existence is analogous to number'[26] so that if his analysis of number statements is on the right lines, then that is the right analysis of statements of existence. And the fact is that existence is analogous to number. For statements of existence are statements of number. As C. J. F. Williams puts it:

> Statements of number are possible answers to questions of the form 'How many A's are there?' and answers to such questions are no less answers for being relatively vague. In answering the question 'How many A's are there?' I need not produce one of the Natural Numbers. I may just say 'A lot', which is tantamount to saying 'The number of A's is not small', or 'A few', which is tantamount to saying 'The number of A's is not large'. If I say 'There are some A's', this is tantamount to saying 'The number of A's is not 0'. Instead of saying 'There are a lot of A's' I may say 'A's are numerous' and instead of saying 'There are some A's' I may say 'A's exist'. All these may be regarded as statements of number.[27]

According to Frege, a proposition like 'There exists no rectangular equilateral rectilinear triangle' states a property of the concept 'rectangular equilateral rectilinear triangle'; it 'assigns to it the number nought'.[28] In that case, something similar is true of 'A rectangular equilateral rectilinear triangle exists', for that is the contradictory of 'There exists no rectangular equilateral rectilinear triangle'. If statements of existence are number statements, therefore, such statements ascribe a property to a concept, not to an object, if statements of number ascribe a property to a concept.

—— II(c) ——

Yet even if we can swallow all that it still seems to me that defenders of the doctrine of divine simplicity need not be unduly alarmed.

(a) To begin with, it is by no means obvious that the express-ions we use to refer to God and his properties cannot be the means of referring to one and the same reality. In this sense God might be identical with his properties and they might be identical with each other. A natural tendency here is to construe such a view as saying that properties which are different are not diffe-rent when God has them and that God is nothing but a prop-erty. That is how Plantinga seems to construe it. But another interpretation of the view is possible. Its defender might accept that ascribing different properties to God is done by means of sentences which differ in meaning. In this sense he might agree that God has different properties. But then he might say that the reality to which our talk of God latches on is not something distinct from its properties and not something with distinct prop-erties. As P. T. Geach indicates, there is a comparison available to us here in the light of mathematical functions. ' "The square of —" and "the double of —" signify two quite different functions, but for the argument 2 these two functions both take the number 4 as their value. Similarly, "the wisdom of —" and "the power of —" signify different forms, but the individualizations of these forms in God's case are not distinct from one another; nor is either distinct from God, just as the number 1 is in no way distinct from its own square.'[29] This is no more than an analogy, of course. But it ties up well enough with the doctrine of divine simplicity. Defenders of the doctrine do not deny that, for example, 'God is wise' means something different from 'God is powerful'. In this sense they can be said to accept that God has different properties. What they deny is that what is signified by 'the wisdom of God' is possessed by God as a property distinct from that of being power-ful. They also deny that 'the wisdom of God' and 'the power of God' refer to something other than what is signified by means of the word 'God'.

(b) Second, it can be argued that writers like Plantinga and Penelhum misconstrue the doctrine of divine simplicity because they treat it as telling us something about God's properties while the doctrine precisely denies that God has properties, at least in one sense. That sounds paradoxical, but what I am getting at is really quite familiar, at least in some circles. With respect to

Aquinas the point has been very effectively made by David
Burrell and by earlier writers such as Victor White and Josef
Pieper:[30] from first to last the doctrine of divine simplicity is a
piece of negative or apophatic theology and not a purported
description of God. I should have thought that this fact was
obvious from even a casual reading of authors like Augustine and
Anselm. It is particularly evident from a reading of Aquinas since
he is quite explicit that in saying that God is simple he is giving an
account of what God is not. This is clear from texts like the
Introduction to *Summa Theologiae*, Ia, 3, where Aquinas describes
what follows (of which the first thing is his exposition of divine
simplicity) as a consideration of 'the ways in which God does not
exist'. What this in turn proves to mean is that Aquinas is not
saying that, for example, God's properties are unqualifiedly identical with each other and that God is unqualifiedly identical with
all of his properties. To cast things in a more modern idiom, the
Thomist doctrine of divine simplicity is an exercise in 'logical
grammar'; its aim is to tell us the sort of conclusions about God
which are not to be drawn. And one thing being said by it is that
God is not to be thought of (cannot be known) as something with
properties distinguishable from each other, or as something we
can conceive of as distinct from the nature we ascribe to it.

(c) Our third reply follows from this. For now I want to suggest
that the conclusion just referred to is not only intelligible but also
true. For if there is a God, then he is the Creator. And this truth
has implications which we can turn to by reflecting for a moment
on the notion of creation.

What does it mean to call God the Creator?

Everyone agrees that it means that God is the source or the
cause of all his creatures, that it is by virtue of his action that they
are there at all, that creatures are 'made' by God. By 'creatures'
here I mean everything other than God, everything that can be
significantly referred to as an individual or object.

But it is important to stress that, in the full theological sense of
the term, to say that God 'creates' is not just to say that he brings it
about that things come to be. That could be taken only to mean
that he causes them to begin to exist, while to say that God creates
is normally to be construed as saying that he is also responsible
for the existence of things since they are made to be by him for as
long as they exist. He is, as we might put it, the cause not just of
becoming but also of being.[31] Hence we find writers who have no
difficulty in supposing both that God is the Creator and that the
created world never had a beginning. As far as the theological
notion of creation goes, it is there being any world at all that

Brian Davies

matters, not just the fact that the world began to be. Thus, for instance, Leibniz in *On the Ultimate Origination of Things* (1697) treats as an irrelevant objection to theism the possibility that things have prior causes going back temporally into infinity.[32] Aquinas takes the same line in his famous teaching that, although the existence of God can be demonstrated philosophically, philosophy cannot disprove the traditional Greek thesis that matter is backwardly eternal.[33]

In the case of God, then, creating is not to be distinguished from sustaining. As H. P. Owen puts it, 'Although we find it natural to distinguish between creation and preservation they are in reality identical'.[34]

And to this one can add another point.

Causes in the world always operate in the context of the world, and they bring things about by changing the world. But the traditional notion of creation rules this out in the case of God. For it asserts that God is the cause of the existence of everything apart from himself. It also states that creation is out of nothing (*ex nihilo*). In that case it follows that creation (God's creating) is not essentially a matter of change. For there is no pre-existing material to be altered by it. As Geach has noted, this can be represented in formal terms and by means of the apparatus of modern logic. We may insert an existential quantifier (i.e. (E), meaning 'For some —') to bind the 'x' in 'God brought it about that x is an A' in two different ways. (I) God brought it about that (Ex) (x is an A) (i.e. God brought it about that, for some x, x is an A). (II) (Ex) (God brought it about that x is an A) (i.e. For some x, God brought it about that x is an A). (II) implies that God makes into an A some entity presupposed to his action. But (I) does not. And we express the supposition of God's creating an A by conjoining (I) with the negation of (II) for some suitable interpretation of 'A'.[35]

So to say that God exists is to say that there is a Creator who, for as long as his creation exists, is the cause of its being, but not by modification of anything. As one might also put it, the continued existence of anything other than God depends on God as a causal agent, but not as one who causes by acting on anything. God, so we might say, cannot make any difference to anything.[36] And this will not be because he is feeble or distant. It will be because he is present to everything as making it to be for as long as it exists.

But what now follows from this? If we are working within the framework of the doctrine of creation, what might we deduce about God *qua* Creator?

To begin with, of course, we will have to deny that God is something bodily. Otherwise he will simply be part of the world

60

the existence of which is said to depend on him in terms of the doctrine of creation.

This, in turn, means that God cannot be comprehensible in terms of what Aristotle meant by 'genus' and 'species'. God cannot be classified as a member of the world; he will be no possible object of research for biologists, zoologists, physicists and chemists.

Nor can he share with things in the world certain of their essential features. He cannot, for instance, be confined in a space, for that presupposes bodily existence and location. Nor can he be something changing or changeable, where 'change' is ascribable to a thing precisely in virtue of its materiality.

So God cannot move around. Nor can he be altered in other ways that depend on or involve bodily changes. He cannot, in fact, be *altered* by anything.[37] To be altered by something is to be on the receiving end of the causal operation of something. It is to be passive to the action of something else. Yet if God is the cause of his creatures being there at all, he cannot be like that. All of God's creatures will be God's effects in that their whole reality will derive from him and will spring from him as making it to be. In this sense the causal relationship between God and creatures must be asymmetrical. In this sense God cannot be altered by anything.

But not only that. For, in spite of what I said earlier, we can also deny that God is an individual.

By this I do not mean that God is in no sense a subject or an agent. I am not denying the reality of God. But suppose one concentrates on the sense of individual (arguably its most common sense) according to which to call something an individual is to imply that there could always be another of the same kind. In that case, so I am arguing, we would be right to deny that God is an individual. We can deny that he can be thought of as sharing a nature with other things.

For how do we distinguish between individuals sharing a nature? How, for example, do we distinguish between one dog and another?

We cannot, to begin with, distinguish between them in terms of their nature as dogs. Their being canine is something they share. They are dogs in precisely the same sense and we cannot appeal to this fact as a means of distinguishing between them.

But nor can we appeal to what Scholastic writers would have called their accidental attributes – differences which can serve to help us distinguish between things of a kind without putting them into different kinds. I mean, for example, that we cannot distinguish between Fido and Rover by noting that one of them has brown hair and the other has black hair, or that one is in the kennel and the other in the field. For to say that is already to presuppose that we have two and not one, that we have *one* and the *other*. It may indeed be that one dog is brown and the other is black. But such differences cannot make the two dogs to be two. The two dogs could not have these varied fortunes if they were not already distinct.

So how do we distinguish between one and another of the same kind of thing? The question is a hard one, but what seems to be going on, I suggest, is that we distinguish between individuals in the world by pointing to them somehow. In the end, as it seems to me, we distinguish between Fido and Rover not just by describing them (by saying what they are by nature or by saying what they look like exactly or where in fact they are and so on) but by simply recognizing that Fido is *this* thing and Rover is *that* thing, that Fido can be located by nodding at *this* parcel of matter, and Rover by nodding at *that* one. 'What makes it one rather than the other of a pair of identical twins that you are in love with? Certainly not some specification blueprinted in your mind; it may be no more than this: it was one of them and not the other that you have met. The theorist may gesture to the description "the one I have met" but can give no explanation for the impossibility of its being outweighed by other descriptions which may have been acquired as a result of error and which may in fact happen to fit the other, unmet, twin. If God had looked into your mind, he would not have seen there with whom you were in love, and of whom you were thinking.'[38]

In other words, we distinguish between individuals in the world because they are material or because they exist in a context of materiality. In this sense to understand something as an individual is to understand it as part of the material world. And in this sense we can deny that God is an individual. For if God is the Creator *ex nihilo*, then, as we have seen, he cannot be anything material.[39]

Another way of putting it is to say that *who* God is cannot be something different from *what* God is. John and Mary are both human beings. But John is not Mary and Mary is not John. They are individual people. And though they are human they do not, as individuals, constitute human nature. Along with many others, they exemplify it. Suppose we express this by saying that they are not as individuals the same as their common nature, that who they are and what they are can be distinguished. Then, so I am arguing, if God is in no way material, who he is and what he is are not distinguishable. We cannot get a purchase on the notion of a class of Gods. In terms of the doctrine of creation, 'God', so we may say, is not the name of any class at all. It has to be construed as the name of a nature, as analogous, that is, to 'Man' and 'Horse' in assertions like 'Man is a rational animal' and 'The horse is a quadruped'.

And to all of this one can add something else. For if everything other than God owes its existence to him, then God owes his existence to nothing. He is underived. If he exists, he is also underivable, for if he could owe his existence to something not himself that thing would have to exist independently of him. And that can be expressed by saying that God and his existence are identical. This is something which it makes sense to say even allowing for the sort of considerations about existence, properties and so on noted earlier. Maybe it is true that existence is not something subsistent. Maybe it is no distinctive property. But if there being a thing depends on its being created (if the existence of x derives from what is not x as creatures are said to derive from God), then the thing and its existence can be distinguished simply on the ground that what the thing is will not suffice to secure its being there. And, by the same token, God can be distinguished from it by saying that this cannot be true with reference to him, or that what he is and the fact that he is are not distinguishable. For if such were not the case, then he too would be created. He too would be such that in the sense just noted he and his existence could be distinguished.

In other words, if we concede the doctrine of creation, there is a case for saying that statements like 'God is his own being' or 'God is subsistent existence itself' are perfectly in order even though at one level they can be challenged. They will serve to remind us that we cannot think of God as something which depends for its existence on the activity of anything outside itself, that God is uncreated and uncreateable.

That, it seems to me, is what Aquinas wants to say. In denying that in God there is *compositio* of *essentia* and *esse* he makes three points in the *Summa Theologiae*. First, he says, the existence of God cannot be 'externally caused'. Second, there is no potentiality in God (i.e. he cannot be changed or produced by anything). Third, God is the 'primary existent' (*primum ens*, the ultimate or first cause of creatures).[40] The upshot would seem to be that, according to Aquinas, to say that God is *esse* is not to assert an identity statement comparable to assertions like 'John Smith is really Bill Jones'. What it seems to be is what, as I have noted, Aquinas says that the whole of his doctrine of divine simplicity is

– an account of what God is not. What it says is that God is neither made to be by anything nor able to be made by anything. And, in spite of what writers like Penelhum argue, this is not to hold that the fact of God's existence is deducible from his nature. The second thesis here is a positive one, while Aquinas's, it seems, is negative. Apart from that, in terms of Aquinas's thinking, if God's existence were derivable from his nature, someone could know what it is that is signified by 'God'. He could also see that it includes what is signified in saying that something exists. 'God' would be in principle definable and 'existing' could be recognized as part of its definition. Yet Aquinas rejects this view. 'God' for him is not definable since God belongs to no genus or species.[41] Even if this were not so, he says, the existence of God could still be denied without contradiction.[42] There is nothing for Aquinas in the meaning of 'God' which entails the truth of theism. According to Aquinas we do not really know what we mean when we use the term. What we can know is the world of creatures, or at least part of it. 'God' is the name given to the unknown source of this. Though that is not to say that 'God', for Aquinas, is a piece of gibberish. His position is as Herbert McCabe has expressed it. 'When we speak of God, although we know how to use our words, there is an important sense in which we do not know what they mean. Fundamentally this is because of our special ignorance of God. We know how to talk about shoes and ships because of our understanding of shoes and ships. We know how to talk about God, not because of any understanding of God, but because of what we know about creatures.'[43] That, in a nutshell, is the drift of the famous discussion of analogy and the like, *de nominibus Dei*, q.13 of the *Prima Pars*. A careful reading of it will reveal, I think, that Aquinas does not subscribe to the Ontological Argument even unofficially. Insofar as he holds that God is a 'necessary being', his point is that nothing can or does create God.[44]

(d) But now for another problem. Suppose we concede what I have been urging. Are we not still left with a decisive objection to the doctrine of divine simplicity? For will it not now be true that God is not a *person*? And if we say that God is not a person, should we not also agree with Plantinga after all? Does not the doctrine of divine simplicity leave us with something other than theism?

Well, why should it be thought that it does? If what I have been saying is cogent, the opposite is true. For what is theism if it is not belief in the existence of God the Creator? And that belief, so I have argued, leads to what can be recognized as the doctrine of divine simplicity.

In any case, must a theist agree without demur that God is indeed a person? Does he need to accept the presumption of people like Plantinga here?

There are certainly reasons for saying that to believe in the existence of God is to believe in the existence of a person. It is held, for example, that God has knowledge and will, and these are commonly and naturally associated with people. So if people are our models for persons, and if God has knowledge and will, it would seem that God is a person. That looks like a perfectly sensible thing to say.

But this kind of argument can be made to cut both ways. For people are also commonly associated with, for example, bodies and parents and food and drink and sex and society and death. Yet God is said to be above such things. He is said to be bodiless and immortal or eternal. So it also seems appropriate to deny that God is a person. If people are our models for persons, then in an obvious sense God, it would seem, is not a person. And this argument can be developed.[45]

Take, for example, the notion of knowledge. People, we might say, are essentially knowers. Something is wrong with them if they do not know things. But how does it come about that people come to know? They learn, of course. And they do so because they are things in the world on which other things in the world impinge. But God cannot be like this. He is supposed to have made the world, and he is not supposed to be part of it. So God, it would seem, just does not know as people know. And if people are our models for persons, and if this implies that God knows as people know, then God is not a person.

Or consider the question of space. People are in space. So they are here and not there, there and not here. Yet God is supposed to be everywhere, which can be taken to mean that he is also nowhere. So again the point can be pressed. If people are our models for persons, and if this implies that God is what people are, then God is not a person. For God is not anywhere, while people are always somewhere.

And so one might go on. I am not denying that God can be called a person. But it can also be said that he is not a person, not because one wishes to say that God does not exist, but because one can be readily struck by the differences between God and the paradigmatic instances of persons provided by the existence of people. If it seems obviously true that God is a person, it seems no less true that he is no such thing.

Nor does this seem something which has to be denied by those anxious to preserve what we might call an orthodox vocabulary about God. The striking fact here is that the formula 'God is a person' is by no means a traditional one. It does not occur in the Bible. It is foreign to the Fathers and to writers up to and beyond the Middle Ages. Nor does it occur in any of the creeds. In Christian circles, of course, one can appeal to the formula of the Trinity: that God is three persons in one *ousia* or *substantia*. But that formula does not say that God is a person or that he is three persons in one person.[46] It says that some persons are God.

What, in any case, would it mean to say that God is one person? It would imply that there could be two of him, that God belongs to a class, the class of persons presumably. Yet that, so I have argued, is a suggestion we can dispute. Members of classes can be individuated as examples of the class to which they belong. But how are we to think of God as individuated in this way? We may call him an individual to indicate his subsistence. We may call him an individual to indicate that he is undivided. But such ways of speaking are not now in question. The problem we face arises from the fact that God is immaterial. If he were something material, the problem would not arise. It would always be possible in principle to point to God. We could say '*That* one is God'. But when we are talking about something non-material, criteria for individuation are in an important sense lacking. What it is and its individuality are not distinguishable. And that, so it seems to me, is true in the case of God. The upshot again is that sense can be made of denying that God is a person.

—— III ——

So there is much to be said for the doctrine of divine simplicity. And this, in turn, means that there is much to be said for classical theism over and against the alternative which I referred to at the outset.

Yet this conclusion clearly raises some major questions. Classical theism, with its doctrine of divine simplicity, evidently goes with the view that God is deeply mysterious. It is an agnostic conception of divinity. If this conception is valid, therefore, how, for example, are we to account for our talk about God? Or is it that we cannot really speak of God at all? And, as many will want to ask, what about the Bible? How does classical theism fit with what the Bible says? Or is it, perhaps, that the two are incompatible?

Such are some of the problems, and I cannot hope to deal with them adequately here. Broadly speaking, however, I have four main things to say about them.

The first is that theists in general have no *a priori* need to be anxious simply because of the unknowability of God. That has been denied on the ground that 'to say that something transcends the human understanding is to say that it is unintelligible', from which it has been held to follow that 'it is impossible for a sentence both to be significant and to be about God'.[47] But there can surely be more than we can understand. And, if I am right, that is what theists are bound to concede. For it follows from the doctrine of creation, which leads in turn to the view that God is simple. And that view entails that in certain ways he is incomprehensible.

The second point is that much of what gets taken as positive assertion about God can equally (or perhaps more usefully) be read as negation. Take, for example, the classical assertion that God is wholly immutable. Is it to be read as a description of God? I should say 'No'. It can be read as saying what God is not, *and no more*. That, at any rate, is what it says on the lips of a writer like Aquinas, who on this point is often badly misconstrued, as he has been, for instance, by process theologians and the like.[48] He holds that God is changeless because God is the non-material cause of all changing beings, the ground of their *esse*.[49] That is frequently read as saying that God is static or frozen or indifferent. Then we are reminded that God is active and loving, and Aquinas is dismissed as unbiblical or un-Christian or both. But that reaction is just unfair. Aquinas's point is that whatever God's life consists in, it cannot consist in him changing in specifiable ways that creatures change. His activity and love is the activity and love of the Creator. To say this is quite different from saying that God is static and so on.[50]

The third point concerns a range of typical positive assertions about God. These, I think, can often be read as positive but inadequate. They are inadequate because they should not be thought to reflect a knowledge of God in himself. But they are positive because they do, in a sense, serve to characterize God.

First the questions of inadequacy. Take, for example, the familiar assertion that God is personal. I have no difficulty with that and I therefore presume that I am committed to saying that God, for instance, has knowledge or will. But I deny that we have a comprehension of something called the personality of God, and I deny that we should talk of God as if he were the man in the next street. Our language for what is personal (and hence our primary understanding of this) comes from our knowledge of human beings. And we ought to be struck by the difference between what it takes to be a human being and what it must take to be

God. Consider again the idea of knowing. Our personal lives as knowers are the lives of users of language who come to know as we are acted on by things in the world. But if God is the Creator, his personal life as a knower cannot be this. His knowledge cannot be that of someone tied to language, nor can it be something acquired because things have some effect on him and by doing so cause him to know. My knowledge is the knowledge of a creature. But God is what accounts for there being any creatures. And that means that though we can say that, for example, God is personal because he has knowledge, this is not to explain what he is. In this sense 'God is personal' is inadequate.

On the other hand it is a natural thing to say and, in this sense, it is true. For the language of personality is naturally applied to God. Only I think it is this not because we know what God is, but rather because we know what he cannot be and because we can sensibly express that in positive terms. God cannot be bodily by nature, nor can he be something whose action is determined by the action on him of things within the world. If that were not the case he would be part of what I mean by 'the world'. Since he is the Creator, however, we are constrained to say that he brings things about. So in this sense he must be active. How, then, can we help thinking of him except as something personal? Given that we are not to think of him as inanimate and as determined by the action on him of things within the world, what else can we say except that the language of personality is somehow appropriate in talking of him? And what do we say there if not that God is personal?

This, I think, is the proper answer to someone who feels that in speaking of God we can only be saying what he is not and that we are in no way saying what he is. There is a sense in which that conclusion is acceptable, for we talk of God with words which first apply to creatures, and these words can always be regarded as inadequate tools for talking of God because of the difference between God and creatures. But, as has often been observed, if our talk of God is simply read as an account of what God is not, then there seems no particular reason for preferring one way of speaking of him to any other, and there is also the danger of departing too radically from anything that could plausibly be called a traditional belief in God. If, for instance, to call God personal is just to say that he is not inanimate, then why not call him square since this can be read as denying that he is round? And if to call him active is just to deny that he is not active, what do we make of talk about the living God who brings things about? On my account, however, these problems do not arise. In my view we can mean what we say about God and it can matter that we apply this term to him rather than that. It is, for instance, true that God is personal and false that he is canine (though that does not mean that he cannot be significantly spoken of as a dog).

On the other hand, in saying what God is we are not comprehending him. The inadequacy of our ways of describing him is as much a fact about them as their truth. We can, if you like, say more about God than we can mean. That, I think, is the point of those who hold that apophatic theology (negative theology) and cataphatic theology (positive theology) are really two sides of a single coin.[51] Both succeed in saying something because each complements the other.

So I am saying that we can speak truly about God. But I am also saying that there is a sense in which we do not know what he is, what the word 'God' stands for. And, coming now to my final point, I have to add that this view seems to me perfectly consistent with respect to the biblical tradition.

This, of course, is widely denied. The God of the Bible is not the God of classical theism, and so on. And, of course, there is something in that. But what is the biblical God if he is not the inscrutable and mysterious Creator of all things beside whom there is no god and whose ways are truly hidden? 'I am the Lord, and there is no other. . . . To whom will you liken me and make me equal, and compare me, that we may be alike?' Certainly the biblical God is spoken of in the Bible as if he were a creature. But he is also spoken of differently.[52] And a significant thing to note here is the sheer range of the resulting imagery. If my line is right, you would expect to find biblical writers revelling in a myriad of conflicting images for God. And that is just what you do find. God in the Bible is everything from a despotic king to a pregnant woman. He is a father and judge, but also an eagle, a lamb, and a case of dry-rot. And if all that is not a mandate for a strong doctrine of God's transcendence, I do not know what it is.

The reply may be that it is positive description of what God is really like. But I hope it will be clear that I need not dispute that. Nor do I wish to deny that the Bible talks of God in concrete terms and that we should do so too. We can cheerfully concede that God is a pregnant woman because nobody will be misled into looking for her husband. The more concrete our images for God, the less they will be taken as fully adequate and the more they can be allowed to work on us and help us to develop a doctrine of God. But if someone says that these images are the end of the story, then he has a curious way of reading the Bible. He may insist that there is still an enormous gulf between the God of classical theism and the God of the Bible since the former is static and remote while the latter is dynamic and involved. But that seems to me an awful misreading of classical theism. As I have indicated with respect to Aquinas, it is not the view of classical theism that God is static. According to classical theism God is active everywhere and in everything precisely because he is the Creator of everywhere and everything and because this is to be distinguished from him observing, interfering, and so on. Aquinas certainly denies that God is passive with respect to the world, so he denies that God can learn from the world or have it as an object of experience in the empiricist's sense. He also denies that God can be affected by the world. But this does not entail that God, for Aquinas, is not involved. On the contrary, for writers like him God is more involved with things than any created thing can be with another. This is because on their view God does not stand outside creation as an entity over and against his creatures. He is not *other* to creatures as they are to each other.[53]

For some people this view will still seem a long way from what needs to be said about God. It will be argued that God is loving and that stress on him being the Creator fails to allow for this fact. But that also seems to me wrong. If to love means to be moved by passion as we can sometimes be when we love, then I should certainly agree that God cannot love. We will not understand the love of God by taking as our paradigm the case of the romantic lover. Yet it is false that love must involve passion. As Christians have recognized for centuries, it can just as well be thought of as a matter of willing what is good for people. And, for classical theists, God certainly does that.

—— IV ——

My conclusion, then, is that we have reason for being agnostic about God, in spite of our need to try to contain him in words, and in spite of the fact that what we say about God can be true and justifiable. *De Deo non possumus scire quid sit.* Here, so it seems to me, we can still learn something from classical theists like Aquinas, though it ought to be emphasized that with respect to our ignorance about God there is nothing at bottom original in what he says. It is orthodox Catholic doctrine. Hence, for example, according to Lateran IV, God is 'eternal, infinite and unchangeable, incomprehensible, almighty and ineffable . . . one highest incomprehensible and ineffable reality'. According to Vatican I, God is 'incomprehensible' and 'ineffably exalted above all things that exist or can be conceived besides him'. Stress on divine ineffability is as much a patristic legacy as anything else. According, for instance, to Justin Martyr, 'There is no one who can give a name to the ineffable God, and if anyone dares to say that there is one, he suffers from an incurable madness'.[54] Elsewhere Justin says something very similar to what I take myself to be saying. 'Anyone who might be able to impose a name on God', he writes, 'would have to be more primordial than God himself. Father, God, Creator, Lord, Master – these are not precisely proper names; the basis for their application to God lies in his gifts and works. . . . The style of address "God" is not a proper name, but rather is a sort of judgement that lies at the core of the human being about a state of affairs that has no other explanation ready to hand.'[55]

That, I think, is really Aquinas's view. It is in this sense that he is an agnostic. But his variety of agnosticism is also, of course, different from that of the usual secular kind. 'While modern agnosticism says simply, "We do not know, and the universe is a mysterious riddle", a Thomist says "We do not know what the answer is, but we do know that there is a mystery behind it all which we do not know, and if there were not, there would not even be a riddle. This Unknown we call *God*. If there were no God, there would be no universe to be mysterious, and nobody to be mystified".'[56]

NOTES

1 Cf. Richard Swinburne, *The Coherence of Theism* (Oxford, 1977, p. 1 and *passim*.
2 For a brief exposition of classical theism, see H. P. Owen, *Concepts of Deity* (London, 1971), chapter 1. In this paper I concentrate on Aquinas as an example of a classical theist.
3 *Summa Theologiae*, Ia, 1, 7 ad 1.
4 *Summa Theologiae*, Ia, introduction to q.3.
5 *Proslogion* XII and XVIII, trans. M. J. Charlesworth, *St Anselm's Proslogion* (Oxford, 1965).
5a *Summa Theologiae*, Ia, 13, 1.
6 Edmund Hill, *The Mystery of the Trinity* (London, 1985), p. 55.
7 Ronald H. Nash, *The Concept of God* (Grand Rapids, Michigan, 1983), pp. 95f. The quotation from Brunner comes from *The Christian Doctrine of God* (Philadelphia, 1950), p. 294.
8 Alvin Plantinga, *Does God Have A Nature?* (Milwaukee, 1980).
9 Plantinga, p. 47.
10 *Ibid.*

11 *Ibid.*
12 Cf. Herbert McCabe OP, 'God: I – Creation', *New Blackfriars* 61 (1980), p. 412; repr. in *God Matters* (London, 1987), chapter 1, p. 6. Cf. my *An Introduction to the Philosophy of Religion* (Oxford, 1982), pp. 46f.
13 This seems to be true both with respect to believers and with respect to unbelievers. Cf. Richard Swinburne, *The Coherence of Theism*, pp. 89ff. and J. L. Mackie, *The Miracle of Theism* (Oxford, 1982), chapter 12.
14 Robin Attfield, 'The Individuality of God', *Sophia* X (1971), p. 20. Cf. Robin Attfield, 'The Lord is God: There is No Other', *Religious Studies* 13 (1977); 'How Not To Undermine Theology', *New Blackfriars* 61 (1980).
15 Robin Attfield, *God and the Secular* (Cardiff, 1978), p. 165.
16 *Summa Theologiae*, Ia, 3, 4 and *passim*.
17 This is a very rough account of an approach associated with writers such as Frege and Russell. For a careful attempt to expound it see C. J. F. Williams, *What Is Existence* (Oxford, 1981). I am much indebted to this excellent book.
18 Cf. *Summa Theologiae*, Ia, 2, 1.
19 There is some reason to doubt that this is actually what Anselm did think. For some discussion of this matter one might consult D. P. Henry, *Medieval Logic and Metaphysics* (London, 1972).
20 Terence Penelhum, 'Divine Necessity', *Mind* 69 (1960), repr. in *The Philosophy of Religion*, ed. Basil Mitchell (Oxford, 1971). I quote from Mitchell's text, pp. 184f.
21 Cf. *Summa Theologiae*, Ia, 39, 5 ad 5.
22 Cf. *Summa Theologiae*, Ia, 3, 3.
23 *An. Post.* 92b, 13–14.
24 For more precision on all of this see Williams, *op. cit.*, chapter 3.
25 Gottlob Frege, *The Foundations of Arithmetic*, trans. J. L. Austin (Oxford, 1980), p. 59.
26 Frege, p. 65. 'In this respect existence is analogous to number. Affirmation of existence is in fact nothing but denial of the number nought.'
27 Williams, *op. cit.*, pp. 54f.
28 Frege, p. 64.
29 G. E. M. Anscombe and P. T. Geach, *Three Philosophers* (Oxford, 1973), p. 122. Cf. P. T. Geach, 'Form and Existence' in *God and the Soul* (London, 1969), pp. 49f.
30 David Burrell, *Aquinas, God and Action* (London and Henley, 1979); Victor White, *God the Unknown* (London, 1956); Josef Pieper, *The Silence of Saint Thomas*, trans. John Murray and Daniel O'Connor (Chicago, 1965).
31 Cf. *Summa Theologiae*, 45. Cf. James Ross, 'Creation', *The Journal of Philosophy* 77 (1980).
32 *Leibniz: Philosophical Writings*, ed. G. H. R. Parkinson (London and Toronto, 1973), p. 136.
33 *De aeternitate mundi contra murmurantes.* For an exposition and discus-

sion of some classical discussions of this matter see Richard Sorabji, *Time, Creation and the Continuum* (London, 1983).

34 H. P. Owen, *Christian Theism: A Study in its Basic Principles* (Edinburgh, 1984), p. 9.

35 P. T. Geach, 'Causality and Creation' in *God and the Soul*, p. 83.

36 It might be replied that God makes a difference to things since he can intervene. But there is a sense in which this is false. For intervention presupposes absence, and, given the notion of creation, it seems true to say that God is never absent from things.

37 By alteration here I am thinking of what Geach alludes to as 'real' change as opposed to 'Cambridge' change. See P. T. Geach, 'God's Relation to the World' in *Logic Matters* (Oxford, 1972), pp. 321f.

38 Gareth Evans, 'The Causal Theory of Names' in *Collected Papers* (Oxford, 1985), pp. 5f.

39 This does not, I think, entail that nothing material can be divine. So I am not to be taken as denying doctrines such as the doctrine of the Incarnation. For some of my views on the Incarnation see my *Thinking About God* (London, 1985), chapter 10. I should also note here that what I am saying does not, I think, entail that there can be no non-material individuals, e.g. angels. My point is that even if there are such things, we cannot pick them out as such as we can pick out things like Fido and Rover.

40 *Summa Theologiae*, Ia, 3, 4.

41 *Summa Theologiae*, Ia, 3, 5.

42 *Summa Theologiae*, Ia, 2, 1.

43 *Summa Theologiae*, Blackfriars ed. (London and New York), vol. 3, trans. Herbert McCabe OP (1964), Appendix 3 ('Signifying Imperfectly'), p. 104.

44 In accusing Aquinas of committing the error involved in the Ontological Argument Penelhum is arguing that, for Aquinas, God is a necessary being in the sense of being a logically necessary being, i.e. a being the existence of which is entailed by its definition. For the meaning of 'necessary being' in Aquinas see Patterson Brown, 'St Thomas' Doctrine of Necessary Being', *The Philosophical Review* LXXIII (1964).

45 It has been effectively developed in recent years by philosophers claiming to be particularly influenced by Wittgenstein. These philosophers are often accused of untraditional teachings about God, but what they say is often quite near to the position of orthodox classical theologians. With respect to such matters, see Fergus Kerr, *Theology After Wittgenstein* (Oxford, 1986).

46 Some accounts of the Trinity quaintly take it to say something very like this. See David Brown, *The Divine Trinity* (London, 1985) and the review of this book by Nicholas Lash in *The Times* (2 November 1985).

47 A. J. Ayer, *Language, Truth and Logic* (Harmondsworth, Middx, 1971), p. 156.

48 I am thinking here of writers such as Charles Hartshorne and Jürgen Moltmann. Cf. Charles Hartshorne, *The Logic of Perfection* (La Salle,

Ill., 1962); Jürgen Moltmann, *The Trinity and the Kingdom of God* (London, 1981).

49 Cf. *Summa Theologiae*, Ia, 9 and 10.

50 As Herbert McCabe argues in 'The Involvement of God', *New Blackfriars* 66 (1985); repr. as chapter 4 of *God Matters* (London, 1987).

51 This is suggested by Andrew Louth in *The Origins of the Christian Mystical Tradition* (Oxford, 1981), p. 178.

52 Isaiah 45:6–7; 46:5. Biblical traditions to the effect that God can be known while he remains hidden are interestingly explored by Robert Davidson in *The Courage to Doubt* (London, 1983).

53 Herbert McCabe, 'The Involvement of God', p. 470 (*God Matters*, p. 46).

54 I *Apol.* 61.

55 II *Apol.* 6.

56 Victor White, *God the Unknown*, pp. 18f.

4

DISTINGUISHING GOD FROM THE WORLD

David B. Burrell CSC

Two features which have shaped philosophical considerations of divinity in Jewish, Christian, and Muslim worlds since the beginnings of such reflection – God's simpleness and God's eternity – have recently been subject to severe questioning. An entire theological movement (so-called 'process theology') has developed to offer an alternative construction of divinity, while an increasing number of philosophers of religion simply proceed as though these features (which are 'formal features') no longer constrained discourse about divinity.[1] While the arguments which theologians offer for rejecting the 'classical doctrine' differ somewhat in perspective from those which philosophers offer for avoiding the 'Anselmian conception' of divinity, there is significant overlap between the two groups.[2]

I shall focus here on the forms of argument philosophers normally adduce for eschewing divine eternity and simpleness, and I shall try to show how alternative routes inevitably jeopardize the cardinal teaching of Jewish, Christian, and Muslim traditions, that of creation. (I have already shown [see note 1 below] how theological alternatives in fact replace creation with a far weaker notion of *creativity* borrowed from Whitehead; I shall merely state here that the tendency which some forms of Christianity have of virtually eclipsing creation by redemption can only weaken the import of redemption itself.) The direction of my constructive argument, then, shows how philosophical theology must answer not only to criteria of consistency but also do justice to practices and beliefs shared in living religious traditions, much as philosophers of science construct models of explanation with a keen eye to laboratory practice. The reference to three distinct 'monotheistic' traditions is meant to offer converging and mutually corroborative testimony, as shall be seen, and not to propose a syncretic common faith.[3]

Philosophers have come to be persuaded that it is impossible to link an eternal God with temporal events (here their arguments often overlap with those brought forward by 'process theologians'), and that the very notion of divine simplicity is freighted with incoherence. Yet the arguments which have persuaded so many of them display little understanding of the roots of the notions being disputed as they were elaborated in the service of the three traditions referred to above. Those dealing with divine eternity invariably settle for its abstract component – *timelessness* – without asking themselves whether that dimension captures the traditional sense of *eternity*.[4] Two recent articles by Norman Kretzmann and Eleanore Stump (on 'Eternity' and 'Absolute Simplicity') can be extremely useful in confronting this current myopia. Each offers constructive ways of recovering the tradition and responding to certain consequences of the traditional notions which many have judged should invalidate them.[5] While indebted to their treatment, I propose to undergird a wider endeavour to understand the central role played by *simpleness* and *eternity* in doing philosophical theology, by showing how these formal features secure 'the distinction' of God from the world.[6]

Without a clear philosophical means of distinguishing God from the world, the tendency of all discourse about divinity is to deliver a God who is the 'biggest thing around'. That such is the upshot of much current philosophy of religion cannot be doubted; that it stems from overlooking the crucial role of these 'formal features' is the burden of this article. The wary will note that talking about a God distinct from the world will involve one inevitably in analogical forms of speech, yet the aversion many philosophers show to this dimension of our discourse can only reflect an oversight of recent explorations of this domain.[7] Or it may stem from an overpowering concern for clear-cut meaning which issues in treatments of God in which little care is taken to do justice to the notion of God as 'the creator of heaven and earth'. If this be the case, the current surge of interest in philosophy of religion may ill serve religion, since (adapting an observation of Aquinas) misleading conceptions of matters divine on the part of believers can only subject the faith to ridicule.[8] Lest my own efforts seem overly pretentious, I am not promising an adequate response to the objections raised to God's eternity and simpleness. I am trying to make the case for grappling with those objections more honestly and directly, after the manner of Kretzmann and Stump, in an effort to capture the role these formal features play in philosophical theology. For disregarding or overlooking the role risks failing to speak of God at all.

INNER CONNECTION OF ETERNITY WITH SIMPLENESS

I have consistently referred to *simpleness* and *eternity* as 'formal features' of divinity, thereby marking them off from attributes or characteristics. It is like determining whether to treat light as particles or waves, after which one may ask about the velocity of the particles or the length of the waves; or whether to adopt an 'event' or a 'substance' ontology. Formal features concern our manner of locating the subject for characterization, and hence belong to a stage prior to considering attributes as such – a stage which will in part determine which attributes are relevant and certainly how they are to be attributed to the subject in question. (Or if one remains wedded to an undiscriminating use of 'property', these would be *ur*-properties.) The order of Aquinas' treatment in the *Summa Theologiae* clearly distinguishes those features the psalmist attributes to God from these formal ones, thereby making a semantic and ontological distinction among what many would indiscriminately call 'divine attributes'.[9] It is my contention, moreover, that it is the formal features which secure the proper distinction of God from the world, thus determining the kind of being (so to speak) said to be just and merciful, and hence establishing critical modifications in those attributes. This complex assertion will be unravelled as we proceed. In short, God's simpleness and God's eternity are part of what assures us we are talking about divinity.

How so? Aquinas' treatment is illustrative here, the more so as one realizes how much he is resuming developments in Muslim and Jewish philosophical theology which preceded him.[10] The first step is to articulate a nominal definition of God suitable to all three traditions: 'beginning and end of all things and of rational creatures especially' (ST, Ia IIae, intro). While this formula would be compatible with an emanationist view like Avicenna's, Aquinas will develop it in an unmistakably creationist manner, following Maimonides.[11] A first step in that direction is to note an immediate consequence of the formula itself: the One who begins and is the end of all things is *not* one of those things. Or as Aquinas put it, 'God does not belong to the genus of substance' (ST, Ia, 3, 5, 1). God is not one of the items in the world of which God is the origin. Avicenna expressed this distinction in terms of *necessary* and *possible* beings, where the First alone exists 'by its essence' (and is hence *necessary*) while everything else – *possible* in itself – derives its existence from the First.[12] Aquinas prefers to mark the distinction by separating what is utterly without composition (or 'simple') from everything else, which is *composed* of essence and *esse* (or existence). The idea for such a division came to him from Avicenna, but his development of it assures a clear creation perspective by insisting that the 'proper effect' of the simple One is the to-be (*esse*) of the cosmos. So the formal feature of divine simpleness is intended to distinguish God from everything else – God's creation. That is, divine simpleness assures God's distinction from 'all things' as well as providing the ground for asserting the gratuity of creation.

What then can *simpleness* mean? And why must one say that God is simple? To reply to the second question first: because we have no other way of assuring ourselves that we are talking about the One from whom all things come. What distinguishes divinity from all that is not divine, in such a way as to be able to characterize that One as the source of all the rest, must have to do with the *nature* of the subject in question and not simply its *attributes*. It will not do to inquire into God's knowing, willing, or moral character without first asking what sort of thing it is to which we are attributing knowledge and will and moral character. The price one pays for adopting such a short-cut is uncritically to presume similarities between God and humans, as in the opener: 'assuming God to be a person . . .'.[13] Or one presumes a univocal understanding of powers (or properties) like knowing and willing, as though the world consisted of such properties, shared by God and creatures according to more or less. Both presumptions can be found in current philosophy of religion, presumably embodying a fear that admitting analogical discourse leaves us conceptually at sea. Yet a vague notion of similarity, coupled with strategic avowals of difference (at least in degree) hardly represents a critical approach to the central issue: the distinction of God (creator) from the world (creation).

How does *simpleness* secure that distinction? To answer this question we must articulate what *simpleness* means. I have noted that Aquinas' elaboration of divine simpleness replaced a distinction which Avicenna had drawn across the field of being (what is) between that which is necessary in itself and that which is possible in itself (and made necessary – in another sense – by another). What is 'necessary in itself' is so because it exists 'by its essence' (*bi-thatihi*). Aware as he was of the many senses of the term 'necessary', Aquinas eschewed using that term as the primary one distinguishing God from all that is not God, preferring to articulate Avicenna's distinction in terms borrowed from him as well: essence and existence (*esse*).[14] What gives divinity the necessity peculiar to it is the formal fact that God's nature is nothing other than its own existence: to be divine is (simply) to-be. That is what *simpleness* means for Aquinas, at any rate, who uses it principally and essentially (*primo et per se*) of God alone (ST, Ia, 3, 7).

There is no doubt that Aquinas' treatment is something of a seamless robe, for one must at least acknowledge the possibility of conceiving existence (*esse*) as he does, on the analogy of act or activity, to allow that such a characterization could capture what we mean by divinity, however remotely or 'formally'. I shall indicate ways in which that can be made plausible when I treat of *simpleness* in relation to creation. For now, some tentative concessions need to be made to allow the main lines of the argument to be sketched out.

So simple a One would exist without needing a cause of its existing, and its being simple would not be a merely negative feature, like lacking parts. Indeed this way of characterizing divine simpleness makes it equivalent to *aseity*, yet goes on to spell that out in terms of its *existing* 'by its essence' (*per se*). Other things that one would be inclined to call *necessary* may therefore be usefully characterized as 'pertaining to every possible world', yet such considerations remain conceptual. Were such things actually to exist as part of *this* world, then they would either pertain to its structure, and so enjoy the simpleness proper to formal structure without a claim to separate existence, or they would be brought into existence, and in that sense be 'composed'. (Aquinas presumed the heavenly bodies and angels to be such objects, so he used his distinction of essence from existence to distinguish them from divinity while acknowledging their everlasting status.)

It should be becoming clear how much Aquinas' specific articulation of divine simpleness as the identity of God's essence with the divine act of existing seems tailored to a characterization of God as creator: the One who bestows existence. Let us first, however, see how *eternity* emerges from simpleness so conceived, by way of necessary implication and as an articulation of the sense of *simpleness* developing here.

This One whose essence is simply to-be cannot be limited by quantity (since it is not bodily) nor by genus or species, since its essence – to-be – 'overflows' both genus and species. So what is simple is also unlimited or, more traditionally, infinite. Nor can such a one be temporal, since it does not come to be, and so is not subject to motion or change, of which time is the measure. So what is simple must be beyond change – not unmoving, as the traditional term 'immutable' is often taken to mean, but beyond the categories of *kinesis* or of *stasis*. (Such an avowal, however necessary as a consequence, will require a notion of *activity* which is not motion if it is to be plausible – again the seamless-garment aspect of this treatment of divine simpleness.)

We have not quite concluded, however, to God's eternity, but only to the fact that divinity, to be the 'beginning and end of all things', must lie beyond change. What does eternity add to this? Boethius' classic definition suggests the answer: 'the possession all-at-once (*tota simul*) of unending *life*'. Whatever is eternal, in the full-blooded sense in which that is intended when claimed as a formal feature of divinity, must be alive – existing or actual, if you will – and not merely the sort of thing to which temporal becoming is irrelevant, as it is to mathematics.[15] God's eternity, then, specifies the modality proper to an activity which is not a movement, and it is this dimension which the variant 'timeless' omits. If God's eternity entails *timelessness*, as derived via the argument that divinity lies beyond becoming, it remains the case that the timelessness entailed is *not* what we associate with mathematical entities or truths. And since 'timeless' is inevitably closely connected with such things as these, to which becoming is irrelevant, it seems at least rhetorically misleading to speak of God as timeless, as it is certainly inaccurate to equate eternity with timelessness.

So God's eternity, on this account, also prepares the way for asserting the One to be creator, as it underscores the fact that God's nature is simply to-be, by recalling that whatever simply is must lie beyond the realm of becoming, of cause-and-effect, and so be eternally. Aquinas' pregnant analogy: 'as time measures becoming, so eternity measures to-be (*esse*)' (Ia, 10, 4, 3), opens the treatment to the act of creation, for the 'proper effect' of what acts in this eternal fashion will be the to-be (*esse*) of things (Ia, 8, 1; 45, 5). So the activity of the eternal One will be conceived, not by analogy with timeless entities impervious to time, but in terms of what makes the world to be. And since 'what is' is *now*, the One who makes things to be will be primarily and essentially (*primo et per se*) present. The metaphor of *presence* can be a useful one to flesh out this analogy to present existence.[16]

Finally, I have spoken throughout of 'the One'. For the conception of divine simpleness which I have been elaborating not only grounds the distinction of God from the world, but also articulates the faith of those religious traditions which have embodied that distinction in a doctrine of creation – that God is one. And not merely in the sense that there happens not to be another answering to the specifications of divinity, as is the case with our sun, but in the sense that this notion of divinity entails uniqueness.

Although the assertion that God is one seems to go without saying since the Athenian philosophers undermined the Acropolis, it remains doubtful (at least to me) whether treatments of God which avoid securing the nature of their subject can do anything more than *presume* there to be but one God. The exposition of divine simpleness offered here is presented as a challenge to anyone purporting to speak of God when treating, say, of divine knowledge. If divinity, and with it the distinction of God from the world, be not secured in some fashion such as this, how will we know we are treating of God? And if not this way, what are the alternatives?

DIFFICULTIES WITH ETERNITY

The difficulties which philosophers have found with eternity are two-fold: (1) arriving at a proper conception of an eternal entity, and (2) relating such a being to temporal affairs. The first difficulty shows up immediately in our language, which appears to be irremediably tensed. Attempts to construct a tenseless verb inevitably founder on relating the action depicted to what is happening now, and sacrificing all connection with the token-reflexive 'now' leaves one with a thoroughly abstract form of discourse – since whatever happens, happens now. Yet it must also be noted that these difficulties have arisen in relation to a purportedly *timeless* discourse. What would happen were one to discriminate God's eternity from timelessness, in the manner suggested?

This eternal being could hardly be thought of as one to which temporal occurrences were irrelevant, since they exist by virtue of its eternal to-be. It follows, of course, that there is only one such – God – and that such a One, as the source of the existence proper to each temporal existent, would better be imagined *inside* the becoming which time measures than *outside* it. There is, to be sure, a specific sense in which the eternal One is timeless (or 'outside time') as well, namely the fact that the present tense applied to such a one never becomes the past, as it does with everything else. So, while there has to have been a first moment in time marking the beginning of the created universe, we cannot properly say that God *created* the world but that God *creates* the world. (The Creed sidesteps this issue nicely by using the noun instead: 'We believe in one God ... Creator of heaven and earth ...'.) Since the reference point, however, is normally not the divine action but its effect, religious language can properly speak of 'the great deeds God has done on behalf of God's own people'.

It is no less true, of course, that *we* cannot speak a language whose present never becomes past, any more than we could function with an idiom pretending to be tenseless. So attempting to construct such a language would produce countless puzzles, as we tried to make it do what our tensed discourse does. Yet there is no need to construct a language for God, but only to draw attention to strategic disanalogies with our tensed discourse. Kretzmann and Stump have been helpful in assembling reminders for discussions of the way God knows what will happen. Often misleadingly referred to as 'the future', as though there were a determinate scenario waiting in the wings, the object of God's knowing what will be the case has spawned more than philosophical puzzles, in provoking acerbic theological controversies. The very thought that God knows what I will do can evoke a frisson of terror, as well, in the religious soul.

Much current discussion of God's knowledge concentrates on whether and how God knows 'the future' without pausing to reflect on the ambiguities in that term – like the hapless soul who gave up a prestigious post for a future one (which 'failed to materialize', as we say). The presumption of a determinate scenario for what the case will be appears to subserve a characteristic form of argument. God must know everything that is the case, for divine omniscience permits no surprises. Cast in terms of knowing which propositions are true, along with the corollary that once something is true, it is timelessly true, God is then said to know what will take place since omniscience requires that God know which side of a disjunction is true, lest God be surprised.

The switch to propositions allows one to let go of one's tenses here, giving the discourse its scrambled air, which becomes further confused as 'true propositions' seem to refer only indirectly to what *is* the case. As a result of these manoeuvres, one can sidestep Aristotle's quandary over future contingent events – a discussion which shaped Aquinas' treatment of the matter. Aristotle, for whom a true statement asserts what is the case, acknowledges sufficient determinacy regarding what might happen to offer a general description with its negation, insisting that one or the other would indeed be the case (the law of bivalence). But no one can know whether the sea battle will occur tomorrow or not (which of the disjuncts 'is' the true one), until it occurs. We can predict, of course, as a BBC spokesman acknowledged in the midst of a news blackout in the Falklands crisis: 'there will have been casualties'. But predictions are not statements. So strictly speaking, no one can know what will take place, so long as we keep true assertion linked to fact. Not even God can, concurs Aquinas, since 'the future' does not yet exist, and what does not exist is not there to be known (Ia, 14, 13).

Holding on to one's tenses, then, seems to be linked closely with keeping true discourse tied to states of affairs: what *is* the case. Those who forgo both, as do proponents of 'middle knowledge', seem caught in a stranger paradox than the one at least some of them thought they were escaping. The paradox they would avoid is the one the wary reader will have associated with Aquinas: since God cannot know what *will* happen, but must know everything, all that was, is, or will be must be present to God eternally. The logic is impeccable, since only what *is* the case can be known to be the case, but one is at a loss to say just how what has not yet happened can be *present* to God. We are faced with an equivocation on 'present' which can be resolved only by articulating the sense proper to an eternal present, plus its relation to the present of tensed discourse – 'what *is* the case' – both of which lie quite beyond one whose discourse is tied to tenses.

How could proponents of 'middle knowledge' be caught in a paradox stranger than this one? Because their presumption of a determinate scenario also requires that what will be the case be present to divine knowledge, yet be so without benefit of the strategic disanalogies with tensed discourse which accompany asserting God to be eternal. As a result, God can be said to know beforehand what the case will be, since God knows which of each pairs of disjuncts is true. But the last 'is' must be a timeless one, so God can be said to know 'the future' even though what God knows has not yet taken place. Chary of a resolution involving an eternity which lies beyond our capacity properly to conceive, they need to rely nevertheless on a notion of *timelessness* which allows them to state something quite inconceivable: namely, *what I will do before I have done it*. Eternity, as one of the terms in the earlier paradox, at least lies *beyond* our powers of conception; while a timeless affirmation of the free actions of an actual subject *while* that subject is yet a possibility defies reason: *de posse ad esse non valet illatio*.[17]

By avoiding characterizing divinity in those ways which assure its distinction from the world and hence entail divine eternity, or else by denying such a formal feature in favour of an everlasting God in time, the claims of divine omniscience have nonetheless forced these philosophers into admitting into divine knowing a quality of timelessness akin to eternity, and also to create an object of knowledge 'midway between' what is actual and what is merely possible. Hence the term 'middle knowledge'. It should be clear how such a treatment prefers propositions to statements

regarding what is the case, so that it can speak of true propositions abstracted from what the case *is*. If proponents of divine
eternity equate that condition with timelessness, then the difference between the two positions may be largely tactical: where one
puts the emphasis. If, however, eternity belongs to God alone as
the One whose essence is simply to-be, and as such is the source
of each thing existing, then the resolution in terms of eternity will
involve an ontology centred on existence and actuality. It is in
these terms that we shall now examine divine simpleness.

THE CASE FOR DIVINE SIMPLENESS

The simpleness proposed offered more than a mere denial of
multiplicity in divinity, but was positively articulated by insisting
that God's nature is simply to-be (*esse*). Aquinas, in his treatment,
offers further reasons why no other mode of composition can be
found in divinity – potency/act, matter/form, genus/species,
substance/accident – but the positive reason underlying every
negation is the identity of God's essence with God's very existing. The greatest obstacle to accepting this account as coherent
lies in trying to conceive what is meant by existing, or *esse*. It
cannot be an accident of substance, since it is presupposed to the
notion of substance as *that which is*, whereas accidents presuppose substance. Nor can it be a merely formal feature like *identity*,
since such features hold indifferently of possible and actual
things, whereas we mean by *esse* the *act* of existing: that which
makes something to be here and now.

Here is where Aquinas' manoeuvre recommends itself. Existing is to be conceived as a constituent feature of whatever is, as
toads are constituted toads by the constituent structure called
toadness. In the case of *esse*, however, this constituent feature is
not merely formal but actual. So Aristotle's analogical complements of potency and act are recapitulated a step beyond matter/
form to allow the essence to be realized in an existing individual.
The analogy of *act* cannot be further analysed, as Aristotle saw,
but can be displayed. What we call actions are paradigmatically
actions of existing subjects, so the *ur*-action, if you will, is the
existing of the acting subject.[18]

One cannot get *behind* this fact of existing, any more than one
can *explicate* why the arrival of a newborn infant is always more
than the sum of the processes which brought it into being. What
now exists is one capable of acting, and in the case of humans, of
taking responsibility for one's actions. That is the surplus which
must be recognized ontologically even when one cannot analyse

it any further. A strategic way to recognize it is to conceive existence as *act* (not *an* act) perfecting the essence as form does matter, by realizing the nature in an existing individual. As the *ur*-act, then, accounting for the constitutive fact that individuals are agents, existing will not be relegated to the status of a mere *given*, or of a presupposition. It will be the source of all further capacities for development and self-actuation which characterize such an individual. (In other words, certain ranges of action are typical of certain types of thing, but only the existing individuals of the species can *do* them.)

This last move is the crucial one. If one accepts it, the account given of divine simpleness can be made quite plausible, whereas without it – with a notion of existence as a mere given or presupposition – simpleness remains a puzzle. If one begins with properties, for example, rather than with an acting individual, one will be puzzled to know how two distinct properties, like knowing and will, could be identified with the divine essence, as simpleness demands, without thereby losing their distinctness in becoming identified with one another.[19] The assertions of simpleness seem incompatible with an elementary application of logic. Moreover, Aquinas' response to this objection appears, from such a perspective, to be a semantic slight of hand: 'the words we use for the perfections we attribute to God, although they signify what is one, are not synonymous, for they signify it from many different points of view' (Ia, 13, 4).

If we assume the primacy of existing individual agents, however, the difficulties can be met and Aquinas' response found to be insightful. For then what we call properties will be located as distinct powers in a subject capable of acting. Where the subject in question is the uniquely divine one, however, which is act without potency, then the distinct acts (knowing and willing) need not be rooted in separate powers. And one should be able to give an analysis of knowing along the lines of the commendation in Genesis 1: 'and God saw that it was good', in which a single knowing act, carried to its term, reaches its fruition in the enjoyment of what is – insofar as it is – then the knowing and willing which are distinct acts for us will be but the articulations of a single act of knowing in God.[20] (The only further premiss required here is the unproblematic one that an act of knowing 'carried to its term' can well be but one act in a mind sufficiently powerful – by analogy with one who 'sees' conclusions quickly.)

What seems more perplexing, in fact, is the multiplication of acts of knowing and of willing by the objects known and loved. It was this hurdle which forced Avicenna and Gersonides (though

85

Muslim and Jew, respectively) to limit God's knowing to the 'definitions and order of things', whereas al-Ghazali and Maimonides knew they had to defer to Qur'an and Torah to affirm God's care of each individual 'without being able to say how'.[21] What can we say? That in knowing God's own to-be, God knows and takes pleasure in bringing forth individuals 'according to their kinds'.[22] If this activity is conceived as a selection among alternative scenarios, it will require a distinct act of will, and the articulation would have to be: in knowing God's own to-be, God knows and takes pleasure in what God *chooses* to bring forth. . . . If the activity is rather understood as a practical knowing, by analogy with doing or making (as *creation* strongly suggests), then no distinct act of choosing will be needed, since the object made is the term of artistic knowing, as the action performed forms the conclusion of a practical syllogism.[23] Choices are entailed, certainly, in human execution, but they subserve the intention coming to realization in the object.

That God's self-knowledge of God's own essence as the to-be in which things can participate in being, after their own fashion, becomes a practical action of creation is of course a free act on God's part, but again, freedom need not (and I contend, ought not) primarily to be considered as freedom of choice.[24] What turns a contemplative *delectatio* into a making defies our articulation, but it need not demand a distinct 'decision' on God's part. In other words, the sense in which creation is at once gratuitous yet utterly fitting, according to the axiom that 'good diffuses itself', reminds us that divine freedom may be better understood on the model of Zen 'resonance' than on that of a western penchant for *decisions*.[25] Or to put it another way, the most significant decisions of our lives seem less *made* than they are 'taken', as most western languages put it. If the good moves us by drawing us rather than by constraining us, so that following the bent of one's nature can be at once natural and free, why cannot creation be similarly understood?

These considerations are meant to persuade us of the plausibility of a simple divine nature whose unitary act of loving knowing of itself issues in a making (creating) of the universe. Many questions remain, of course, and proper arguments need to be supplied as needed, but enough has been said to suggest that the effort to supply them is worthwhile. The articulation of simpleness as an essence identical with its to-be (or 'act of existing') is clearly the critical piece in the pattern. For without the premiss that the to-be of a thing is the source of all its activity (and hence of whatever perfects it), we would not be supplied with a unitary perspective or with the heightened sense of *act* needed to speak of creation as the free culmination of divine loving knowledge of itself. We shall see in a moment that this same premiss offers fruitful links both with mystical aspirations and with subsequent trinitarian developments in Christian theology. For the moment, however, it is worth warning that such a simpleness also entails a divinity that is radically unknowable. The very attempt to conceive the *esse* which comprises divinity will have alerted many; the fact that a normal subject/predicate sentence will *ipso facto* be ill-formed of God clinches the matter. At this point, the analogous reaches of our discourse have to be pressed into service, yet the fact remains that they are there to be so.[26]

Without some such attempt to articulate what distinguishes God from the world of which God is the principle and free bestower of its being, we seem to be left with mere assertions that God is without cause, or *a se*.[27] It does not help to insist that God commands all, for one can still wonder whether the being capable of commanding all is in fact creator of all. And if the sense in which God 'necessarily exists' is left to compete with that of necessary truths – if one fails to distinguish existential from logical truth – then God can be made to look much like Plato's demiurge, fashioning the world according to the forms. Whereas on the pattern of a God whose essence is to-be necessary truths assume a properly formal role as the manners in which created things can participate in such *esse*.[28] The critical fact remains, however, that a treatment of divinity which looks only to divine attributes (or properties) without attempting to articulate the uniqueness of the divine nature – announced in the faith-claims of Jew, Christian, and Muslim that God is one – should leave one wondering whether one is discussing divinity or not. And if the tenor of the discussion, besides, leads readers to suspect one to be referring to 'the biggest thing around', then the suspicion may well indicate a fatal flaw in the enterprise.

SIMPLENESS, ETERNITY, AND RELIGIOUS LIFE

'Process theologians' regard a divinity beyond change (and hence eternal) who is 'pure act' to be inherently unresponsive and so antithetical to the God presented to Jews and Christians in the Bible. Some would even hold this 'classical doctrine of God' responsible for secularism in the west, since no sensitive individual could respond to such a God.[29] Perhaps enough has been said here to suggest that the 'classical doctrine' they revile bears little relation to a thinker as classical as Aquinas. In fact, once one takes *esse* to be the source of all perfections, one finds divine activity to be thoroughly 'intentional' in character, relating to itself and its creation with an understanding love which is the quintessence of responsiveness. Moreover, in the measure that the animating spark of one's own being can be said to be a participation in the very to-be of the One from whom all existence flows, there can be said to be in each of us what John of the Cross calls the 'centre of the soul'.[30]

One way to God, then, could be by way of disciplines of mind and heart directed to that 'centre' or source of one's life. Moreover, the understanding profferred of eternity as itself at the heart of temporal existence rather than removed from it, suggesting the metaphors of *presence* and *present* life, underscores how God's simpleness – conceived as pure *esse* – can open the way to an invitation to live present to God in the present of one's life, in a way mindful of spiritual disciplines in diverse traditions. And for Christians, the fact that the divine to-be expresses itself in a knowing which becomes a *delectatio* opens the way to exploiting the analogies for triunity offered by Augustine and developed by Aquinas, wherein Father, Son and Spirit are likened to the articulation of our knowledge in a word which brings intrinsic enjoyment as it expresses what is good, true, and beautiful.[31]

All this by way of suggestion, since the process theologians' criticism is taken even if it mis-identifies its target. Philosophical considerations regarding divinity will fail in their ultimate aim of clarification if they end up presenting a God to which one cannot respond with one's whole person. For if divinity means anything, it must mean 'the beginning and the end of all things, and especially of rational creatures', and nothing less than 'the love which moves the sun and moon and all the stars' (Dante) can present itself as the ultimate end of rational creatures. Such at least is the claim of every religious tradition, and something which many rational creatures come to appreciate in their lifetime. In the Islamic tradition al-Ghazali's criticism of the writings of 'the philosophers' came pointedly to this: that they (and especially Ibn-Sina) offered a scheme culminating in a God whom one could not worship, for the One presented could not properly be called Creator or Lord.[32] Similarly, my concern in this article has been to offer the sketch of a way in which philosophers treating of divinity might so distinguish God from the world as to assure that the One from whom all things come would also be the One to whom rational creatures could wholeheartedly respond.

NOTES

1 On 'formal features', see my *Aquinas: God and Action* (University of Notre Dame Press, Notre Dame, 1979), pp. 14–17, where I acknowledge my indebtedness to Eddy Zemach.

2 Schubert Ogden refers to 'classical theism', following Charles Hartshorne, while Tom Morris speaks of 'the Anselmian conception': 'The God of Abraham, Isaac, and Anselm', *Faith and Philosophy* 1 (1984), pp. 177–187.

3 'Monotheism' is of course an abstraction, though useful in identifying a family of faiths; on the proprieties of speaking of a 'common faith', see my review of Wilfrid Cantwell Smith's recent publications: 'Faith and Religious Convictions: Studies in Comparative Epistemology', *Journal of Religion* 63 (1983), pp. 64–73.

4 A common starting point for philosophers is Nelson Pike's *God and Timelessness* (Routledge & Kegan Paul, London, 1970), which presumes the identification: see my 'God's Eternity', *Faith and Philosophy* 1 (1984), pp. 389–405. Characteristic arguments against the notion of divine simplicity can be found in Alvin Plantinga, *Does God Have a Nature?* (Marquette University Press, Milwaukee, 1980). I prefer 'simpleness' to 'simplicity' for rhetorical reasons: see *Summa Theologiae*, vol. 2: *Existence and Nature of God*, trans. Timothy McDermott OP (Eyre and Spottiswoode, London, 1964).

5 Norman Kretzmann and Eleonore Stump, 'Eternity', *Journal of Philosophy* 78 (1981), pp. 429–458; 'Absolute Simplicity', *Faith and Philosophy*, forthcoming.

6 For 'the distinction', see Robert Sokolowski, *God of Faith and Reason* (University of Notre Dame Press, Notre Dame, 1983).

7 See James Ross, *Portraying Analogy* (Cambridge University Press, Cambridge, 1981); Patrick Sherry, 'Analogy Reviewed', *Philosophy* 51 (1976), pp. 337–345; 'Analogy Today', *ibid.*, pp. 431–446.

8 Most notable are treatments of divine knowledge which proceed, quite innocent of the creator/creature relation, to presume God to be an omniscient onlooker.

9 See my *Aquinas* (note 1), chapter 2, and Mark Jordan, 'Names of God and the Being of Names' in *Existence and Nature of God*, ed. Alfred J. Freddoso (University of Notre Dame Press, Notre Dame, 1983), pp. 161–190.

10 See my *Knowing the Unknowable God* (University of Notre Dame Press, Notre Dame, 1986).

11 The crucial difference between these perspectives is of course the gratuity of the universe; hence Josef Pieper insists that creation is 'the hidden element in the philosophy of Aquinas': *Philosophia Negativa* (Kösel, Munich, 1953).

12 *al-Shifa: al-Ilahiyyat* I, ed. G. C. Anawati and S. Zayad (Cairo, 1960), chapter 8, section 4 (p. 346, line 11).

13 This statement is particularly ambiguous from within the Christian tradition, which has appropriated the term 'person' to express divine

triunity. That our discourse about, as well as our address to, God is *personal* cannot be gainsaid; yet asserting God to be *a person* begs a number of critical questions.

14 For the story of that borrowing and subsequent transformation on the part of Aquinas, see Armand Maurer, *On Being and Essence,* 2nd revised ed. (Pontifical Institute of Medieval Studies, Toronto, 1968); and my 'Essence and Existence; Avicenna and Greek Philosophy', *MIDEO* (1985), as well as *Knowing* (note 10).

15 Hence Kretzmann and Stump distinguish *eternity* from mere *atemporality*: 'Eternity' (note 5), p. 432.

16 See John S. Dunne's evocative treatment in *House of Wisdom* (Harper and Row, New York, 1985).

17 See the observations of Anthony Kenny in *God of the Philosophers* (Clarendon Press, Oxford, 1979), pp. 70–71.

18 A further way to display that activity which characterizes the being of an individual is to attend to the way in which judgement crowns the activity of knowing: see my 'Essence and Existence' (note 14) or *Knowing* (note 10).

19 See Alvin Plantinga (note 4), pp. 37–38.

20 Such is the thesis of Bernard Lonergan, whose *Verbum: Word and Idea in Aquinas* (University of Notre Dame Press, Notre Dame, 1967) articulates Aquinas' epistemology in such a way as to allow it to develop Augustine's mental analogy for the trinitarian processions in God.

21 The formula 'without [being able to say] how' (*bi-la kaifa*) is a classic recourse of al-Ghazali in such matters: see Simon van den Bergh, *Averroes' Tahafut al-Tahafut* (Luzac, London, 1969), pp. 151–152, which incorporates al-Ghazali's original *Tahafut al-Falasifa,* ed. Suliman Dunya (Dar al-Ma'arifa, Cairo, 1980), pp. 153–154. For the others, see my 'Maimonides, Aquinas and Gersonides on Providence and Evil', *Religious Studies* 20 (1984), pp. 335–351.

22 Edward Booth OP, *Aristotelian Aporetic Ontology in Islamic and Christian Writers* (Cambridge University Press, Cambridge, 1983) shows how Aquinas' ability to formulate God's creative activity in so neat a fashion relies on his appropriation of pseudo-Dionysius.

23 James Ross makes this fruitful suggestion, among others, in 'Creation II' in *Existence and Nature of God,* ed. Alfred Freddoso (note 9).

24 Kretzmann and Stump concur, with a careful presentation of Aquinas' strong alternative views on freedom, in 'Absolute Simplicity' (note 5).

25 Such a strategy would suggest ways of responding to Norman Kretzmann's quandary regarding Aquinas and the gratuity of creation, in 'Goodness, Knowledge and Indeterminacy in the Philosophy of Thomas Aquinas', *Journal of Philosophy* 80 (1983), pp. 631–642. For similarly fruitful suggestions, see Etienne Gilson, *Le Thomisme,* 5th ed. (J. Vrin, Paris, 1938), pp. 183–185.

26 This is the burden of Ross's *Portraying* (note 7). For a theological application, see Roger White, 'Notes on analogical predication and

speaking about God' in *Philosophical Frontiers of Christian Theology*, ed. Brian Hebblethwaite and Stewart Sutherland (Cambridge University Press, Cambridge, 1982), pp. 197–226.

27 Here is the weakness of al-Ghazali's critique of Ibn-Sina, in his *Tahafut* (note 21), pp. 191–192.

28 See *Knowing* (note 10), chapter 4.

29 This is a subsidiary thesis of Schubert Ogden in *Reality of God* (Harper and Row, New York, 1966).

30 John of the Cross, *The Living Flame of Love*, Stanza 1, pars 9, 14; Stanza 4, par. 3; cf. *Collected Works*, trans. K. Kavanaugh and O. Rodriguez (Institute of Carmelite Studies, Washington DC, 1979), pp. 582, 584, 643.

31 See Bernard Lonergan, *Verbum* (note 20).

32 al-Ghazali, *Tahafut*, pp. 148–149; van den Bergh, pp. 124ff.

5

FEUERBACH, MARX AND REDUCTIVISM

Denys Turner

In this paper I propose to confront directly the accusation, frequently made against the work of some liberation theologians, that any theoretical alliance between Christianity and Marxism is bound to have, or at least contains inherent dangers of, reductivist consequences for Christianity. So stated, the accusation is false. This is not to say, however, that no forms of liberation theology and no forms of theological alliance with Marxism are reductivist, but if any are I shall not consider them, simply because I do not know of them. Still, in its 1984 statement warning of the dangers of liberation theology, the Vatican's Sacred Congregation for the Doctrine of the Faith seems to think that some forms of liberation theology are, to use its term, in danger of 'immanentism' and those in peril of this ailment are so because of their infection by Marxism. For my part I happen to think just about exactly the opposite of this, namely that the dangers to Christianity of reductivism still come chiefly from Feuerbach and that a good dose of Marxism is the best antidote there is.

Rather than consider the writings of the liberation theologians in detail, therefore, I wish to examine in this paper what I take to be a rather general and formal assumption which underlies the Vatican's fears. That assumption could be briefly formulated thus: that the attempt to think through and construct a theological standpoint on the basis of accepting *as true* the fundamental theoretical positions and practical commitments of Marxism is bound to be destructive of Christian faith.

In so formulating this assumption I wish to emphasize the word 'true', for the following reason. I happen to think that, taken broadly as the theory and practice of the critique of capitalism and as the theory and practice of the revolutionary transformation of capitalist society, Marxism is true. That is to say, I think that Marx's critique of capitalism is true; I think it is true to say that the only serious alternative actually on the agenda of available historical alternatives is some kind of post-capitalist possibility of socialism; and I think it true to say that socialism could be brought about only on the sort of conditions which Marx specifies, namely the waging and winning of a class-war by the forces of wage-labour. Finally, I think that what Marx has to say about the relationship of Christianity to these theoretical and practical projects is, broadly, true.

However, none of this do I think true *because of* my Christian beliefs, which I also think true. I do not think, for example, that the Bible, Exodus or Amos, or even the Gospels, give me *reasons* for thinking that Marxism is true; nor even do I think that Christianity supplies any *motives* for believing Marxism to be true, for example that it would be helpful, in the attempt to grapple with the meaning of Christian faith in the modern world, if Marxism were true. Again, I think the very opposite on both counts: first, that theological life for the Christian would be a great deal easier if one could safely assume that Marxist claims were false; and secondly, at the level of entailments, I am as aware as anyone that, *prima facie*, the boot is generally regarded as being on the other foot: it is generally thought that if Marxism is true it follows that Christianity is false, most spectacularly on the question of theism itself. So, for my part, I am certainly not saying that I am a Marxist *because* I am a Christian. More nearly, I am saying that I am a Christian in spite of being a Marxist.

I am inclined therefore to think that there are *no* specifically Christian reasons for being a Marxist. But I also want to say that you cannot be a Christian, sound in theological wind and limb, unless you are a Marxist and for this proposition there can be only *one* good reason, namely that Marxism can be shown to be true on its own grounds of social, economic, political and historical theory. Though naturally, in a paper concerned with the consequences for theology of accepting this proposition, I cannot dwell on the evidence for believing Marxism to be true, it is worthwhile saying that sometimes theologians shirk their responsibilities here: while broadly speaking rejecting Marxism overall as false, or irrelevant, or dated, they are nonetheless sometimes to be found rummaging through the theoretical rubble of the collapsed edifice of Marxism for decoratively enhancing or even structurally useful bits and pieces, the odd 'insight' here, the odd 'category' there, wherewith to shore up their own theological structures.

I do not doubt that this sort of piecemeal picking-over of Marxism is a titillating pursuit to be engaged in; an archaeological

Marxism can give pleasing refreshment to the theologically sated mind. And there are, after all, some seductive analogies and verbal parallels between Christian and Marxist talk. It is not hard to get some of these analogies to do theological work for you, once you have stretched a few categories of Marxism into metaphors for theological propositions, so that the proletariat becomes the *anawim*, liberation does duty for salvation or redemption, alienation becomes original sin and even, I once read, the Leninist revolutionary leadership becomes the Roman Catholic priesthood. Well, evidently, the Sacred Congregation for the Doctrine of the Faith fears such rhetorical equations for their reductivist, particularly for their politically reductivist, consequences. It instances – and I select randomly – the reading of Exodus not as a figure of Baptism, but as a symbol of the political liberation of the people (X, 14), the disinclination to see the Eucharist as the real sacramental presence of the reconciling sacrifice but rather to see it as a 'celebration of the people in their struggle' (X, 16), the search for the unity of the Church in terms of the class struggle (*ibid.*) and, more generally, it notes

> the tendency to identify the kingdom of God and its growth with the human liberation movement and to make history itself the subject of its own development, as a process of the self-redemption of man by means of the class struggle (IX, 3).

Some liberation theologians, it adds,

> go so far as to identify God himself with history and to identify faith as 'fidelity to history' (and) as a consequence, faith, hope and charity are given a new content. They become 'fidelity to history', 'confidence in the future' and 'option for the poor'. This is tantamount to saying that they have been emptied of their theological character (IX, 4, 5).

'Affirmations such as these', the document concludes, 'reflect historicist immanentism' (IX, 3).

It is worth noting, as a kind of unimportant aside, that some of us in Britain (and I am sure that elsewhere in Europe and in North America the experience has been the same) have already lived through a little bit of the history of the Vatican's difficulties with this kind of verbal synthesizing of Christianity with Marxism. In a moment of self-criticism, one of the leading British Christian-Marxists of the 1960s, Terry Eagleton, remarked how he, along with others

> in the good old days of . . . the Christian left . . . con-
> sistently made a category mistake about Marxism and
> Christianity – we thought they were more or less the
> same kind of thing, and dazzling homologies could be
> drawn between them.[1]

Eagleton himself no longer thinks this, but it is, I guess, a natural
inclination within the Christian left in the Northern world to
think of Christianity and Marxism primarily as discourses in
parallel, never, perhaps, meeting quite in matters of substance,
but analogically sufficiently similar as to allow a relatively free
traffic from biblical metaphor to political category and back again.
But, Eagleton goes on, Marxism and Christianity

> are not synchronous discourses, they can't be trans-
> lated into one another without a great deal of merely
> idealist acrobatics. Marxism is the theory and practice
> of resolving the contradictions of class society; it isn't
> a humanism, or an anthropology, or an eschatology,
> and it thus doesn't situate itself on the same ground as
> the Christian Gospel.[2]

Nonetheless, though not 'situated on the same ground', Marxism
and Christianity do, according to most Marxists, meet in head-on
collision epistemologically, for, on their account, Marxism is a
form of genuine knowledge and Christianity but a bastard form,
it is ideology, the medium of an inherently miscued relationship
with the real world. Marxism makes of Christianity an object of its
general critique of ideologies and so, as the atheist-Marxist Francis Barker puts it

> There is something radically problematical about the
> idea of a science *debating* with what is potentially its
> object *as if* it were an epistemological equal. This is one
> of the reasons why this debate is perennial, and as a
> *debate* cannot be resolved.[3]

Which, we might add, is, in turn, one of the reasons why many
Marxists propose to resolve the matter of Christianity *without*
debate.

All the same, that the temptations to explore the parallels of
discourse between Christianity and Marxism persist among some
theologians can in part be laid at the door of Marx himself. Such
passages as the following are not hard to find at least in Marx's
early writings:

Where is there, then, a *real* possibility of emancipation...?

This is our reply. A class must be formed which has radical chains, a class in civil society which is not of civil society, a class which is the dissolution of all classes, a sphere of society which has a universal character because its sufferings are universal, which does not claim a particular redress because the wrong which is done to it is not a particular wrong but wrong in general. There must be formed a sphere of society which claims no traditional status but only a human status ... a sphere which, finally, cannot emancipate itself without emancipating itself from all the other spheres of society, without, therefore, emancipating all these other spheres, which is, in short, a total loss of humanity and which can only redeem itself by a total redemption of humanity. This dissolution of society, as a particular class, is the proletariat.[4]

It is difficult to read passages such as these with an ear completely insensitive to the Christian rhetoric which it mimics. The Marxian discourse reads as if it were but a collapsing into material, political categories of already familiar, independently established theological meanings. If, as for example, Professor Lash does in his book *A Matter of Hope*,[5] you in any case regard Marxism as but a form of secularized Messianism, a sort of Feuerbachian inversion of theological categories, then it will be an understandable irony if Christians seek to turn the tables in the form of a sacralized Marxism, in an attempt to find a purchase for theological language on the world of actual history and society.

In all this wild oscillation on the Christian political left between a view of Marxism as Christianity secularized and a view of Christianity as a Marxism sacralized, there is revealed, I think, a deeper, systematic ambiguity about how to handle the relations in general between the sacred and the secular. It is as if the sacred and the secular were opposed to one another as mirror-images of one and the same object are opposed to one another. Or, to switch metaphors, it is as if the sacred and the secular stood merely at opposed ends of the same semantic continuum, that they are in relations of trade-off with one another, so that the more you give to the secular the more you take from the sacred and vice versa. Nonetheless, on this picture in *either* case the sacred and the secular are opposed across the same semantic continuum, for it is in terms of that semantic continuity that the parallels and analogies between them are made possible. But this, it will not be hard to see, is pure Feuerbachianism; and if they sit ill as bed-fellows, Eagleton and Ratzinger are surely right, it is undoubtedly a form of reductivism – or, as Ratzinger insists on calling it, 'immanentism'.

It seems that here we get somewhere near the heart of the problem, for at the centre of the debate about reductivism lies a concatenation of problems about the sacred and the secular, the transcendent and the immanent, the vertical and the horizontal, the divine and the human, the religious and the political; and in our disagreements about these relations it is Feuerbach who has fixed the terms of the debate: to one and the same property, whether that of love, or infinity, or omniscience or whatever, you can either attribute a divine significance, in which case you evacuate it of human significance, or else you can attribute a human significance, in which case you evacuate it of divine significance, and so on, going down the list, the Feuerbachian dialectic replicates the oppositions. Nonetheless, it is essential to realize that the Feuerbachian oppositions of the transcendent and the immanent are oppositions across an essential continuity. It is the *same* essence which is reified in God, fully realized in the species-being.

If it is possible to identify a kind of Feuerbachian reductivism within some versions of the Christian-Marxist synthesis, this will be no surprise. What is, however, a little less obvious is that the Feuerbachian *dialectic* can also be identified in what ought to be the polar opposite of that reductivism, the fideism of the theological right.

Don Cupitt, no doubt, would not be amused to hear his theological views so characterized. And yet they should be, for the fideism of his views about religious language shares curious features in common with the Anglican conservatives with whom he is so regularly in conflict, for example, the ecclesiastical historian and implacable opponent of liberation theology, Edward Norman.

But to begin the story at the beginning. In *The Myth of God Incarnate*, Cupitt, along with John Hick, argues that the traditional doctrine of the Incarnation is not just an extremely implausible doctrine (which of course it is), nor even that it is a false doctrine (which is very plausible), but that it is a self-contradictory proposition. Hick puts it most succinctly. It is, he maintains, as contradictory to say of one and the same person that he is both God and man as it is to say of a shape that it is both a square and a circle. Cupitt, as clear as Hick is about this conclusion, is, however, more forthcoming about the grounds from which it is supposed to follow. For Cupitt, traditional Christology

> suggests a synthesis and continuity between things divine and things of this world[6]

whereas Christianity's

> proper subtlety and freedom depends upon Jesus' ironical perception of *disjunction* between the things of God and the things of men.[7]

Cupitt, of course, links this conclusion with a premiss concerning the transcendence, the complete *otherness* of God from man. That transcendence is such, he claims, that it is necessary to ask, of anything whatever, whether it has the nature of the divine *or* the nature of the human. It cannot have both. For that is the proper character of a disjunction: either/or, not both/and. It follows that it is a contradiction in terms to say of anything whatever that, being a creature, it is also truly divine.

Now this is all extremely odd. It is not in the least odd to want to emphasize the transcendence of God and in the name of that transcendence, to deny that there can be any semantic continuity between the things of God and the things of the human. What is odd is to seek a formulation of this transcendence and discontinuity in terms of a difference between God and creatures as mutually excluding each other, for this is a quite self-defeating way of putting it. As a matter of fact it is a simple matter of logic. Entities which exclude each other cannot be all *that* different from each other because there has to be some *common* space from which they exclude each other. As Herbert McCabe has well put it,[8] Hick's circles and squares exclude each other only within the common territory of shapes. To be opposed, there must be something which circles and squares are opposed *as*, namely, shapes. Likewise, what is a sheep cannot be a man because, in the common territory of animals, sheep and men exclude one another. In logic, a statement which contradicts another statement occupies the same semantic space as the statement it contradicts. If I assert any proposition you choose, say p, and you assert not-p, your statement contradicts mine if and only if you deny what I assert. Suppose, then, I say 'Jesus is man' and you say 'Jesus is God', what you say contradicts what I say if and only if 'Jesus is God' entails 'Jesus is not man'. But 'Jesus is God' can entail 'Jesus is not man' only if there is something in common between being God and being man, some space which God and man both occupy in relations of mutual exclusion, as circles and squares occupy the territory of shapes in mutual exclusion. And this, as I say, is a very odd proposition to get from someone who wishes to assert the otherness and transcendence of God. For surely, the transcendence of God implies the very opposite of this, namely that there is no class of things to which God and man both belong, even in relations of exclusion, for there is nothing at all which God and man could be opposed *as*. They are *utterly* unlike, as Cupitt says. Just for that reason, then, there can be no disjunction between the things of God and the things of men.

No apologies should be demanded for this minor excursion into a matter of elementary logic, for it directly concerns our argument. It is evident that, in Cupitt's Christology, there is the same Feuerbachian dialectic at work as in the reductivist case. For the same assumption is made that the transcendent and the immanent are distinct from one another as are terms which are opposed against a background of semantic continuity. Moreover, it is possible to identify this same dialectic at work yet again in the proposition of the politically conservative theologian, that Christianity and politics, to put it popularly, are like oil and water, for the one is concerned with the spiritual things of God and the other with the material things of man. It is admitted, of course, that Christianity is concerned with the things of God *in* this world of man, but where they occupy the same world they exclude each other as oil and water do. And so that notable conservative Edward Norman[9] holds that the politicization of Christianity is the denial of its transcendence, of its otherworldliness, as if the affairs of this world and the affairs of the next could not coincide without the destruction of either the one or the other.

For this reason the concerns of the Christian, *qua* Christian, are those to be found within an individualist spirituality. But in Norman's terms there can be no way forward for the Christian. Only increasingly rapid secularization is possible at the price of an increasingly vapid spirituality. Christianity cannot, any longer, as Norman admits, aim at the reconquest, the resacralization of territory long since lost to the secular. Consequently, as Norman concludes, Christianity can only aim at a truce with secularization along lines of demarcation drawn far back down the continuum where it occupies a position of merely spiritual, therefore individual and so non-political significance.

On a crucial point of epistemology, therefore, it seems that both fideism and reductivism are playing the same game, both according to Feuerbachian rules. For both, it seems, theological language is locked into an account of the relations between the transcendent and the immanent on which they are opposed to

one another against a common background. They differ only in
the emphasis they give, the one, fideism, stressing the discon-
tinuities but in a way which can only imply a semantic continuity,
the other, reductivism, stressing the continuities, but in such a
way as can only entail the evacuation and extinction of the one by
the other. It was of Engels, the reductivist *par excellence*, that the
following comment was made, though it is as apt of Edward
Norman: Engels

> put religion on trial before a rather Kafkaesque tribun-
> al: insofar as religion is sincerely religion, it is a set of
> abstract platitudes, at best useless, at worst harmful to
> the advancement of humanity; insofar as it says any-
> thing about the social and political reality of the time, it
> has ceased to be religion.[10]

Now it is central to my case about the relations between Marxism
and Christianity that, while true of Feuerbach, it is *not* true of
Marx that, as Professor McGovern has put it recently,[11] having
accepted the proposition 'what one gives to God one must take
away from humans . . . Marx saw no choice but to opt for
humanity'. Far from this being true of Marx, he decisively rejects
that Feuerbachianism which plays God and the human off
against one another and so affirms 'man' only indirectly through
the negation of God:

> Atheism, as a denial of this unreality (of theism) is no
> longer meaningful, for atheism is the negation of God
> and seeks to assert by this negation the existence of
> man. Socialism no longer requires such a roundabout
> method. . . . It is positive human self-conciousness, no
> longer a self-consciousness attained through the nega-
> tion of religion.[12]

He saw through this atheism as being as firmly rooted in the
theological conception of the universe as is its mirror-image, a
theism which affirms God only via the negation of man. In fact
what Marx negated was the antithesis, 'either God or man'. From
this negation I do not think any known humanism, even a post-
theistic humanism, can be derived, because to negate the antithesis is to negate that whole intellectual and cultural world for
which the abstraction 'man' exists: namely, that world in which
'man' is invented to stand in polar opposition to God. As much as
anything else, Marx's opposition to Feuerbach resided in his
hostility to this abstract, de-historicalized 'man' who only existed
for Feuerbach via the negation of God. In the name of actual

populations of men, women and children – history's real products – Marx protested equally against a theological and an atheist
denial of real historical people living under specific historical
conditions, products and agents of their own history. It was the
'real individuals' of *The German Ideology* whom Marx wished to
emancipate, whether they were crushed beneath the weight of an
overwhelmingly dehumanizing God or by their subsumption
under the Feuerbachian abstraction, 'the species-being'. In short,
Marx invokes a plague upon the houses of both 'God' and 'man'.

Many Christians who rightly for their own part deny that
Christianity is caught up into this Feuerbachian antithesis,
wrongly take it for granted that Marx is implicated in it. In effect
this is to reduce Marx's atheism to Feuerbach's, which is to miss
the point of Marx's. This is a pity, for Marx's response to Feuerbach's antithesis is to isolate what he, Marx, takes to be the
shared theological instinct which binds Feuerbach to his Christian opponents: the instinct, that is to say, that there is a place to be
occupied at the centre of the universe of meaning and value by
some being or other from whom all meanings and values derive;
that instinct which led Sartre the atheist to assert that if God does
not exist there must be some being to give meaning and value to
things; that instinct which leads fideistic and reductivistic Christians alike to suppose that, if God and man compete, there must
be some common territory for them to dispute. As I have argued
elsewhere, it is the instinct to say that 'insofar as God is centred,
man is decentred. Insofar as man is centred, God is decentred'.[13]

It is therefore with some sense of irony that we can welcome
Quentin Lauer's description of Marx's atheism both *as* a descrip-
tion of Marx's atheism and as an unconscious debunking of a
Feuerbachian Christianity. He asserts

> there is no conceivable God that would be acceptable
> (to Marx, for) any being in any way superior to man is
> simply inconceivable.[14]

Taken strictly for what it says, this is a proposition with which *any*
good Christian should heartily agree, though for my part I can
conceive of entities superior to human beings, being somewhat
less sure that any such exist – namely, angels. If it is possible to
conceive of a being superior to humans, however, the one thing
such a being could not be is God, for in the Christian view God is
not a conceivable being. God is not a possibility (essence) instantiated. God is not a kind of thing, even a 'wholly other' thing
(a quite senseless conjunction of attributes). In fact, for the
Christian, there is no conceivable God. That is why no Christian

can accept the terms of the debate which Feuerbach imposes, for both the assertion and the denial of the Feuerbachian answer are false. In fact, of course, it is only a *conceivable* God who could be in that way superior to humankind, in which, in the words of the arch-Feuerbachian Don Cupitt, he stands 'crushingly over-against' the human.[15] To think of God as being 'superior' to humans is to suppose that there is some standard of comparison in terms of which God's superiority to humans can be judged. That supposition is, of course, idolatrous. It is useless to protest that for the Christian God is *infinitely* superior to the human being, for, as Marx saw, this is merely to say that God crushes humans into nothing at all.

If God were something we could conceive of as superior to humans, then the game would have to be conceded to Feuerbach. A conceivable, infinite God displaces the world and denatures humanity, not by virtue of some utter transcendence but, on the contrary, by virtue of being nothing more than humans, displaced from their material, contingent history and projected upon the infinite degree *of the same scale* – in short, by being all too *immanent*. It is this idolatrous conception of God which generates the theological problem of 'either God or human', and Feuerbach accepts it. Consequently, he quite naturally abandons that God – but in the name of the corresponding polar opposite, the abstraction, 'human being'. However, Marx rejects the problematic itself, and with it he rejects one of the most pervasive sources of Western ideology. That he also *consequentially* rejects God may be put down to the fact that there were few Christians and little enough good theology available to him which could have convinced him how sound his own theological instincts were. Knowing what we do about Marx's acquaintance with theology, this should not surprise us in the least. What should surprise us is that there are, evidently, other theologians than Cupitt today who seem to think by implication that, if there is no conceivable God who is in some way superior to humankind, then God does not exist.

It would be inappropriate here to expand on these condensed and arcane remarks. Suffice it to say that many Christian accounts purporting to be of Marx's atheism are in fact accounts of Feuerbach's and that many attempts to wed Marx and Christianity fail (and are bound to) because they are in fact attempts to marry Christianity off with Feuerbach. It is crucial to observe the radical gulf that exists between Feuerbachian reductionism and the Marxist critique. The Marxian critique is, in my view, a criticism of a kind of idolatrous religion which is bound always to create ideological distortions even within the authentic socialist movements whenever, rarely, it seeks alliances there. It is not my point that a nonidolatrous Christianity need expect no trouble from Marx. It is, rather, that, without a radical integration of the Marxian critique into the theological and practical project of Christianity, we are unlikely ever to expunge from it the corroding effects of Feuerbach and so of his idolatrous God. To know God we must do justice to Marx.

NOTES

1 Terry Eagleton, 'Marx, Freud and Morality', *New Blackfriars* (January 1977), p. 22.
2 *Ibid.*, p. 23.
3 Francis Barker, 'The Morality of Knowledge and the Disappearance of God', *New Blackfriars* (September 1976), p. 404.
4 Karl Marx, *Contribution to the Critique of Hegel's Philosophy of Right, Introduction*, in *Karl Marx: Early Writings*, ed. and trans. T. B. Bottomore (London, 1963), p. 58.
5 Nicholas Lash, *A Matter of Hope* (London, 1981), p. 55.
6 *The Myth of God Incarnate*, ed. J. Hick (London, 1973), p. 140.
7 *Ibid.*
8 H. McCabe OP, 'The Myth of God Incarnate', *New Blackfriars* (August 1977), p. 353; repr. in *God Matters* (London, 1987), chapter 5, p. 57.
9 E. R. Norman, *Christianity and the World Order* (Oxford, 1979).
10 J. Maguire, 'Gospel or Religious Language: Engels on the Peasant War', *New Blackfriars* (August 1973), p. 350.
11 A. F. McGovern, 'Atheism: Is it Essential to Marxism', *Journal of Ecumenical Studies*, vol. 22, no. 3 (1985), p. 496.
12 Marx, *Economic and Philosophical MSS*, in Bottomore, pp. 166–167.
13 'De-centring God', *Modern Theology*, vol. 2, no. 2 (January 1986), p. 138.
14 Quentin Lauer, 'The Atheism of Karl Marx' in *Marxism and Christianity*, ed. Herbert Aptheker (New York: Humanities Press, 1968), p. 48.
15 Don Cupitt, *Taking Leave of God* (London, 1980), p. xi.

6

AQUINAS ON KNOWLEDGE OF SELF

Anthony Kenny

In striving, over many years, to reach understanding of Aquinas' philosophy of mind, I have profited greatly from discussions with Herbert McCabe, and I am glad to have this opportunity to express my gratitude to him.

Aquinas has a problem in giving an account of how a human intellect knows itself. Intellectual knowledge, for him, is immaterial; but matter is the principle of individuation. Hence, he concludes, intellectual knowledge is primarily only of universals; individuals can be known only secondarily and indirectly by the intellect. How, then, can a human intellect be immediately aware of itself, since any such intellect is itself a particular individual? The present paper attempts to outline how Aquinas tried to solve this problem, and to assess how far he succeeds in doing so.

In Aquinas' account of these matters, a crucial role is played by the relationship between the intellect and the imagination. According to article 7 of question 84 of the first part of the *Summa Theologiae*, the two faculties are intimately interrelated. The issue raised in the article is whether the intellect can exercise intellectual activity using only the intelligible species in its possession without turning to phantasms.[1] The answer given is that in the present life the intellect cannot exercise intellectual activity upon anything at all unless it turns itself towards the phantasms.

Let us begin by decoding the arcane terminology. Aquinas' *intellectus* is fairly enough translated by the English word 'intellect': it is the capacity for understanding and thought, for the kind of thinking which differentiates humans from animals; the kind of thinking which finds expression especially in language, that is, in the meaningful use of words and the assignment of truth-values to sentences. But English does not have a handy verb, 'to intellege', to cover the various activities of the intellect, as the

Latin has the verb *intelligere* for what the intellect does. To correspond to the Latin verb one has to use circumlocutions, as above I used 'exercise intellectual activity' to correspond to *actu intelligere*. An alternative would be to use the English word 'understanding' in what is now a rather old-fashioned sense, to correspond to the name of the faculty, *intellectus*, and to use the verb 'understand' to correspond to the verb *intelligere*. In favour of this is the fact that the English word 'understand' can be used very widely to report, at one extreme, profound grasp of scientific theory ('only seven people have ever really understood special relativity') and, at the other, possession of fragments of gossip ('I understand there is to be a Cabinet reshuffle before autumn'). But 'understand' is, on balance, an unsatisfactory translation for *intelligere* because it always suggests something dispositional rather than episodic, an ability rather than the exercise of an ability; whereas *intelligere* covers both latent understanding and current conscious thought. When Aquinas has occasion to distinguish the two he often uses *actu intelligere* for the second: in such cases the expression is often better translated 'think' than 'understand'.

What, next, are 'intelligible species'? These are the acquired mental dispositions which are expressed, manifested, in intellectual activity: the concepts which are employed in the use of words, the beliefs which are expressed by the use of sentences. My grasp of the meaning of the English word 'rain' is one kind of species; my belief that red night skies precede fine days is another kind of species. The most natural English word to cover both concepts and beliefs is 'idea', and in some contexts 'idea' makes an unproblematic equivalent for *species*. But in the present context it might be misleading, since the British empiricist philosophers used the word 'idea' for mental images, which are something quite different from *species intelligibiles*.

Mental images are called by Aquinas 'phantasms' (*phantasmata*). A visual image, called up when one's eyes are shut; the words one utters to oneself *sotto voce* in the imagination: these are clearly examples of what he means by 'phantasm'. How much else is covered by the word is difficult to determine. Sometimes straightforward cases of seeing events in the world with eyes open seem to be described as a sequence of *phantasmata*: it is not clear whether this means that the word is being used broadly to cover any kind of sense-experience, or whether Aquinas held a regrettable theory that external sense-experience was accompanied by a parallel series of phenomena in the imagination. For our purposes it is not necessary to decide between these alternatives:

when Aquinas talks of *phantasmata* we can take him to be speaking of occurrences taking place either in the senses or the imagination. For what he is anxious to elucidate is the role of the intellect within the sensory context provided by the experience of the sentient subject.

According to Aquinas, phantasmata are necessary both for the acquisition and for the employment of *species*. At birth the intellect is pure capacity, void of concepts and beliefs; these are acquired by abstraction from phantasms (Ia, 85, 1). (Again, the analogy with the British empiricists suggests itself; again the analogy is misleading.) When a concept has been acquired, or when a belief has been formed, the intellect has taken a step from potentiality towards actuality; it is no longer a *tabula rasa*, but has a content; it is in possession of *species*. But this, according to Aquinas, is not sufficient to enable the intellect to operate unaided: phantasms are needed not only for gaining possession of species but also for making use of them.

Why so? Aquinas puts to himself the following objection:

> It would seem that the intellect can exercise intellectual activity without turning to phantasms, simply by using the species in its possession. For the intellect is placed in a state of actuality by a species informing it. But for the intellect to be in a state of actuality is precisely for it to exercise intellectual activity. Therefore species suffice to enable the intellect to exercise intellectual activity without turning to phantasms (Ia, 84, 7, obj.1).

The answer is to be found by distinguishing two stages of actuality. Possessing a concept or a belief is different from being totally uninformed; but it is different again from exercising the concept or calling the belief to mind. I may know French without, on a given date, speaking, reading, or thinking French; I may believe that the earth is round even when my thoughts are on totally different things. The distinction, in terms of actuality and potentiality, may be made in more than one way. Knowing French is an actuality by comparison with the state of the newborn infant; it is a potentiality by comparison with the activity of actually speaking French. Sometimes Aquinas, and often later scholastics, distinguish the three stages as pure potentiality, first actuality, and second actuality. In these terms, the thesis of Ia, 84, 7 is that phantasms are needed not only to take the intellect from potentiality to first actuality, but also from first actuality to second. Without the jargon, the thesis is that intellectual thought is impossible apart from a sensory context.

It seems to be possible to bring out the truth of this thesis even if one takes a starting point very different from that of Aquinas. According to one strand of modern philosophy, thought is essentially operating with symbols; and symbols are signs that bear meaning. Whatever account we are to give of the way in which meaning can be attached to signs, we cannot dispense with the signs to which the meaning is to be attached. The signs may be uttered sounds, or marks on paper: entities perceptible by the senses. Or they may be items in the imagination, such as the words of a fragmentary interior monologue. Either way the signs will provide the sensory context for the intellectual thought.

Any thought must have two essential features: it must be a thought with a content, and it must be a thought with a thinker: it must be somebody's thought, and it must be a thought of something. What makes a thought a thought of something is its meaning, its intentionality; what makes a thought somebody's thought is its being an item in *his* mental history rather than someone else's.

One may think by talking, whether aloud to others or in silence to oneself. What gives the thought its content, in such a case, is the meaning of the words used; and it is because we grasp that meaning that thinking is an activity of the intellect, which is, precisely, the ability to confer and understand meaning. When I think thus, what makes the thought *my* thought is, in the standard spoken case, that it is I who am doing the speaking; in the case of my talking to myself, it is the fact that those images are part of *my* mental history. It is thus that the occurrence of something perceptible by the senses, or something occurring in the imagination, is necessary if I am to have a thought; it is thus that intellectual activity involves *conversio ad phantasmata*.

Aquinas' own arguments for his thesis are rather different. He says that since the intellect is a faculty which uses no bodily organ, its operation could not be impeded by bodily injury unless some other faculty were involved. But human beings cannot use their minds if they are in a state such as a seizure or a coma. This must be because the intellect cannot act without the aid of the senses and the imagination which do have bodily organs (Ia, 84, 7, c).

Several things seem wrong with this argument. First, we want to know why Aquinas says that the intellect has no bodily organ. Why do not the phenomena he cites tell as much in favour of the thesis that the intellect has a bodily organ as in favour of the thesis that the intellect has need of the imagination? Aquinas might argue that the intellect does not have an organ in the way that the faculty of sight has, because there is no part of the body that one brings to bear in order to understand better, in the way that one moves and focuses one's eyes to see better. If so, it can be replied that in precisely the same sense of 'organ' there is no organ of imagination either: there is no part of our body which we bring to bear in order to imagine better. But 'organ' may be used in a broader sense, to mean any part of the body which is intimately related with the exercise of a faculty; so that, in this sense, the visual cortex would be an organ of sight no less than the eye. If so, why should we deny that there is an organ of the intellect? Is not the brain just such an organ?

Moreover, Aquinas' argument makes it appear as if the need for thought to take place in a sensory context is a contingent matter. This is something which is not uncongenial to him, since he wishes to defend the possibility of thought in disembodied souls. But if the considerations outlined above are correct, the connection between thought and imagination seems to be a necessary rather than a contingent matter.

Aquinas' second argument for his thesis also seems flawed. It goes thus:

> Everyone can experience in himself, that when someone tries to understand (*intelligere*) something, he forms for himself some phantasms by way of examples in which he can, as it were, look at what he is trying to understand. That is also why when we want to make someone else understand something, we offer him examples from which he can form phantasms for himself in order to understand. . . . If it is to exercise its proper activity about its proper object, the intellect must turn to phantasms, to intuit the universal nature existing in the particular (Ia, 84, 7, c).

The line of argument here suggests that the relation of species to phantasm is the same as that of universal to particular. But this is not so, for several reasons. I can have a concept of horse which is not the concept of any particular horse; but equally I can have an image of a horse which is not an image of any particular horse. When I use instances and examples to help grasp a difficult proposition, the instances and examples may be general no less than particular. Thus, suppose I am wondering about the correctness of the logical principle:

> If every x has the relation R to some y, then there is some y to which every x has the relation R.

In such a case I will no doubt call up instances and seek for counterexamples. But the propositions I would call to mind – 'Every boy loves some girl', 'every road leads to some place' – though less general than the logical principle I am using them to test are none the less universal and not particular.

But though Aquinas' arguments seem doubtful, his conclusion seems, as I have already argued, to be correct. Moreover, in answering the third objection to his thesis, he makes a qualification to it which removes the most obvious argument that might be brought against it. The third objection runs thus:

> There are no phantasms of incorporeal things, because the imagination does not go outside the world of time and the continuum. So if our intellect could not operate upon anything without turning to phantasms, it would follow that it could not operate upon anything incorporeal.

This conclusion would be, of course, quite unacceptable to Aquinas since he believed that we could have some understanding of God and immaterial angels. In his reply he explains that this understanding, though genuine, is limited. Incorporeal substances are known negatively and by analogy.

> Incorporeal things, of which there are no phantasms, are known to us by comparison with empirical bodies of which there are phantasms ... to understand anything of things of this kind we have to turn to phantasms of empirical bodies, even though there are no phantasms of them.

Aquinas is perhaps too pessimistic about the possibility of there being images of non-bodily things. After all, surely Michelangelo's Sistine creation *does* contain an image of God. What is true is that the image of a non-bodily thing is not an image of it in virtue of resembling it. But there is good reason to believe that what makes an image of X an image of X is *never* its resemblance to X, even if X is bodily. Be that as it may, Aquinas' answer to his objection does make the valid point that even if it is true that one cannot think of anything without an image, it does not follow that one cannot think of X without an image *of X*. When we think by talking to ourselves, if we talk to ourselves about X, the most common image which will be the vehicle of our thought about X will not be an image of X (visual, say), but an image (most likely auditory) of the word for 'X'. But of course it may be an image of many other things too, and there are many ways of thinking

109

about X which do not involve talking to ourselves.

According to the thesis defended in article 7 of question 84, imagery, or a sensory context, is necessary for thought of any kind, including the most abstract, metaphysical, or theological thought. But when we turn to consider thought about concrete individuals – the kind of thought expressed by a proposition such as 'Socrates is mortal' – then the senses and the imagination are involved in an even more intimate way. This is spelt out in two stages. In article 3 of question 85 Aquinas asks whether our intellect knows what is more universal before it knows what is less universal; in article 1 of question 86 he asks whether our intellect knows individuals.

There is, as we have said, a special problem for Aquinas about intellectual knowledge of individuals because of his thesis that individuation is by matter. Some philosophers have thought that an object could be individuated by listing the totality of its properties. Since to have a property is to fall under some universal – to be square, for instance, is to be an instance of the universal 'square' – if an item can be individuated by its properties, all we need to identify an individual is to list the universals under which it falls. But Aquinas rightly rejected this: in theory, however long a list of universals we draw up, it is always logically possible that more than one individual will answer to the list.

One of Aquinas' clearest statements on this topic occurs in the second question of *De Veritate*, in article 5, where the topic is God's knowledge of singulars. According to Avicenna, Aquinas says, God knows each singular in a universal manner, by knowing all the universal causes which produce singulars.

> Thus, if an astronomer knew all the motions of the heavens and the distances between all the heavenly bodies, he would know every eclipse which is to occur within the next hundred years; but he would not know any of them as a particular individual, in such a way as to know whether or not it was now occurring, in the way that a peasant knows that while he is seeing it. And it is in this manner that they maintain that God knows singulars; not as if he intuited the singular nature of them, but by positing the universal causes.

But this account, Aquinas maintains, is quite inadequate, for the following reason.

> From universal causes nothing follows except universal forms, unless there is something to individuate the

forms. But however many universal forms you pile up, you never make them add up to anything singular. For it always remains possible to think of that totality of forms as being instantiated more than once.[2]

All this is well and clearly said, and it underlines Aquinas' problem. If the intellect – human, no less than divine – is a faculty for grasping universals, how can there be intellectual knowledge of a singular individual? The theses which set the problem are boldly stated in the discussion, in Ia, 85, 3, of whether intellectual knowledge of the more universal is prior to intellectual knowledge of the less universal. The first thing to be said on this topic, according to Aquinas, is this.

Intellectual knowledge in a certain manner takes its origin from sense knowledge. And since the object of the sense is the singular, and the object of the intellect is the universal, it must be the case that the knowledge of singulars, in our case, is prior to the knowledge of universals.[3]

We know the singular before the universal (for instance, when we are babies innocent of language); but our *intellect* can be said baldly to have as its object the universal alone. This seems correct. A child sees dogs long before it acquires the concept 'dog'; seeing is of the individual, because one cannot see a dog that is not any particular dog; the concept is of the universal, because there is no theoretical limit on the number of things which may fall under the description 'dog'.

But both in the case of the senses and of the intellect, Aquinas says, more general precedes less general knowledge. From a distance you can tell that something is a tree before you can tell that it is a beech; you can spot a dog without being able to decide whether it is a labrador or an alsatian; you can see a man coming before you can recognize him as Peter or Paul. Here Aquinas appeals to the authority of Aristotle:

Thus, at the beginning, a child distinguishes man from non-man before distinguishing one man from another; that is why, as Aristotle says, a child begins by calling all men 'father' and only later distinguishes between each of them.

The illustration is not really very helpful, because one wants to know how Aristotle decides whether the child (a) means 'man' by 'father' or (b) means 'father' and believes that everyone he sees is his father.

111

The fact seems to be that in the case of a faculty such as a sense, which is a faculty for discrimination, the precise discrimination is, logically, subsequent to the imprecise discrimination; progress in discrimination is progress from the less determinate to the more determinate. But in the case of the intellect it seems we cannot make the same generalization. Sometimes we proceed from the more general to the less general, and sometimes in the opposite direction. We may acquire the concept 'tree' before learning the different kinds of tree; on the other hand, a child may have mastered 'dog' and 'cat' before he has the more general term 'animal', and in adult life it may take a degree of sophistication to regard both heat and light as species of a common genus.

But genus and species are related as more general and less general within the realm of the universal; according to the doctrine enunciated in the *De Veritate*, the relation between species and individual is quite different from that between genus and species. There is one surprising passage in article 4 of question 85 where it almost seems as if Aquinas had forgotten this. He says:

> If we consider the nature of genus and species as it is in individuals, we find that it stands in the relation of formal principle with respect to individuals; for the individual is individual because of its matter, it belongs to a species by virtue of its form. But the nature of the genus is related to the nature of the species in the manner of a material principle; because the nature of the genus is taken from what is material in a thing, the specific element from what is formal; as animality is derived from the sensory part, and humanity from the intellectual part.[4]

At first sight, this looks as if Aquinas is suggesting that genus is related to species as species is related to individual. This would be quite wrong, on his own principles: the two relationships cannot be treated as parallel instances of the relation of indeterminate to determinate. Genus is related to species as indeterminate to determinate, indeed, but species is not related to individual as indeterminate to determinate; as Aquinas spelt out in the *De Veritate* passage above, no collection of determinations will individuate a particular.

But Aquinas is not saying that the individual is related to the species as determinate to indeterminate. He is saying that in a given individual the matter can be regarded, like genus, as something indeterminate. Just as there is no animal that is not a particular kind of animal – no animal which belongs to the genus but to no species of the genus – so too there is no matter which is not matter of a particular kind, matter informed by a specific form. But it would be wrong to say that matter is to form as indeterminate to determinate; the truth is that matter is to informed matter as indeterminate to determinate.

It is in the brief article 1 of question 86 that Aquinas finally gives his answer to the question whether our intellect knows individuals. 'Directly and primarily' he says 'our intellect cannot know individuals among material things.'

> The reason is that the principle of individuation in material things is individual matter, and our intellect, as said before, operates by abstracting intelligible species from that kind of matter. But what is abstracted from individual matter is universal. Therefore our intellect has direct knowledge only of universals.

There was a time when I found this thesis shocking and incredible. Shocking, because if it is impossible to have intellectual knowledge of an individual, it must be equally impossible to have spiritual love for an individual; for the will can only relate to what the intellect can grasp. Hence love between human individuals must be mere sensuality. Incredible, because one of the time-honoured paradigms of intellectual activity is the formulation of syllogisms such as 'All men are mortal; Socrates is a man; therefore Socrates is mortal'. But one cannot formulate singular propositions, in a real case, if one cannot understand what is meant by the individual terms which occur in them. How much preferable to Aquinas' teaching, I used to think, is the belief in the Scotist tradition that each individual has a *haecceitas*, a unique essence, which can be grasped as such by the intellect!

Later, however, I have come to see that Aquinas was right to maintain that our knowledge of material individuals cannot be something which is purely intellectual. This can be made clear if we reflect that the intellect is, above all, the human capacity to master language and to think those thoughts which are only expressible in language. There is no way in which we can uniquely identify an individual in language without going outside language itself and latching on to the context within which the language is used.

When I think of a particular human being, there will be, if I know her well, many descriptions I can give in language to identify who I mean. But unless I bring in reference to particular times and places there may be no description I can give which would not in theory be satisfiable by a human being other than the one I mean. As Aquinas emphasized in the *De Veritate* passage, I cannot individuate simply by describing a list of attributes. Only perhaps by pointing, or taking you to see her, can I settle beyond doubt which person I mean; and pointing and vision go beyond pure intellectual thought.

Similarly, if I bring in spatio-temporal individuating references I have left the realm of intellectual thought; from the point of view of a pure spirit there would be no such framework. It is only by linking universal intellectual ideas with sensory experience that we know individuals and are capable of forming singular propositions. And that is what Aquinas says.

> Indirectly, and by a certain kind of reflexion, the intellect can know an individual; because, as said above, even after it has abstracted species it cannot make use of them in intellectual operation unless it turns towards the phantasms in which it grasps the intelligible species, as Aristotle says. Thus, what the intellect grasps directly by the intellible species is the universal; but indirectly it grasps individuals which have phantasms. And that is how it forms the proposition 'Socrates is a man'.

We come, then, finally to the question how, within this theoretical framework, to account for knowledge of the individual self. The question of self-knowledge can be put in more than one way. We may ask: how does a human individual know himself? Or we may ask: how does the human intellect know itself? Aquinas prefers, in question 87, the second formulation. This is perhaps surprising in view of his correct insistence elsewhere that it is a human being who thinks and understands, just as it is a human being (and not, say, an eye) which sees. Equally surprisingly, the first question which he puts to himself, in connection with the intellect's self-knowledge, is whether the intellect knows itself by its essence. We may well wonder whether talk of the essence of an individual intellect does not, in the end, involve Aquinas in believing in something very like a Scotist *haecceitas*.

Let us postpone, for the moment, the question of the essence of the individual intellect, and consider what St Thomas thought about the essence of an individual human being. One might first try to distinguish a Thomist individual essence from a Scotist *haecceitas* by saying that it includes matter. But according to St Thomas the essence of a human being does not include any individual matter (*materia signata*); no particular parcel of matter, only some matter or other. The essence of a human being is what makes him a human being, which includes having a body; but the essence does not include having *this* body, or a body composed of *this* matter. For St Thomas as for Scotus there are individual essences; but whereas for Scotists it is the *haecceitas* which individuates, for the Thomist it is the other way round: the essence is individuated by its possessor. My soul, my essence, my intellect are the soul, essence, intellect they are, are the individual items they are, because they are the soul of Anthony Kenny, who is *this* body. Even if, as Aquinas thought, they can survive my death, they are still the individuals they are because they belonged to this *body*.

If we bear this in mind, we realize that my soul does not have an essence except in the sense that it is the spiritual aspect of *my* essence. If Aquinas asks whether the intellect knows itself by its own essence, it is not because he believes that it has an independent essence, but because that was what was believed by those Platonists whose view he is attacking here. If the human intellect were a pure spirit in contact with some world of pure Ideas, then its self-knowledge too would no doubt be some spiritual self-translucence. But *our* minds are not like that, at least in the present life.

> Our intellect becomes the object of its own intellectual activity in so far as it is actualized by species abstracted from empirical things by the light of the active intellect. . . . So it is not by any essence of itself, but through its activity that our intellect knows itself (Ia, 87, 1).

But intellectual self-knowledge is of two very different kinds. There is the individual's self-knowledge: Socrates perceives that he has an intellectual soul by perceiving his own intellectual activity. But there is also the human race's knowledge of what human understanding is: this is something gathered painfully by philosophic toil, and many human beings never rightly acquire it. The first kind of knowledge, Aquinas says, presents no such problem.

> In order to have the first kind of knowledge of the mind, the mind's own presence is sufficient, since it is the principle of the act by which the mind perceives itself.

We may wonder, however, whether, on Aquinas' own principles, matters ought to be as simple as this. The intellect is a faculty for the grasping of universals: what is this 'perceiving' that we are now told is one of its activities? If it is a perceiving involving knowledge of an individual – namely the mind itself – it seems that it must operate indirectly, through reflection on phantasms. But we are given no account of how reflection on phantasms helps the mind to knowledge of that individual which is itself. Aquinas has explained that what makes a thought the thought of an individual object is its relation to phantasms which are related to that object. But what makes the thought the thought of an individual subject: i.e. what makes my thoughts *my* thoughts? It is not as if this – at first sight bizarre – question was not one which occurred to Aquinas. As I wrote a few years ago in a popular work on Aquinas:

> The question was a very lively one in Aquinas's time and the subject of much controversy between Latin and Arab interpreters of Aristotle. Aquinas insisted, against the Averroists, that such a thought is my thought, and not the thought of any world-soul or supra-individual agent intellect. But to the question what makes them *my* thoughts his only answer is the connection between the intellectual content of the thought and the mental images in which it is embodied. It is because these mental images are the products of my body that the intellectual thought is my thought. This answer seems unsatisfactory for many reasons. Wittgenstein, who reawoke philosophers to the importance of the question of individuating the possessor of a thought, was surely better inspired when he urged us to look at the expression of a thought to supply the criteria for individuating its possessor. Aquinas has nothing of value to offer in the search for such criteria: his significance for the modern reader here is that he alerts one to the existence of the problem (*Aquinas*, p. 94).

Herbert McCabe protested against this passage. The account which I rejected, he said, was indeed unsatisfactory; but it had been rejected even more forthrightly by Aquinas himself in his *De Unitate Intellectus* when he dismissed the Averroist account of human thought. Averroes, Aquinas says, held the receptive intellect to be a substance quite separate from any human being; an intelligible species was the form and act of this intellect, but it had two subjects, or possessors, namely the receptive intellect and the phantasm of an individual human. Thus, the receptive intellect is linked to us by its form by means of the phantasms; so that when the receptive intellect understands, an individual human being understands. But this account, says Aquinas, is empty: *Quod autem hoc nihil sit, patet* (*De Unitate Intellectus*, ed. Keeler, sections 63–64).

Of the three reasons which Aquinas gives to prove the futility of the Averroist position, the following is the most persuasive. It is true, Aquinas says, that one item may have more than one subject or possessor: a wall's looking red to me may be the very same event as my seeing the redness of the wall. So there is no objection in principle to the idea that a species may be both a form of the receptive intellect and something which belongs to the phantasms. But that would not make the human being, whose phantasms these are, be an intelligent subject.

> The link between the receptive intellect and the human being, who is the possessor of the phantasms whose species are in the receptive intellect, is the same as the link between the coloured wall and the faculty of sight which has an impression of that colour. But the wall does not see, but is seen; it would follow therefore that the human being is not the thinker, but that its phantasms are thought of by the receptive intellect (*ibid.*, section 65).

The positive account which Aquinas sets against the Averroist account is that the thoughts I think are *my* thoughts because the soul which thinks them is the form of *my* body.

McCabe is perfectly correct that this is Aquinas' official position. However, it seems that what Aquinas says elsewhere prevents him giving a convincing answer to the question 'What makes my thoughts *my* thoughts?' He maintains that the soul can exist, and think, without the body. But, given the general Aristotelian hylomorphic theory to which he is committed, if X is the form of Y, then operations of X are operations of Y. Of course Aquinas denies that thinking is the operation of any bodily organ, and in that he is correct, if we are thinking of organs in the sense in which the eye is the organ of sight. But though thinking is not the operation of any bodily organ, it is the activity of a body, namely the thinking human being. That is to say, the manifestations, expressions, of my thoughts are the movements of my body, just as in general the manifestation of my knowledge of a language such as English consists in the movements of my speaking lips, my reading eyes, my writing fingers, my acting limbs. Hence it is not enough to say that my thoughts are *my* thoughts because the soul which thinks them is the form of my body: it is necessary to spell out the way in which it is my body which expresses the thoughts if the thoughts expressed are to be my thoughts.

But are there not unexpressed thoughts, the thoughts which pass through our minds in private, unvoiced thinking? Indeed there are, and we may well ask: what is it that makes these thoughts my thoughts? It may seem unhelpful, though it is true, to reply: they are thoughts which, if they were to be expressed, would be expressed by me. To make this answer seem less vacuous, and to convince ourselves that even in this case the criterion for the possessor is still bodily, we should reflect on cases of alleged telepathy or thought-reading.

Suppose that at a thought-reading session, or seance, the thought-reader or medium says 'Someone in this room is thinking of Eustace'. Here, *ex hypothesi*, the occurrence of the thought has been ascertained through means other than normal bodily communication. Even here, the way we would seek to decide whether what the thought reader claimed was *true* would involve appeal to bodily criteria. What settles the matter is whose hand goes up, whose voice confesses to the private thought. And *whose* the hand is, *whose* the voice is is determined by looking to see which body is involved.

Let there be no misunderstanding here. It is not being suggested that it is by observing actual or conjecturing hypothetical movements of my own body that I decide which thoughts are my own thoughts. Aquinas is indeed right that we 'perceive', that is to say know without any intermediary, what we are thinking. There is no state of mind in which I know that certain thoughts are present, and wonder whose thoughts they are, mine or someone else's. It is not by bodily criteria that I know which thoughts are mine, or know what I am thinking, because it is not by any criteria at all that I know these matters. But what it is that I know, when I know that certain thoughts are mine, is the same thing as other people know; and what I know, and what they know, is something to which the bodily criteria are necessarily relevant.

To sum up, then, the residual, unresolved, difficulty which vitiates Aquinas' account of self-knowledge: it is correct, as Aquinas says often (e.g. Ia, 75, 6) that my thoughts are my thoughts because they are operations of the form of my body. But the only account which he gives of the way in which my body is involved in the operation of the intellect is his account of the way in which the phantasms are involved in our present life, at every level, in the exercise of thought. It is only by reifying the intellect, by treating form as something separable from matter, that he is able to avoid the Averroist account of the relation between intellect and imagination which, as he rightly says, is sheer nothingness.

NOTES

1 Utrum intellectus possit actu intelligere per species intelligibiles quas penes se habet non convertendo se ad phantasmata.
2 Si quis astrologus cognosceret omnes motus caeli et distantias caelestium corporum, cognosceret unamquamque eclipsim quae futura est usque ad centum annos; non tamen cognosceret eam in quantum est singulare quoddam, ut sciret eam nunc esse vel non esse, sicut rusticus cognoscit dum eam videt. Et hoc modo ponunt Deum singularia cognoscere; non quasi singularem naturam eorum inspiciat, sed per positionem causarum universalium. Ex causis universalibus non consequuntur nisi formae universales, si non sit aliquid per quod formae individuentur. Ex formis autem universalibus congregatis, quotcumque fuerint, non constituitur aliquid singulare; quia adhuc collectio illarum formarum potest intelligi in pluribus esse.
3 Cognitio intellectiva aliquo modo a sensitiva primordium sumit. Et quia sensus est singularium, intellectus autem universalium; necesse est quod cognitio singularium, quoad nos, prior sit quam universalium cognitio.
4 Si autem consideremus ipsam naturam generis et speciei prout est in singularibus, sic quoddamodo habet rationem principii formalis respectu singularium: nam singulare est propter materiam, ratio vero speciei sumitur ex forma. Sed natura generis comparatur ad naturam speciei magis per modum materialis principii: quia natura generis sumitur ab eo quod est materiale in re, ratio vero speciei ab eo quod est formale; sicut ratio animalis a sensitivo, ratio vero hominis ab intellectivo.

7

SOME SEVENTEENTH-CENTURY DISAGREEMENTS AND TRANSUBSTANTIATION

P. J. FitzPatrick

Contributing to this Festschrift is for me not only a pleasure but the payment of a debt, for in 1972 and 1973 I found an exchange of views over transubstantiation with Herbert McCabe in *New Blackfriars* very useful.[1] My purpose here is not to revive the debate, but to try to place a little more clearly the distinctions and terms that are used in accounts of transubstantiation. It is customary nowadays to say that philosophical distinctions in the Aristotelian tradition – distinctions between substance and accident, or between matter and form – were given eucharistic adaptation (abuse, I would contend) by theologians like Aquinas. What I want to explore here is the sense of the phrase 'philosophical distinctions'. And I want to do this by accumulating texts, not just from Aquinas, but from some of his medieval predecessors, and from some of the seventeenth-century scholastics. To give an account of debates over transubstantiation in that century would be a vast undertaking; I have been working on some themes in it, and what follows is something of a progress report on only one of them. To sum it up in a way that I shall end by calling misleading, what did scholastics of that age think they were doing with the distinctions they drew? What relationship do those distinctions bear to the tradition they inherited from the Middle Ages, and what relationship did they bear to the new sciences that were then springing up? The investigation leads down by-roads, but I think it brings out things that deserve emphasis.[2]

I begin in the next section with a brief account of the scholastic analysis of change, and follow it with something even briefer on the eucharistic employment of that analysis. I state here once for all that the account is nothing more than a sketchy reminder of what I have written elsewhere, such as in my exchange of views with Herbert. But I do add something that will fill out the sketch – it concerns Aquinas and some of his medieval predecessors, and

120

it brings out what we might call the *status* of the vocabulary and distinctions he uses.

From all these medieval sources I turn to a range of authors from the seventeenth century. I deal first with the nature of the claims made by them for the reality of forms, and then with arguments over the origin of forms. All these texts exhibit what to our view is an ambiguity, and the ambiguity is most perceptible in what occupies the section after that – a rejection of prime matter altogether. This I take as in its way characteristic of the century; I give reasons, and I try to spell out what changes are exhibited then among scholastics. And in the last section of all I draw some general conclusions about the relation between present and past. If the essay has a moral, it is that saying how things were in the past involves a claim, implicit or explicit, as to what 'saying how things were' amounts to. It is one of the peculiar virtues of the seventeenth century that it obliges us to face problems like this.

1. THE SCHOLASTIC ACCOUNT OF CHANGE

First then for a very brief exposition of the terms in which Aquinas, in the Aristotelian tradition, discusses change. If I rub a small cube of Blutack between the palms of my hands I get what the geography primers used to call an oblate spheroid. The account Aquinas gives makes the Blutack to be the *subject* or *matter* of the change, and the successive shapes to be *forms*. The matter was to start with *actually* cubic but *potentially* spherical; the spherical form was *educed* from the potentiality of the matter. Two comments need interposing before we go further. The first indicates the *limits* of the account – it does not explain why, if we rub the ball of Blutack in the same way, we do not end up with a cube of the stuff. The second points to the need to respect the terms used in the account. The account offers a formulation of the change in shape undergone by the Blutack when pressed. If we treat the shapes themselves as such, or the matter itself as such, as *things*, if we *reify* them, then we shall fall into paradox and confusion. And reification here is easier than we might suppose. We might wonder what shape the Blutack is all the time; answer that it is of no particular shape all the time; and take the answer to mean that the Blutack is in itself in some topological limbo, and given shapes only by its successive forms. Or we might ask where the shapes come from, answer that they come from the Blutack when I press it, and take the answer to mean that the various shapes which the stuff might be are already in it in some peculiar

121

fashion. (And if the supposition seems too absurd to be entertained, we might ask ourselves how near it is approached by some recent speculations about 'possible worlds'.)

Dangers like these become more pressing when we consider changes of a more radical sort. Pressing the Blutack left it Blutack; but burning it presumably leaves something highly messy and unpleasant. Let us call it 'Sludge', and see how the account already given is extended to cover changes like this, changes which leave us with a different *kind* of stuff from that with which we started. The Aristotelian tradition calls the change in shape *accidental*; the Blutack is a *substance* which is qualified first by the accidental form of being cubic and then by the accidental form of being spherical. When it is burned, the same pattern is offered. The two extremes of the change are qualified by the forms of being Blutack and being Sludge; but these are not accidental but *substantial* forms, they do not qualify this or that sort of thing, they *are* what it is to be this or that sort of thing. And, just as the two accidental forms successively qualified the Blutack, so the two substantial forms successively qualify the matter.

It is not difficult to see why the dangers of reification are here more pressing. For some reasons we shall have to wait, but others can be noticed at once. 'What shape is the Blutack all the time?' is a badly-put question, but it at least has a recognizable stuff to be put about. 'What is it that is first Blutack and then Sludge?' has not even that. (If we prefer a less malodorous example, we can consider a carafe of wine that has turned to vinegar, and ask what was in the carafe all the time.) To this confusion another can be added – confusion over the order of 'each' and 'some', the confusion that tempts us to pass from 'every journey has an end' to 'there is one end to all our journeying'. The confusion can now tempt us to pass from 'in every substantial change, matter is qualified first by one substantial form and then by another' to 'there is something, namely matter, which in every substantial change is qualified first by one substantial form and then by another'. And if we do make that move, we are taking 'matter' as some primal material – *materia prima*, to use the scholastic term – which is a featureless and infinitely adaptable substrate, almost like some cosmic plasticine, that is actualized to this or that kind of thing through being informed by this or that substantial form.

2. THE ACCOUNT ADAPTED EUCHARISTICALLY

It is not my concern here to ask whether loss outweighs gain in the extension of the formulation used in accidental change to provide a formulation of substantial change. We shall see in due course that the various dangers I have noticed do present themselves in medieval and in seventeenth-century thought and that we have more at stake in them than fallacies in reasoning. For the present, let us see, again very briefly, what use was made by Aquinas of these accounts of change in what he wrote of the Eucharist, and what sense can be made of it. Once more, I write to recall things to mind, not to give them the account they deserve – *that* I hope to do elsewhere.

Aquinas insists that the eucharistic change comes under no natural classification – so he does not claim that the account so far given can offer an adequate description. Rather, he sets the change apart from others, and we can start from a natural change to show how. During his earthly life, Christ ate and digested bread, a change which is substantial – what was bread is now absorbed by him, it is now informed with his substantial form. But this will not accommodate the Eucharist, for it would make the bread used at Mass an *ingredient* of Christ's Body. Natural changes are limited to the forms of things, accidental or substantial; God's almighty power extends to the whole substance of the bread, matter as well as form, and it is this that passes over to the Body of Christ. The change is obviously not accidental (that would leave us still with bread); we have seen it is not substantial either; it is transubstantial (ST, IIIa, 75, 4; 75, 8).

Some recent theologians have complained that expressing eucharistic belief in terms of transubstantiation confines that belief too closely to Aristotelian categories. My own complaint is quite different: what we have here is no more than a nonsensical abuse of terms derived from the Aristotelian tradition. For better or worse, that tradition formulated its account of change in terms of a subject or matter informed first one way and then another. But the whole point of transubstantiation is to *deny* that there is any subject common to the bread and to Christ: how can it have any sense or coherence when it combines terms in order to exclude what it was their purpose to affirm?

All it can do is what it does. It gives a semblance of content to statements by treating the distinctions drawn between form, matter, substance and accident as if they were *dissections*, as if we were dealing with the constituents of the bread. Once that is done, transubstantiation becomes an admittedly miraculous re-shuffling of these constituents, and we can discuss it in terms of divine power when we ought to be discussing it in terms of intelligibility. The scholastic account of change was, as we saw, already open to abuse by reification of its terms, but reification is of the very essence of talking in terms of transubstantiation. The crudity of picturing substance as concealed beneath accidents, or accidents as entities normally but not always supported by a substance: such crudities – repudiated though they be – are all that enable the account even to appear to make sense. The account ties belief to Aristotelian categories only in the sense that forged money depends upon an already accepted currency. A philosophical tradition offered an account of change that may be philosophically debated; all we have here is what Aquinas calls in another context *discohaerentia terminorum* – the terms of the account are put together in a way that will not let them cohere.

3. AQUINAS AND EARLIER ACCOUNTS OF THE EUCHARIST

Such is my argument sketched, and I stand by my arguments. What interests me here is rather asking what 'philosophical' means. The question will turn out to lead us a long way, and I begin answering it by considering some texts in which Aquinas examines eucharistic theories of his medieval predecessors. I am glad here to acknowledge my debt to the German scholar Hans Jorissen, whose monograph is invaluable for its copious quotation of a variety of sources, many still in manuscript only. Texts I know from his book only I cite by 'J' and page-number.[3] And I begin with some passages in the *Summa Theologiae*.

The first considers the opinion (Abelard's in fact) that after the consecration, when the substance of the bread has been converted into the substance of the body of Christ, the surviving accidents of the bread take the surrounding *air* as their subject. To this very 'physical' account, Aquinas puts two objections that are just as 'physical': air cannot receive such accidents, and, if it did, moving a consecrated host would drive the air away (ST, IIIa, 77, 1). The second opinion on which he passes judgement asks what becomes of the substance of the bread at the consecration, and suggests that it is resolved into its elements (like the Star of the Magi, some added; J 29). Aquinas objects that, were this the case, the elements would still have to be moved away from under the surviving accidents, for there must be nothing under them except the Body of Christ (ST, IIIa, 75, 3). A third text of Aquinas surveys and evaluates several earlier opinions about the fate of the water that is mixed with wine in the chalice at Mass. It cannot remain unaltered (nothing must be there but Christ); it cannot be changed into the water that flowed from the side of Christ (that would call for a separate consecration); it seems best to say that it is first transformed into wine, and then transubstantiated into the

Blood of Christ (ST, IIIa, 74, 8). The oddities in these texts should not obscure for us the fact that all three are concerned with the behaviour of recognizable physical objects – air is incompatible with some accidents, and is easily moved; the elements of the bread's substance will need moving away; water undergoes a change into wine before the eucharistic conversion takes place. We are in all three cases in the order of physical reality and of its properties and activities; we are certainly in the order of the miraculous; but we are not in some 'philosophical' order removed from a general attempt to make claims about the way in which things in the world behave.

The authors cited by Jorissen have just as 'physical' a view of the eucharistic change. The analogies they offer to it reveal their cast of thought – hay into glass, the Egyptian magicians' rods into serpents, water into wine at Cana, Lot's wife into a pillar of salt (J 87, 123, 77 etc.).[4] Indeed, one of the earliest uses of 'transubstantiate' I have seen (it is not mentioned by Jorissen), that by John Belethus (*c.* 1165) in his *Rationale Divinorum Officiorum*, is in a picturesque setting that is even more physical. Some shepherds one day recited the words of consecration over some bread and wine in the fields (their 'bait', presumably); it was transformed 'and perhaps transubstantiated, if I may so speak, into the Body of Christ' and they were all struck dead (PL 202, 52; the point of the story is to explain why the words of consecration are said inaudibly). Yet another group of texts given by Jorissen concerns the capacity of the Eucharist to *nourish*. Appearances, it would seem, cannot nourish, and the difficulty was felt all the more because some writers, such as the author of a *Sententiae Divinitatis* of between 1142 and 1147, denied any reality whatever to the appearances, and reduced them to the status of the perennial 'bent stick in water' (J 78). (And this opinion, we shall see, won a new lease of life in the seventeenth century.) An analogy was used to suggest the possibility of a solution: some Indians live off the smell of apples, and the smell of wine has been known to intoxicate (J 93; the source is Peter Cantor's *Summa de Sacramentis* of the mid-1190s). The reason Aquinas offers for rejecting the analogy is just as physical, as well as a testimony to his good sense – activities of the sort can give no more than momentary solace, the body needs something more (ST, IIIa, 77, 6). Aquinas, like his predecessors, saw the terminology employed in a euchar-istic context as borrowed from a general concern with the be-haviour of physical objects like air, water, food, hay and the rest. Neither he nor his predecessors took the distinctions as borrowed from a piece of philosophical speculation that stood apart from the particular ways in which physical objects behave.

So to say that transubstantiation is a theological abuse of philosophical distinctions already looks a little odd. Think as we will about what Aquinas and his predecessors wrote about the Eucharist, we must admit that their terms and examples and analogies were of a piece with how they speculated about the perceptible world and tried to make sense of its changes. Shall we say then that transubstantiation abuses *scientific* terms? Trying to answer this question will take us further still – and takes us at once into the seventeenth century.

4. THE REALITY OF FORMS

The *viva* of the medical candidate in the last act of *Le Malade Imaginaire* has entered the folk-lore of philosophy. Asked why opium induces sleep, he replies that there is in it a *virtus dormitiva*, a soporific power, whose nature it is to calm the senses; and the answer wins the new doctor loud applause for his eloquence, he is the *novus doctor qui tam bene parlat*. Molière made the gibe he did to poke fun at an inherited wisdom among doctors. The inheritance was more than medical, and included the scholastic tradition we have been considering. So we can first notice the same charge being made by a writer at odds with that tradition. Antoine Legrand was the author of a vigorously written account of Descartes' philosophy, just as vigorously Englished in 1694 as *An Entire Body of Philosophy According to the Principles of the Famous Renate Des Cartes*. In Part IV, c. 3, he treats 'Of the Nature and Constitution of Matter'. Here, Legrand charges talk of substantial forms with being as vacuous as saying 'fire is fire, and water water'; and asks what we should say to anyone who explained the phases of the Moon or Venus, and other astronomical phenomena, by saying that they proceed from their inward principles: should we call him an interpreter of nature? Further objections from Legrand, and the significance of the examples he has offered here, will concern us later.[5] Meanwhile, what would we ourselves make of the objection he has just proposed? Bearing in mind the Blutack example, we should reply that the account was not meant to answer questions about why the Blutack yields such a shape on being pressed, or such a Sludge on being burned; we should take the objection as missing the point. That things were otherwise in the seventeenth century can be seen from what another author of Cartesian sympathies writes and quotes.

Pierre Cally, in his *Institutiones Philosophiae* (1674), asks why it is that the scholastics call for a *substantial form* in things, and gives the standard answer offered in the commentary on Aristotle (1625) by the Jesuits of Coimbra (the 'Conimbricenses'): there is the same matter in all things; matter has no force in itself; so the differentiation of things by their peculiar characteristics – thinking for a man, neighing for a horse – must have another cause; and that cause is the substantial form (Lib. I, c. 9). And Cally takes this claim to mean that those who, like the Conimbricenses, hold to the scholastic tradition believe that there is produced something in change, namely the form, over and above the arrangement of constituents (*compositio elementorum*) in what changes (Cally, *Secunda Pars*, p. 119).

Nor is it just Cartesians who regard substantial forms and matter in this way, the scholastics themselves do. A popular manual, French in origin, was the *Summa Philosophiae* of Eustachius a Sancto Paulo, which was given a Cambridge printing in 1649.[6] Writing in the section of *Physica* devoted to prime matter, Eustachius describes it as an incomplete substance capable of assuming all forms; he argues for it on the ground that, since nothing can come from nothing, when, say, fire turns into air, the air must come from something pre-existent which remains in it when it has come to be – and this is prime matter (*De principiis*, Quaest. II; p. 119). This picture of a passive and indefinitely adaptable matter specified by forms is confirmed by an argument employed against the Cartesian denial of it. For Cartesians, a uniform matter was distinguished only by its shapings and movements, nothing more was allowed than a purely mechanical explanation. Against this, the *Metaphysica Scholastica* (1675) of William Ayleworth (a Jesuit from Monmouthshire who taught in their College at Liège) makes the riposte that, if the Cartesians are right, how are the unity and constancy in things to be explained? (The terms used by Ayleworth suggest both material cohesion and what speculations over Induction have called 'The Principle of Limited Independent Variety'.) A vigorous Thomist, the Dominican Antoine Goudin, argued for substantial forms in his work of 1692 on the grounds that compounds possess qualities superior to those simply produced by the compounding of their elements. Plants provide one example, while other examples are drawn from minerals, such as the attractive power of a magnet, and the capacities of jasper to staunch blood and of jade to ease pain (Tom. III, Pars 3: 'De Generatione et Corruptione').

These scholastic accounts give substantial forms a job to do for which evidence can be offered: their specifying and unifying functions show themselves in the emergence of effects that simple collocation of elements could not produce. And the very hesitancies of some scholastic writers do as much. To understand these, we must bear in mind that the classic example of a substance for Aristotle is a living being – it is living things that combine a physical unity and purposive behaviour with the capacity to change their material content over a length of time. The biological background to the notion of substantial form was supplemented by the Christian doctrine of the immortality of the soul. The need for substantial forms seemed met by a proof of their reality – the soul can survive the dissolution of the body. Yet for some thinkers the privileged position of human beings set them and their substantial forms apart, and an opponent of scholasticism like Jacques Rohault, in his *Traité de Physique* (1676), contended that the independence of the rational soul proved nothing as to the existence in purely material things of substantial forms, 'real substances, and so possessing an existence distinct from that of matter' (c. xviii). And as I said, even defenders of the scholastic tradition thought that not all was as it should be. The Oratorian J. B. de la Grange wrote, also in 1676, that he had never found satisfactory proofs from scholastics that inanimate objects have substantial forms. Authors who attempt a proof take for granted the reality of *accidental* forms; they assume that heat, light, knowledge and truth (a significant list!) are real things that are irreducible to the movement of particles. It is with proving this that any proper treatment should begin. We may notice at once that contentions by scholastics for the 'reality of accidental forms' are always obscured by the ulterior motive of the contenders – real accidental forms are the kind of entity that supposedly can exist without a substance. Having noticed that, I put it aside in favour of one of the examples offered by La Grange – the persistence in movement of projectiles, which is irreducible to mechanical pushes or pulls (*Les Principes de la Philosophie*, p. 160: the general thesis is stated in La Grange's Introduction to his book). Some readers will have encountered Leibniz's arguments over this persistence, but all will easily recognize that the unease felt and the example offered bear witness to how scholastics of the seventeenth century regarded forms, whether substantial or accidental – they regarded them as contributing something specific, something not reducible to what the elements can do, or to what can be done by impulse of one body against another.

I close this first series of texts with two more examples. One illustrates the uncertainties of scholastic writers, while the other declares outright that Molière's joke is by way of being a compliment.

J. B. Duhamel (1624–1706) filled his long life with an interest in experimental work, and with labours appreciated in high places. He visited England in 1668 and was encouraged in his work by Boyle, and Colbert had recommended him two years before for the Secretaryship of the Académie des Sciences. He is taken in his writings to be seeking reconciliation between older and newer opinions. It would be fairer to say that he had an Emersonian disregard for consistency, and that his use at times of dialogue-form enabled him to hedge his bets. In his *Philosophia Vetus et Nova*, he adopts after some hesitation the view that there is nothing in inanimate objects distinct from the *elementorum temperatio*, the blending of the elements. It is not so with living beings: here substantial form is not so reducible. *Elementorum temperatio* is for Duhamel as for others a rival to substantial form, and one argument he uses shows what kind of work he expected the form to do. Scholastics objected that the *homogeneity* of objects called for a substantial form; Duhamel denies the objection's presupposition; things are *not* homogeneous – 'anything can be disintegrated by chemistry' (*Physica Generalis*, Tract. 1). He is more sympathetic to forms in another work, *Commentarius in Universalem Aristotelis philosophiam* (1705), where substantial and accidental forms are presented as respectively primary and secondary principles of activity. An artificial object like a clock has only external form; a natural thing contains a principle that is internal and substantial.

I think it is characteristic of Duhamel that he should offer *translations* from one idiom into another. In his earlier work, talk of substantial forms can be translated into talk of *temperatio elementorum* – which sounds as if belief in the forms does not commit believers to much. But in the later work, while still allowing translation between scholastic and Cartesian terminology, it is the scholastics he favours, precisely because a form is seen as an *internal* principle of what the object does, not merely an *external* principle – one of the mechanical sort Cartesians favour. Duhamel's preference goes here with a choice of language that we should notice, the distinction between *metaphysice* and *physice* – 'metaphysically' and 'physically'. *Physice*, the two kinds of explanation are the same – that is, as far as their effects go; it is only *metaphysice* that they differ. The distinction seems to suggest proximate and remote explanations, and perhaps it is the same distinction that gets drawn later. There, we are told that natural phenomena could be explained *metaphysice* in a Cartesian way, but not *physice*; for an explanation *physice*, a natural explanation, they need a principle that is internal; that is, a substantial form. Duhamel's distinction, if I understand it aright, does what the other texts have done; it claims that substantial forms are needed on the ground that *elementorum temperatio* is not enough, and that there must be an internal principle of what a thing does. That the forms are not required absolutely, not *metaphysice*, stresses the perceptible job they have to do; they are part of an explanation of how things behave.

We shall be returning to Duhamel. Let us now examine the much more rollicking work *Lettre d'un philosophe à un cartésien de ses amis* (1672), prepared for publication by the Jesuit I. G. Pardiès. He acknowledges that the Cartesians blame the schoolmen for saying things such as that a key opens a door because it has a *virtus aperitiva*, an 'opening power'. But what is wrong with this? Are not the Cartesians over-particular in their investigations? Is not enquiry about the mechanical operations of wards and levers in a lock scarcely *digne d'honnêtes gens*? Are not such questions useless? Do they not turn an *école de philosophie* into a locksmith's shop, *une boutique de serrurier*? Must gentlefolk be obliged to acquire such knowledge? Is it not like obliging the ladies of the Court to learn carpentry? Is it not enough to say that the key is made in a way that allows it to open the door – that, in other words, it has a *virtus aperitiva*? (p. 167). And so on – the work invites endless quotation by its mixture of verve and snobbery.

5. THE ORIGIN OF FORMS

For all this spirited rejection of what is done by those who soil their hands, the general line of argument adopted by defenders of forms keeps very close to the specific behaviour of material things. Forms specify a passive matter; give stability and cohesion; account for properties that go beyond a *temperatio elementorum*, and by means of an intrinsic principle. Given that forms are so seen by those who favour them, we may perhaps not be surprised to learn that their *origin* occupied minds also. For the adversaries of forms, it was the problem of their origin that was the biggest argument against accepting them. Legrand, the Cartesian already cited, puts the point clearly; scholastics hold substantial forms to be more substantial than the matter with which they are united, and the changing character of the world obliges us to believe that many such forms come to be and pass away each day. But what is their origin? Are we to suppose that fresh acts of creation by God attend upon every substantial change? And where do they go when they cease to inform the matter? Is God expected to annihilate them? And if they survive, how do they work without matter to inform? (IV, 7; p. 102. Cally argues in the same way, *Secunda Pars Philosophiae*, p. 119.)

This line of objection may well bring to a head the unease that readers may have felt in what has been said and cited here about forms. Surely this is all no more than one long missing of the point? Surely it is simply that *reification* against which a warning was given earlier? Treat forms as things, and you will end in paradoxes – and both Aristotle and Aquinas have said as much.

But an examination of texts will show that there is more to it than paradoxes due to faults in logic. Scholastic writers need to be seen in the concreteness of what they actually wrote, and what they wrote shows that the origin of forms was for them a real problem, with empirical consequences. Thus, the Jesuit Pereira wrote in 1591 a work against superstitious practices, and devoted a section to the alchemists' claim to make gold. He records the opinion of Aquinas (In II *Sent.* 7, 3, 1 ad 5) that while art can 'induce some forms into matter', it cannot induce all. The alchemists' fire cannot induce the substantial form of gold, which has to be induced by the heat of the Sun, *per calorem Solis*.[7] Pererius adds that, were alchemists right in claiming that sulphur and mercury are the matter of all metals, they ought to be found in veins of silver and gold, whereas they are not. See how forms are 'induced', and how there is no break here between talk of matter and form and claims about mining; and how the origin of the induction of forms is seen as a genuine question, to be answered one way or another.

Still more problems were held to be raised by the origin of the forms of *living* beings – not surprisingly, given the ultimate origin in Aristotle of talk about substantial forms. Duhamel, after stating that the origin of forms is the hardest of all questions, retails an argument of 'Fernelius' (this is Jean Fernel [d. 1558], physician to Henri II) that the forms of animate beings are celestially induced. When spontaneous generation takes place, the matter there cannot provide life; so it must come from the heavenly bodies (the Sun breeds maggots in a dead dog, as Hamlet pointed out). But higher animals must have no baser origin than things like maggots. Ergo. To this view (popular in the Middle Ages and lingering on in astrology), Duhamel puts an objection that is at least ingenious – the first chapter of Genesis has grass and green things (that is, animate things) springing up on the third day, while the Sun and the rest do not make their appearance until the fourth (*Philosophia vetus et nova, Physica Generalis*: 'De formarum origine'). But the distinctive character of what is animate seemed to some to call for a distinctive origin of their forms, and when Micraelius, in a popular philosophical lexicon (1653 etc.), denied that they were induced by the heavenly bodies, he also denied that they were educed from the matter. Rather, they were created along with it in the beginning (*Lexicon Philosophicum*, s.v. 'Forma').

The phrase 'educed from matter' in Micraelius is of course scholastic in origin, as we have seen (p. 121). Let us see then what scholastics made of the notion that forms are 'educed from the potentiality of the matter': what they did make of it is, once more, bound up with noticing the specific behaviour of things. Eustachius a Sancto Paulo says that forms cannot be more than potentially in the matter – or we should feel the fire in wood even before igniting it (*Summa Philosophiae*, 'De Forma', Question vi). Aylesworth argues for the reality of accidents on the grounds that, if there were no need of accidental forms (like heat) to prepare for the emergence of the substantial form (of fire), how could so violent a form be enclosed within so weak a prison as combustible matter? (*Metaphysica Scholastica*, Tract. I, Disp. 3, c. ii). Aylesworth's successor at Liège was Francis Sanders, who dictated a set of notes on scholastic *Physica* and *Metaphysica*.[8] Sanders gives a section to 'Descartes and other atomists' and discusses there the Cartesian view that extension is of the essence of a body. All I point to here is his remark *en passant* that a difficulty for the Cartesian view lies in the sudden expansion (i.e. greater extension) that follows the exploding of gunpowder by a spark. For all these authors, the origin of forms is a question to do with something empirically verifiable, something that makes gold, gives life, can be spoken of as 'in the prison' of a material object, suddenly emerge thence, be potentially there. We have more here than reification, or confusion over what Aristotle wrote about change.

That we do have more is well illustrated by two difficulties discussed in the seventeenth century. One concerns accidental forms, the other substantial. The former nicely combines points of logic and of experience, and the latter will lead us to the next stage of our argument.

A popular objection raised against belief in the reality of accidental forms was that making them real went with believing that they can migrate from one substance to another. But this is impossible, for it would show that a given accident did not after all depend completely upon the substance it originally informed – it survived its migration from it. So the real accident would in truth be a substance, not an accident at all (Legrand, c. viii). Now to be sure, the objection is in part a logical blunder, as can be seen if we take an example of this 'migration'. Suppose that a red-hot poker is plunged into a glass of Guinness (yielding a warm and palatable beverage, regularly prepared at one time by my grandmother). The heat of the poker can indeed be nowhere else than in the poker – for the simple reason that, if it *is* anywhere else, it is not the poker's heat. The difficulty is no more real than the inability of anyone but me to hit myself (as opposed to me) on the head; and the confusion here vitiates much said by Cartesians against the reality of accidents. But there is more than confusion to the problem. Clearing up the point of logic does not get us any nearer explaining *how* the heat is transmitted from the metal to the stout. And the late arrival of a satisfactory theory of heat shows that the explanation was not easily come by, and shows that Leibniz's perplexity at the difficulty was a perplexity that touched the whole problem of explaining interaction – as notoriously was the case for Leibniz.

So much for the difficulty concerning accidental forms. The difficulty concerning substantial forms is analogous to it, and is also redolent of the violence and wars of the seventeenth century. Suppose a soldier is killed with a sword-thrust. There he lies, with all his scars upon him, still recognizably D'Artagnan or whoever else he was. When alive, D'Artagnan hàd these distinguishing marks; but D'Artagnan was alive because his matter was informed by his soul, his substantial form, the 'first principle of existence and activity' as Duhamel called it; and D'Artagnan's features, scars and the rest were secondary principles, dependent upon the substantial form. The soul has now departed; how can these dependent and secondary principles survive its departure? The difficulty is considered by the Thomist Goudin, and one cannot but admire how he bites on the bullet. The accidents do *not* survive, because the departure of the substantial form involves the cessation of all accidental forms and the reduction to prime matter – which is now informed by a new form, the *forma cadaverica* or 'corpse-form'. The corpse may present all the evidence of being that of D'Artagnan, but the distinguishing marks are not identical with what once distinguished the musketeer, they are just similar. And if we infer from the similitude that they are the same, we are making the kind of mistake made when we confuse one twin or one egg with another. It may be objected, Goudin adds, that what kills D'Artagnan has to produce the *forma cadaverica*, and that this cannot be – for how could a sword produce eyes of such a colour, scars of such a shape, and the rest? To which he replies that the main cause of the new form is not the sword, but 'universal activities' – *agentia universalia*. These preserve the form of the living being as long as they can; when the right dispositions for the form have been destroyed (in disease, wounding, and so on), the *agentia* induce another form, suitable to what dispositions there are.

It would be hard to imagine a more vivid example of the mixture of what we should now call logic and physical science. D'Artagnan's corpse is not D'Artagnan, and so the scars on it are not the musketeer's either; and yet it was he upon whom they were inflicted, and if the corpse is not he it is his and no-one else's. We can imagine the distinctions that could be drawn, but they are not distinctions that are to be identified with observations of dead bodies. The physical structure of bodies is not irrelevant to questions of identity, but the relevance does not amount to the way in which for us Goudin lumps two kinds of problem together.

6. AN OBJECTION TO PRIME MATTER

Another writer of the seventeenth century considers the problem – indeed, Goudin must have read him. This is the Capuchin Valerianus Magnus, in his *Philosophia Virgini Deiparae dicata* (1648), whose consideration of it is in the setting of objections to the whole concept of prime matter and of the eduction of forms from it.[9] And what Valerianus writes will enable us to bring out just what is the ambiguity about forms that has run through all the texts we have been considering.

Valerianus states the 'corpse' problem vividly, even adding the passage from the *Aeneid* in which the dead Hector appears to the hero, and is, of course, at once identified by him. Given that prime matter is supposed to lack any determination or specificity, is it not absurd to suppose that from this total indeterminacy there can be educed a form precisely similar in all details to the form that has departed? Is not the whole notion of prime matter bound up with a belief that all the elements of things are transmutable into each other? (I take Valerianus to be making here the point I make on p. 122 about a 'cosmic plasticine'.) And is not the notion incompatible with what change and the world are really like?

Valerianus had earlier conducted experiments with a vacuum, and he laid particular stress upon the fact that a ray of light can pass through it, so that we have there a sensible form which is independent of any subject – *Demonstratio ocularis* (1647?). His contention in *Demonstratio ocularis* was attacked on the grounds that the absence of a subject makes the light's ray amount to creation, since only God can make something from nothing, that is, without a pre-existent subject. But Valerianus denies that Christian belief commits us to holding that 'nothing can come from nothing': God alone indeed can be the absolute cause of a thing's existence, for He alone can create; but secondary causes, always dependently upon Him, can produce something without a pre-existent subject. And that principle, declares Valerianus, experimentally demonstrated by sending light across a vacuum, can be applied to the origin of forms. Just as the Sun produces light in the air, not by educing it from the passive potentiality of the air (it cannot be so for Valerianus, or light would never cross a vacuum, where there is no air), but rather inducing it from the fruitfulness of its own light, so do natural agents work upon matter. There is matter; these agents work upon it, and from their own fertility produce many effects in it – but these effects are not educed by the agents from the matter's potentiality (*Philosophia*, Pars II, c. vii). By thus denying the pattern of 'form and subject', Valerianus deliberately sets himself apart from the majority of his scholastic predecessors. His aim is to reject a 'prime matter' that would (to use the phrase we found in Eustachius a Sancto Paulo) 'be capable of assuming all forms', and so to reject the notion that forms are educed from the potentiality of the matter. We might describe his move as being against the notion of matter as a 'reservoir' of forms, and in favour of the power and fertility of *agentia naturalia*.

And it is here that the recurrent ambiguity in our texts is most palpable. In one way we can, of course, no matter what Valerianus says, continue to use the terminology of eduction, by whatever means a change takes place – we simply include all active principles under the general heading 'potentiality of the matter'. In doing this, we are making no claim about how or by what the change is effected. Let us call such a use of 'eduction' its use *as a formulation* – that is, we use it and cognate terms for a general way of expressing change. But this is not the only use. We may be concerned with means of achievement, and shall in that case acknowledge that some changes need far more 'contribution from outside' than others. And here we shall find the vocabulary of eduction more suitable in cases like moulding the Blutack than, say, in cases like the fertilization of an egg. Let us call this other use of eduction its use *as a recipe*. And now we can say that Valerianus is concerned with the terminology as a recipe, and is complaining that the recipe it offers gives too prominent a place to the stuff from which things are composed, and too small a place to activities that can be exercised upon them. But we can also say that, in so dealing with the terminology, he was not missing the point of how his contemporaries wrote of forms, how they defended them, what functions they assigned them, and what they judged their origins to be. All had recipes on their minds.

But what are we ourselves to say of these writers? That question will turn out to be concerned with its own posing, as well as with what they wrote in the seventeenth century.

We have seen substantial and indeed accidental forms defended on the ground that this or that effect or unity calls for more than a blending of constituents in a compound, a *temperatio elementorum*. And what we must say as we look back is that the Latin phrase is very vague. Think of several tasks we might be set: to separate grains of rice from a heap of mixed grains; to pour out some mercury from a bottle; to extract mercury from an amalgam; to extract mercury from cinnabar. All four compounds have a *temperatio elementorum*, but the practical processes involved in extracting are very different. As for *explaining* those differences, that calls for successively more complicated notions in physical science; those notions took a long time to devise; and now that they have been devised, the use of a phrase like *temperatio elementorum* has become, quite apart from its antiqueness, too generic to be useful. In the seventeenth century this was not so. Chemical theory was in its infancy, despite the multitude of practical skills and rules of thumb discovered over the centuries. Cartesian speculations encouraged a general persuasion that all explanations could be couched in terms of extension and motion. At such a time, to talk in terms of forms – in terms that appealed ultimately to the biological pattern of unity in diversity favoured by Aristotle – could be a useful corrective. More precisely, it could encourage (even eccentrically) a *variety* in thought, so that it was not unreasonable for Leibniz to characterize his theories of dynamics as in effect using Aristotle to go beyond Descartes. But as knowledge of physical things and processes increased, so did this implicit appeal to a biological paradigm become less important. The sheer *complexity* of the material world made phrases like *temperatio elementorum* or 'extension and motion' seem vacuously generic: opposition to them inevitably fared as badly.

I pointed to what Valerianus Magnus wrote, not because of any special profundity in it, but because he wanted to give pride of place to *activity*. Whatever he himself made of the notion, we can certainly see it as setting the seventeenth century apart from what had preceded it. It was not by accident that I cited Legrand on 'the phases of Venus' (p. 126), or Pardiès on turning philosophy into a *boutique de serrurier* (p. 130). The two phrases point vividly to the change. The phases of Venus had been observed by Galileo – telescopic observation and the elucidation of the concepts of motion were shaking the foundations of the ways in which belief was expressed about the physical world. 'Locksmith's shops' can sum up the mass of experimental activity, from magnetism to navigation, that was forcing itself on the inhabitants of Europe, whether *honnêtes gens* or not.

There is evidence of awareness of the change that was taking place. Some of it, of course, is simply a rejection of what is new, but cast in a form that has the capacity to amuse. La Grange, whose work against the innovators I have already mentioned, blames in the introduction the Cartesians for destroying 'the ordinary philosophy', which Catholic theologians 'have in a manner consecrated by their use'. And the Carmelite Augustinus a Virgine Maria states in the Preface to his *Philosophiae Aristotelicae-Thomisticae Cursus* (1664) that a profound knowledge of Aristotle is required because the rules of his congregation demand that its members 'follow Aristotelian principles to the extent that the Catholic faith allows'. Four hundred years earlier, medieval Popes and bishops had been handing out condemnations of theologians for *following* Aristotle, in furious and bad Latin. They must have been turning in their graves. Other reactions were more serious. Duhamel, in expounding different views of change, states the scholastic account of eduction in a way that we should take to be treating it 'as a formulation'. But having done so, he adds at once an objection that shows him to be treating it 'as a recipe': a compound cannot have only a single substantial form, for if it did, how could its constituents ever be extracted from it? That the objection is being put by one who has made and then dissolved compounds in a laboratory is clear by what else he says – the Aristotelian tradition neglected sense experience and despised what was obvious, in favour of 'figments of reason' (*De consensu veteris et novae philosophiae*, Lib. II; 'De peripateticis'). He adds a use of 'metaphysical' that is pejorative: the matter of a human being in the obvious sense is his organic body; in the ultimate sense it is the four elements; 'if you go further, you leave physical things for metaphysical'. A similar use of the word is given by Cally, who claims that Aristotle did not write specifically about matter but only 'metaphysically'. The sense of the word he brings out by a pleasingly contemporary analogy: all can cite Aristotle in their favour, just as in an audience-chamber the Prince's picture has its eyes so painted that each one feels them directed on himself (*Secunda pars philosophiae*, pp. 119, 131).

Texts also show an awareness that the changes were affecting disciplinary boundaries. Once more, Duhamel can provide an example. The second book in the second volume of his collected works is *De Fossilibus*: 'Mining and Minerals' might be the best translation. One speaker in a dialogue, when the discussion of 'salt' is opened, asks why a philosopher should soil his hands with potter's clay. To this Pardiès-like objection, the answer comes that in the first place *medici* and *chimici* have wrongly taken over much of *physica* for themselves, when in justice the former profession should be concerned with healing, not theory, and the latter limited to the practices of distillation and retorts (? – *infusoria*). But the answer goes on to deny that it is beneath a philosopher's dignity to investigate what is obvious and of practical use: he must be confined neither to pure speculation nor to chemical apparatus; his discipline lies in theorizing (*aestimatione*), but must not stand wholly apart from activity of practice. He must neither betake himself to the laboratory (*laboratorium* – the word is apologized for) nor refuse to consult those who work in them.

But more important even than these acknowledgements was the sheer *bulk* of what was novel. Elucidation of the laws of motion was an activity far removed from the close natural observation that was one of Aristotle's strengths, and far removed from the teleological explanations he favoured. As the century advanced, ever more topics were being considered that the scholastic tradition had never asked at all. At the very least, the questions it had asked were now only part of what occupied those who engaged in speculation about the nature of things.

7. THE PRESENT AND THE PAST

And it is here that our examination of some seventeenth-century texts points to conclusions of a much wider import. Philosophers nowadays discuss the status of what they call 'Cambridge changes' (the term is Geach's, and the reason for the nomenclature does not concern us here). Butter undergoes a Cambridge change when it goes up in price (as opposed to when it is melted), and so does Socrates, when Theaetetus grows up and overtops him. Cambridge changes raise all manner of problems, and my only concern here is to notice the odd relationship between them and creations of the understanding. We find it natural to say that Socrates has changed when he grows taller, but odd to say that he has changed because Theaetetus has grown taller. Yet, if one intellectual activity is succeeded by another, things are not as clearly set apart. The place of the earlier activity in our judgement is changed 'retroactively' by what has succeeded it. Our descriptions and estimates of the past are touched by something of which those there we strive to understand were not aware – the years that have intervened.

We touch here a general difficulty in interpreting the past; and in our own case the difficulty is compounded. The general difficulty lies in the fact that questions like 'what did they mean by " . . ."?' or 'did they think they were engaged in — or . . .?' are always liable to be unanswerable. Questions of that sort among our contemporaries get answered, not just by inspection, but by a process of interrogation and response. But neither interrogation nor response can always be protracted when we are dealing with a past activity at all removed from our own. Of course, the difficulty is a matter of degree: but then everything is a matter of degree. What the difficulty means is that we can find ourselves, sooner than we should like to think, having to admit that the words and concepts in which we frame our understanding might not have been recognized by those whose beliefs we are interrogating. To this problem there is no recipe for an easy answer. (Indeed, the word 'recipe' reminds me that some writings on the subject fall into exactly the ambiguity we have been meeting – they use terms such as *Verstehen* or the like, terms essentially *formulations*, as if those terms were *recipes*.) Negative advice is more helpful, such as letting the past's vocabulary and its exigencies work as uninterruptedly as we can (I have sedulously avoided translating words like *physica*, nor have I attributed words like 'physical science' to any of our authors). Again negatively, we must respect not only their formulation of questions, but where their questioning stopped. We are not just concerned with repeating their words, but with understanding them, with endeavouring to see the inner connexions and boundaries of their interests and enquiries, and the relationship between those enquiries and our own. Respecting the distinctiveness of what they did means going outside our own customary patterns of thought; but it offers the reward, not only of seeing something alien and intelligible, but of being more aware of what is our own distinctiveness.

None of this dispenses from hard work, and the work is all the harder here for a reason to do with our specific topic. Whatever we think of the ultimately Aristotelian notions we have been investigating, it is Aristotle's vocabulary, given a Latin dress by Cicero and Lucretius as well as by the schoolmen, that still lies behind the words we use in talking about the nature of things. 'Matter', 'form', 'substance', 'category', 'potentiality', 'principle', 'physics', 'nature', 'philosophy': if Whitehead was right in saying that all European philosophy is footnotes to Plato, he should have added that the notes are written in Aristotle's language. We know that the pattern and use of the words has changed; and so the very words we now have to use to express the change are themselves witnesses to it. The web of words and concepts and concerns we have inherited is both the means and the object of our investigation. 'Were they doing physics or philosophy?', apparently a question about the past, is itself a testimony to what both links us with that past and keeps us distinct from it. It does not stand outside what it interrogates; there is no sharp distinction here between object-language and metalanguage.

But we can go further. We now see disagreements in the seventeenth century more clearly, because we know what took place in the intervening years; and so we can exhibit ambiguities in texts with an ease that their authors could not. Indeed, I venture to join two idioms whose separateness we over-estimate, and put it thus: if a text offers a multitude of paths going off in every direction, we know where some of them led, and the authors of our texts did not. Why we can go further is that what they themselves were doing brought out in its turn an ambiguity that goes back much further, to Aristotle himself. Here I must be assertoric because I have no room left to be anything else. A reading of texts from the *Physics* and *Metaphysics* reveals for me an initial uncertainty between what I have called 'formulation' and 'recipe'. In *Physics* A, his use of 'principle' (*archē*) covers too much to be comfortable, and it is significant that in the same book his pronouncement that change does not take place 'at random' (which arouses expectancies of talk about the regularity of things) is filled out simply by the observation that, if a change occurs, the terminal points of it can be expressed as not-F and F. And in *Metaphysics* Z, where the quest for the 'primary reality' (*ousia*) is made, the quest is conducted largely in terms of predication, but reaches its goal in terms of activity, in terms of a principle of unity in living objects.

This is no more than assertion, but I go on to notice that the ambiguity was of no great moment in an age when theoretically ordered experiment was unknown (and where the merits of Aristotle's conceptual analyses could still be acknowledged). When what we might call the age of activity came, with its phases of Venus and its locksmith's shops, things were changing. Valerianus Magnus, by regarding eduction from prime matter as a recipe he did not like, can be seen as embodying the change. And, as we have seen, changes like this have a retroactive effect upon what has preceded them.

Now when an ambiguity is resolved, the resolution often calls for a decision as to how what has been distinguished is to be treated. Molière's gibe about *virtus dormitiva* shows one way in which the older tradition tended to react: it treated its statements as if they were of the same type as statements being made in the new sciences. The candidate who appeals to 'dormitive power' is thus doing more than paraphrase the question, more even than remembering to behave like a gentleman, as Pardiès advised. He is doing more than he could ever have done in the days before the new sciences, because he is claiming to give a reason that underlies whatever might be said by the new sciences about the particular constituents of opium and their effect on the nervous system. 'Forms' are now *rivals* to other explanations, because other explanations are a growing family: it is no wonder that Leibniz, expressing unease at one time about forms, termed them *deunculi*, 'mini-gods'. And if this seems unfair, we can notice that, from the very beginning of the neo-scholastic revival, some authors have regarded modern physical science as concerned with accidents only, leaving substances to philosophers.[10]

And to theologians as well, of course, who habitually award themselves a philosophical degree *ad eundem* in these matters. I have submitted that reification is an abuse that is always a temptation with the Aristotelian account of change; and submitted that reification here is all that gives transubstantiation its appearance of content. Theologians whose concept of substance and knowledge is sound will never be at ease with the theory in the way those will who remove substance from any link with the ordered investigations of physical science. For the latter, things run much more smoothly. Their speculations touch the order of substance only, which is for them untouched by anything outside theology or metaphysics. In such a *terra incognita* they may, as Bottom put it, 'rehearse more obscenely and courageously'.

But their more sensible colleagues have their own share of fallacies to avoid. The revival of scholasticism came when physical science had made advances beyond any conception of the medievals: what were scholastic philosophers to say who took the progress seriously? One view is that propounded in great detail by the Dutch Jesuit Pieter Hoenen: the Aristotelian tradition represented by Aquinas is a necessary philosophical complement to physical science, as it can do justice to notions like potentiality and unity in a way that a mechanistic philosophy cannot. I have expressed in my contribution to Copleston's Festschrift my reservations, not so much about the defensibility of the move as about its content. Here, I simply point to a lack of clarity as to the criteria by which the Aristotelian heritage has been purified of unwanted elements (such as natural place, celestial matter and so on). And I notice that the lack of clarity extends to the presupposition that this act of filtration will leave what comes through it unaltered. Details here are unimportant, it is the general position adopted that matters. In a sense, the lack of clarity is a left-handed tribute to these neo-scholastics' faithfulness to their tradition, because if there is inevitably one gap for us in medieval thought, it lies in the limitations of its sense of historical understanding. Unfortunately, we have lost our innocence in such understanding, we have no choice but to place what we read. The authors of the seventeenth century we have examined faced an enlargement of human knowledge and activity that Aquinas had not known, and their attitudes to the scholastic inheritance prove this: they had choices to make that he had not. We in our turn cannot avoid acknowledging the temporal spread of the words and ways in which people have tried to make sense of the world around them. It is not an accident – Aristotle again! – that the words we use for that purpose are the inheritors of the words he used. But the manner of inheritance needs acknowledging in all its complexity. 'Cast out the obsolete physics, but keep the philosophy' is not like the instruction given by the husbandman to the reapers in the Parable of the Wheat and the Cockle. It is a move inside the temporally spread process, not a comment from the outside upon it.

I must leave further details of the process in the seventeenth century for treatment elsewhere. If the investigation is made more difficult by the deceptive endurance of the words involved, it is helped by the fact that transubstantiation was then a topic on which anyone was liable to offer an opinion, and that so many themes then debated met in it. For Leibniz, the questions of unity between soul and body, and the objectivity of extension; for some scholastics, the interpretation of eucharistic appearances as impressions divinely produced in the eye of the beholder – a view for which, to the annoyance of others, texts from Aquinas could, with only a modicum of violence, be cited; for the same scholastics, the need to interpret and to domesticate conciliar utterances that seemed to say the opposite; for one optical theory, a challenge from transubstantiation; and, perhaps most shrewdly of all, the contention of one Cartesian that the real problem raised by the theory is not ontological but epistemological – Catholic belief both appeals to historical evidence, and yet disregards evidence in what it says of the Eucharist. Of all this and much else, much remains to be said; I hope that what has been written here will at least make the terms of the problem a little clearer.

NOTES

1 Reprinted as chapters 11–13 of *God Matters* (London, 1987).
2 What I write here has some overlap with my contribution (about a recent debate on transubstantiation) to F. C. Copleston's forth-coming Festschrift, and some with an essay of mine (on medieval theories of eucharistic sacrifice) in the volume on Sacrifice edited by Stephen Sykes and to be published by the Cambridge University Press. I hope to be able to draw all this material together in a book on eucharistic belief to be published there too. This will be a drastically born-again version of the book I was writing at the time of the exchange of views in *New Blackfriars*.
3 His work, published in 1965, is *Die Entfaltung der Transubstantiations-lehre bis zum Beginn der Hochscholastik* (Münsterische Beiträge zur Theologie, Heft 28, 1; Aschendorffsche Verlagsbuchhandlung). I do not always share Jorissen's estimations of his authors, or of Roman Catholicism, come to that. But I regard his work as a lucid and permanently valuable piece of scholarship, and wish it had less of a mouthful for its title.
4 Hay into glass *is* natural, whatever some modern authors cited by Jorissen may think. My colleague Dr D. M. Knight tells me that Sir Humphry Davy investigated the beads of glass found when hay-stacks burn down (hay contains silicon).
5 I have given seventeenth-century citations by chapter and section wherever possible, since pagination differs from edition to edition. Readers who would like to tackle these texts themselves will find the topics discussed under headings like *de forma substantiali, de qualitati-bus, de materia prima*, and so on. They must be prepared to read in bulk if they are to make any sense of the stuff, and should put little trust in page-headings or indices.
6 A full study of English printings and translations of Continental philosophical books during the seventeenth century would, I think, yield much of interest. Legrand and Eustachius are not the only authors we shall meet who crossed the Channel, but the latter surely wins the prize for unexpectedness: a manual of scholastic philo-sophy, written by a French Cistercian, gets printed in Puritan Cam-bridge, and in the year of Charles I's execution! I possess myself a Latin translation of the Port Royal Logic, printed in London in 1682, and containing an extra preface in which are rejected examples offered in the Logic of supposed errors among the Reformers.
7 'Saint Malachy's Prophecy' makes the present (John Paul II) Pope be *De calore solis*: since the unit of Polish currency is the złoty, which means 'gold', the forecast can be deemed accurate. But presumably he has already been flattered yet again by someone or other with the

thought that, Thomistically speaking, the motto makes him a twenty-four-carat Pontiff.

8 I recently discovered these dictates in the University Library at Durham. Their provenance (here I am grateful to Miss Elizabeth Rainey) can be traced to the library of the Tyneside antiquary John Trotter Brockett (d. 1842). The (professional?) scribe is one 'T. Durham'. I hope to say more of these dictates elsewhere. I record here that Ushaw College, Durham, possesses a variety of dictates, made at Douai and at Lisbon. The College Librarian, the Revd Michael Sharratt, has prepared an admirable transcription of material here, and I am indebted to him for help and information. Sanders also translated a spiritual book of yesteryear, Rodriguez' *Christian Perfection*. I do not know any more of his activities with gunpowder.

9 This is the Papal envoy Valeriano Magni who appears in Piero Redondi's *Galileo Eretico* – a book, incidentally, whose value goes far beyond any disagreement over its main thesis. Neither Redondi nor anyone else I have read seems to have spotted that Magni is the originator of the famous *mentiris impudentissime* of the *Provincial Letters* – see Pascal's Fifteenth, and see Magni's *Contra Imposturas Iesuitarum*.

10 I give references in 'Neoscholasticism', my contribution to *The Cambridge History of Later Medieval Philosophy*. An example of it in practice I discuss in the item in Copleston's Festschrift, already mentioned.

8

FAITH, OBJECTIVITY, AND HISTORICAL FALSIFIABILITY

Hugo A. Meynell

There has been a vast amount of discussion in theological literature about the bearing of historical investigations of Jesus on
Christian faith. But it does not seem to me that the issues are
always seen clearly for what they are. The following statements
seem to me to be rather obviously true; but they are denied
explicitly or by implication in a great deal of modern theological
writing – this has been done very commonly by Protestants for
well over a century, and by Roman Catholics for the last couple of
decades.

1. If 'the theological Christ' is not in the relevant sense identical
   with the historical Jesus, Christianity in its traditional sense is
   based upon a mistake.
2. The two can be thus identical only if the gospels are roughly
   accurate from a historical point of view.
3. How far the gospels are historically accurate cannot be settled
   a priori, but only by detailed historical investigation.

To insure oneself both ways on the results of historical investigation, however tempting it may be under the shadow of historically sceptical investigations of the gospels, leads inevitably, I
believe, to a religious subjectivism which is incompatible with
traditional Christianity. Here it is above all important to bear in
mind the Popperian maxim, that only what is in principle falsifi-
able can be corroborated; and the close connection of truth with
the possibility of such corroboration.

As Sir Karl Popper sees it, the function of the scientist is to be
fertile in hypotheses, and to be at once stringent and ingenious in
attempts to falsify them. The best scientific hypothesis, the one
with the greatest 'verisimilitude',[1] is not the one which cannot be
falsified *sans phrase*; it is the one which, while it might conceivably
be falsified in all kinds of ways, turns out not to be so. The story

about Popper's *contretemps* with Alfred Adler illustrates the point very well. Popper was doing social work under Adler, and in the course of this encountered a family whose behaviour seemed totally to contradict what one would have expected if Adler's theories were true. When Popper reported the matter to Adler, Adler tried to explain how the family situation supported his theory after all. It suddenly struck Popper that Adler could have shown any conceivable family situation to be in accordance with his theory, and thus that the theory had no content. Freudianism and Marxism, Popper thought, were tarred with a similar brush; just by dint of their capacity to cover every conceivable eventuality, they explained nothing. In this they differed sharply from the theories of, say, Einstein, where it could readily be pointed out what observations or experiments would tend to falsify them.[2]

Popper never intended his principle of falsifiability to be a criterion of meaningfulness, like the verification principle of the logical positivists; he only meant it to be a criterion of demarcation between what merited the dignity of the name of science and what did not.[3] But in *The Retreat to Commitment*, W. W. Bartley applied Popper's analysis to religious doctrines. He objected to the practice of many theologians, particularly Karl Barth and Paul Tillich, of insulating the doctrines which they promulgated from conceivable falsification, especially by historical arguments.[4] It seems to me that Bartley was on firm ground in applying Popper's principles in this way, for all that Popper himself did not do so. Christianity, as traditionally understood, stands or falls with the truth of a set of historical propositions, particularly about the acts and words of the historical Jesus. These propositions, furthermore, are properly speaking 'historical' by virtue of the fact that how far they are liable to be true or false may be established by an objective investigation which does not presuppose a conclusion one way or the other. So far as Christianity is shorn of such historical truth-conditions, and consequent vulnerability in principle to falsification, it tends to be reduced to merely a subjective framework imposed *on* the world and human destiny by certain persons, rather than a matter of certain things being the case *about* the world and human destiny whether people are inclined to use such a framework or not. To put it rather brutally, for a 'Christianity' without historical truth-conditions, and hence without liability in principle to falsification by historical investigation, whether Jesus Christ is the redeemer of humankind is not an all-important question of fact, but a relatively trivial one of temperament and taste. Jesus Christ is the redeemer of humankind insofar as you are the sort of person who happens to feel that way, because of your cultural environment and constitution. This may be desirable in a pluralistic society; but it is hardly the faith once delivered to the saints. It may well be argued that, owing to the requirements of comparative religion or New Testament scholarship or both, we may be driven into a position in which this sort of 'Christianity' is the only one which is available for intelligent, honest and informed persons; but it will not do to identify this too closely with 'Christianity' as it has traditionally been conceived, whether by its adherents or by its opponents.

One might have supposed that this point was obvious, had not the positions of so many theologians implied a denial of it. That of the late Rudolf Bultmann is perhaps the most well-known of these. According to Bultmann, Christian preaching is concerned with the Christ of faith, who is the act of God by which we are judged and forgiven in the present; the Jesus of history is quite a different matter, to be known about, should we wish to know about him (he is not essential to faith), by a kind of inquiry into the first three gospels which presupposes that miracles never occur, and that there are no demons. As he sees it, the freedom of Christian faith from testability by any kind of empirical inquiry is what constitutes its difference from what he calls 'mythology'.[5] What 'mythology' means in this context is something on which we will have to touch briefly later on. But it may be noted immediately that it is just what Bultmann holds would free the faith from 'mythology' that would, if I am right, deprive it of any objective content. That is to say, it would render it such as no longer to include, in the way that it always has done, belief about *how things are*; it would reduce it to a set of ideas and conceptions *brought to* the real world, unquestionably of profound aesthetic and moral significance, but with no claims to be literally true *of* that world. One might say that what traditionally *differentiates* Christianity from such a subjective position is belief that things *will* turn out (eschatologically) and *have* turned out (historically) in one set of ways rather than another. As the Creed expresses it, Christians 'look for the resurrection of the dead, and the life of the world to come': they believe in Jesus Christ who 'was incarnate of the Virgin Mary, was crucified . . . under Pontius Pilate', and 'on the third day . . . rose again'.

The arguments on this issue, about the relation of faith to historical investigation, by the proponents of the so-called 'new quest of the historical Jesus', seem to me to be vitiated by a number of flaws.[6] I have already briefly described Bultmann's position; it was as a reaction to this that the 'new quest' arose. It is often said that the 'old quest' of the historical Jesus, which took place in the nineteenth century, ended in failure. The comment on this by C. H. Dodd is worth pondering: he suggested that exclusive concentration on the narratives of the first three gospels, to the exclusion of the fourth, led to a one-sided, distorted and ultimately incredible view of the historical Jesus.[7] My impression is that it is characteristic of the proponents of the 'new quest' that they want at once to affirm, against Bultmann, that the historical Jesus is essentially relevant to the Christian faith, and to avoid the full consequences of doing so. They are apt to maintain that one cannot *prove* the truth of the Christian faith by historical investigation, and to accuse members of other schools, especially those who were engaged in the 'old quest', of attempting to do so. Such an attempt, they say, if it succeeded, would make faith in the proper sense dispensable.[8]

But what seems to have been overlooked here is the curious parallel between this issue and scientific method in general. It is generally agreed by contemporary philosophers of science, on grounds that were stated at least as early as Hume and have been emphasized by Popper, that one cannot strictly speaking *prove* any scientific theory by citing the empirical evidence supposed to support it. Yet one can certainly *corroborate* it in the manner which I have described; if one finds that the relevant empirical evidence, while it *might* very well have falsified the theory in question, and *does* falsify rival theories, in fact does *not* falsify it. Similarly, it is indeed logically possible that objective historical investigation could converge on the proposition that Jesus was not at all the kind of person that traditional Christians have presupposed him to be – but rather perhaps the politically motivated trickster alleged by H. S. Reimarus in the eighteenth century, or the polymorphously-perverse conjuror who seems to emerge from the work of Morton Smith.[9] To conclude on this matter – that faith cannot literally be *proved* by historical inquiry does not necessarily imply that it cannot be *falsified*, or alternatively *corroborated*, by it; and if faith cannot be thus corroborated, and hence might not conceivably be thus falsified, its claim to be essentially dependent on the existence of a historical person (such as Jesus) or a historical event (such as the crucifixion of Jesus) must be illusory. I do not think that the main representatives of the so-called 'new quest of the historical Jesus' have sufficiently pondered this fact and its implications.[10]

It appears to me that there is what writers on education would call a 'hidden curriculum' in many courses of theology and religious studies; that is, a general perspective on what is being taught which is put over to the student, without it ever being clearly and distinctly stated that it is being put over. The thesis which the student is surreptitiously being invited to accept is that the truth of traditional Christianity does *not* entail the substantial historicity of the gospel narratives. I do know for certain that the implementation of the 'hidden curriculum', where it does occur, causes a great deal of anguish to students. The issue is very often blurred by being conceived as one between what is called 'fundamentalism' on the one hand, and scholarly enlightenment on the other. But it is one thing to insist on historical accuracy in every detail, another to insist on substantial historicity. Again, no matter of *fact*, so to say, is directly involved; only one of *implication*. What is subverted by the 'hidden curriculum' is not belief in the (substantial) historical accuracy of the gospels; it is the incompatibility of rejection of this belief with Christianity in its traditional form. So far from implying 'fundamentalism' in any useful sense, the thesis subverted would be perfectly consistent with *rejection* of Christianity *on the ground that* its historical truth-conditions did not stand up to objective scrutiny. As has been trenchantly remarked, men who told as many lies as the evangelists did on Bultmann's account are not to be taken seriously on any matter whatever.[11] The possibility, if one grants it, that they may have been deceived in good faith, does not really mend matters.

How is the issue resolved, one might ask, by Catholic biblical scholars who attend to the theological consequences of their inquiries? According to Joseph Fitzmyer, 'the guarantee that is implied in biblical inspiration concerns truth, but the truth that is involved is often not literal but analogous and differs with the literary form being used: poetic truth, rhetorical truth, parabolic truth, epistolary truth, even "gospel truth" – apart from historical truth itself'.[12] Elsewhere, he informs us that 'the evangelists were moved by the Holy Spirit to compile, edit, and write down the accounts as they did. This inspiration guarantees their Gospel-truth, which is free from error'.[13] He points out that neither the official Church nor theologians 'have ever taught that the necessary formal effect of inspiration is historicity'; the consequence of inspiration is rather 'immunity from error in what is affirmed or taught in the sacred writings for the sake of our salvation'.[14] I must confess that Fitzmyer's use of the expression 'gospel truth' leaves me a little queasy. The cynic might infer that 'gospel truth' had about the same relationship to truth as fool's gold has to gold. His inference might be thought to be justified, so far as 'gospel truth', even if it does not have to entail historical accuracy in every particular, does not involve at least substantial historical truth. But what relation Fitzmyer supposes there to be, if any, between 'gospel truth' and historical truth, does not seem to be made clear. And if there is little or none, rather than ringing the changes on 'rhetorical', 'poetic', and 'parabolical' truth (I have no notion what Fitzmyer means by 'epistolary truth'), would it not be less disingenuous to declare outright that the gospels are not on the whole *true*, but have, say, the profound relevance to life exemplified by the greatest poems and novels and (other) great myths?

I have been trying to argue that for Christianity to be true is for the gospels to be at least approximately historically accurate; and for the gospels to be approximately accurate is for them to tend to be corroborated rather than falsified when subjected to rigorous historical criticism. On some accounts, my statement of the historical truth-conditions of Christianity is very minimal and pusillanimous. Why cannot we have the 'good, brash hypothesis', as Antony Flew would say, of fundamentalism? The Bible, as any Christian would admit, is in some sense the Word of God. It contains a great many statements which are at first sight of a historical import over and above those concerning Jesus. If one means anything by calling the Bible the Word of God, presumably one implies that it contains no erroneous statements of fact, as it would seem to follow from its doing so that God was either deceived or a liar.[15] I can only counter this position with the rather lame excuse that *if* these are the logical consequences of Christian faith, then I believe that they and it have been falsified as conclusively as is possible by the nature of the case. I cannot quite believe that the biblical criticism which has grown up over the last two centuries, however many incidental blunders it may have made, can be totally mistaken in its conclusions, accepted as it is so widely now by *savants* both Protestant and Roman Catholic. From a philosophical point of view of the kind inspired by Popper, it is very inconvenient for Christians that fundamentalism is not true. It would make life much easier for them if, whenever objections of a historical or scientific nature were made to Scripture, subsequent investigations always tended to show that the objections were mistaken. However, to the best of my knowledge this does not happen. Yet fundamentalists and Popperians are agreed in opposing the pernicious maxim which has dominated so much recent theology, that the less committed you are to the *prima facie* meanings of your assertions, the more intellectually respectable you are.

Should one admit, after all, that fundamentalism and unbelief are the only self-consistent alternatives; and consequently, given

150

that fundamentalism is not a live option, opt for unbelief? I think, or at least hope, that these stark alternatives do not exhaust the field. It has been taken for granted by traditional Christians that the revelation enshrined in the Old Testament is fulfilled and consummated in the New. Why should not some of the Old Testament, then, anticipate the definitive revelation of God which took place through the historical Jesus Christ, in myth, legend and so on rather than in strictly historical narrative? Still, even if it is acknowledged that, for Christians, the heat may be taken out of controversies as to the historical details of the Old Testament, the problem comes up all the more forcefully, if my earlier argument is sound, in the case of the New.

It has become fashionable recently to emphasize the status of the biblical narrative, both in Old and New Testaments, as 'story'. Someone might argue rather as follows. Is it not enough that the biblical narratives, especially those about Jesus, are profoundly enlightening and expressive of the nature of the human condition? At this rate, is it not merely vulgar to insist that the narrative must have literal historical implications which are important for believers – that Jesus really did walk on the surface of a lake, or multiply loaves and fishes, or turn water into wine? Would not someone show crassness of a comparable order, if she would not take *King Lear* seriously, until she had established to her satisfaction the probability that there really *was* a king of that name and description who once ruled over Britain? Such a question seems to me to overlook the distinction between necessary and sufficient conditions – not a rare oversight, one might say, in contemporary theology. It is, I believe, a necessary condition of the truth of Christianity that the narratives of the Bible, and especially those about Jesus, should be significant for human living in something like the way that the greater Shakespeare plays are.[16] But it should be noted that the stories characteristic of *all* the great religions have this kind of depth and resonance to them; they are vehicles, as one might express it, of 'profound truth'. But it by no means follows from this that, for Christianity to be true in anything like the traditional sense, the stories about Jesus in the Gospels do not have to be by and large literally true as well. Short of this, it is very difficult to make any sense of the claim that Christianity is in any way unique. Perhaps we wish to withdraw this claim; but if we do, it is as well to be absolutely clear and above board about what we are doing.

It might still be argued that there is no organic connection between belief in the historicity of the gospels on the one hand, and the rest of Christian faith on the other. But I do not think it is too difficult to show that such an organic connection exists. Christianity might be said to involve three fundamental beliefs: that the world was created by God, that humanity is somehow estranged from God, and that God has acted uniquely through the life, words, acts and fate of Jesus to rectify this estrangement. As to the nature of this 'estrangement', if there is anything which is common to nearly all religions, it is the intuition that there are better possibilities latent in human life than are in fact realized; more concretely, that we human beings are both more wicked and more unhappy than we might be. Christianity appears in the world as one of several rival proposals as to how this plight of humanity is to be remedied.

Two obvious questions arise at this point. Would the remedy, assuming that it had been provided, actually meet the problem? And assuming that it would, has it actually been provided? The first question has traditionally been dealt with by theories of the atonement. Among such theories, two have been conspicuous; first, that Christ saves us from sin and damnation by setting us an example to follow; second, that Christ lets us off the consequences of our sin by undergoing the punishment which we deserve. The first, which was put about by Abelard, and by Liberal Protestants in modern times, has seemed to most people to be right as far as it went, but to go nothing like far enough. But the second, which has commended itself to many as the only viable alternative, has been stigmatized as implying an utterly immoral or irrational conception of God; it may be guessed that many have rejected traditional Christianity on the ground that it has such implications. Suppose Smith has been cheated by Jones, and vents his annoyance and frustration at this by giving Robinson a black eye. It may be that Smith stops feeling angry with Jones as a result of his aggressive act; but no good light is thrown on Smith's character by this. If Smith really thinks that taking it out on Robinson atones for the fault of Jones, granted Jones was at fault at all, he is immoral or irrational in doing so. And how does the 'substitutionary' theory of the atonement differ essentially from this?

I believe that a number of types of specifically modern knowledge and enquiry throw light on how the atonement ought to be understood; what is surprising is that more account has not been taken of them by theologians.[17] Among the fields of knowledge from which one might argue what Catholic theologians used to call the *convenientia* of the Christian doctrine of the atonement are political and social theory, comparative religion, and comparative mythology and literature. With regard to the first, no-one would disagree that very many if not most human beings, whether for constitutional or environmental reasons or a mixture of the two, are disposed to be militantly aggressive against other members of their species; or that this constitutes one of the most difficult problems in the conduct of human affairs. Konrad Lorenz suggested that four factors above all were needed in the control of militant aggression – a group, an enemy, a cause, and a leader.[18] Now, granted that God *has* acted in such a way as to deal with the moral plight of humankind, would it not have been appropriate for God to have provided those very things? Orthodox Christianity in effect claims just this – that we have as leader a God-man, who alone is able to carry the immense load of adulation which human beings are apt to heap on their leaders; that we have as community the Church, loyalty to which cuts down to size our devotion to other communities; for the cause of the advancement of truth and goodness as such (the Kingdom of God), against the enemy which is falsehood and evil as such, as opposed to the human beings who are their slaves and dupes.

As to comparative religion, R. C. Zaehner remarked on the 'hunger for an incarnate God' which seems such a widespread factor in the religions of the world, so much so that Muhammad and the Buddha have tended to get turned into incarnate gods by some of their more heretical followers, in flat contradiction to what they themselves claimed or wished. On the other hand, divine incarnations seem two a penny in Vaishnavite Hinduism, as indeed in ancient paganism; but none of these putative incarnations appears to have a sound historical basis. Only in Christianity, he suggests, among the great religions, does this seem to have been of the essence of orthodoxy from the very first, since apparently Jesus both was a real person, and claimed to be the unique son of God.[19] Mircea Eliade among others has pointed out that it is rather usual for so-called 'primitive religion' to acknowledge a remote God who has created the world and promulgated the moral law, but to be more directly involved with a human or semi-human cult-hero whose story is repeated in 'myth' and re-enacted in ritual. Again, both of these features are directly paralleled in Christianity.[20]

Similar considerations arise from comparative mythology and literature. The 'myth of the hero' is world-wide, and traces of it are easily found in literature right up to our own times. That the fourfold gospel has the overall shape of this 'myth of the hero' – with its story of a babe of mysterious origins, who survives deadly dangers soon after his birth, who develops precociously, who performs miraculous deeds when he grows up, who dies early and tragically, who undergoes a symbolically significant manner of death, who rises again after death – is obvious to the most superficial examination, however embarrassing the fact may have been to many Christians.[21] But would it not suit their book very well indeed if the gospel were, as one might put it, the one 'historical myth' in which God does for humanity what humanity has tried to do for itself through the profound but literally false 'deep stories', as one might call them, which are 'myths' properly speaking?

It is of considerable interest in this connection that, when C. S. Lewis first became convinced of the existence of God, he did not embrace Christianity because he could make no sense of the doctrine of the atonement. He could well understand how humankind as a whole might be so enslaved to sin that only a miracle could save it, rather as an individual might be thus enslaved to drugs or to alcohol. What he could not comprehend was how the life and death of one human being, however good, could constitute a remedy. At about this time he had a long conversation with J. R. R. Tolkien and Hugo Dyson, who pointed out to Lewis that he was very sensitive to myth when he encountered it in any context other than the Christian one. Lewis had indeed written a few months before, *à propos* of *The Winter's Tale*, how he was moved more and more by literary works through which the structure of myth could clearly be seen. Tolkien and Dyson suggested to him that the gospel was as it were God's myth rather than man's, operating on our sensibilities at the profoundest level in the way myths do, but with the wonderful difference that this time *it had really happened*. Lewis ultimately admitted that he could make very good sense of the doctrine of the atonement on this basis, and duly became a Christian.[22] I think it is fairly obvious how the kind of argument which convinced Lewis could have been reinforced by the two other kinds of consideration, from the nature of politics and of society on the one hand, and from the nature of religions on the other, which I have mentioned. Of course any number of such considerations would never amount to a 'proof' of Christianity, if indeed anyone, moved by Protestant tendencies to fideism or Catholic polemics against 'rationalism' in the tradition of the First Vatican Council, should object in principle to such a thing. But I must emphasize that this kind of understanding of the atonement will only work if the gospels are approximately true as a matter of history. To revert to my earlier suggestions about the essence of Christianity – not only must the proposed cure for human estrangement from God be such that one might expect it to work, but there must be some reason for thinking that God has actually provided it. And of what nature could this be other than some kind of historical confirmation?

For all its obvious promise, investigation of Christianity as 'the true myth' has been oddly neglected by recent theologians and apologists. The main reason for this, I believe, is the ambiguity of the term 'myth' and its cognates. Theologians of such very different opinions as Rudolf Bultmann, Karl Barth and Karl Rahner have all insisted that genuine Christian faith can have nothing in common with myth, and that any element of myth which it may incidentally have or appear to have must be excised from it.[23] But the trouble here is that two very different things are or may be meant, when it is maintained that a narrative or a set of propositions or whatever is 'a myth' or 'mythological'. It may be implied on the one hand that it is false; and on the other hand that it is profoundly moving and expressive of important aspects of human life and fate. To say that Christianity is 'myth' in the former sense is just to say that it is false. Yet nothing is more obvious to any but the most prejudiced eye than that it is thoroughly 'mythological' in the second sense. Both in basic structure, and in matters of detail, the gospel narratives show again and again parallels with what everyone would call myths. To denude it of these would leave virtually no remainder; and what is more would deprive Christianity of precisely those elements which seem to have made it the power in human life that it is.

I have argued at length that the truth of Christianity depends on the substantial historical veracity of the gospels. How does this stand up under unprejudiced examination? Divergences between respectable scholars on this matter have been and are startlingly wide; but I think one can urge that those who maintain sufficient historicity in them to support the traditional faith are not obviously biased or defective in their methods of argument. I shall outline five possibilities as to the relation of the historical Jesus to the gospel narratives, and mention some developments of scholarship in relation to them.

1. The stories about Jesus' words and acts are almost entirely legendary.
2. Jesus preached about the fatherhood of God and the brotherhood of humankind, but said and did nothing that implied unique nature or status for himself.
3. Jesus did say and do what implied unique nature and status for himself, but the terms in which he did this are not those which we find in the gospels.

4. What Jesus said and did to express his unique nature and status has on the whole been preserved faithfully by the first three (synoptic) gospels, but not by the fourth (John).
5. Jesus' character, self-consciousness, and way of speaking and acting are on the whole faithfully preserved for us by the four gospels.

Of these five positions, I should say that the first two were clearly incompatible, the third at best questionably compatible, with traditional Christianity; 'the theological Christ' turns out not to be, as traditionally assumed, 'the historical Jesus' envisaged from points of view different from those available to people in Jesus' place and time, but someone quite different. I do not think that it is possible to say at exactly what point historical scepticism about the gospels becomes beyond the pale for traditional Christianity; but it remains that some historical conclusions are definitely so. Here is yet another application of Aristotle's wise remark, that the educated person expects in a subject only such precision as its nature permits.[24] The first position was in vogue around 1910, but is not now much in favour; though it appears that whenever someone claims that no respectable historian will defend it, one proceeds to do so. Also, the tide of scholarship, quite apart from the *Zeitgeist*, does seem to have set pretty heavily against the second position, which has been claimed not implausibly to be ideologically motivated; the scholar, as it has been expressed, looking down into the well of history only to see the reflection of his own face.

Now it is obvious that consciousness by Jesus of his unique nature and status, which differentiates the third, fourth and fifth positions from the second, is affirmed with special clarity by John.[25] So it was only to be expected that an alliance should have grown up between the second position on the one hand, and on the other belief that the synoptic gospels were theologically garnished history, John more or less pure theological fiction; and the alliance has been quite influential right up to the present.[26] However, the twentieth century has seen two independent developments in scholarship which have tended to subvert the alliance. It has appeared that the synoptic gospels should be interpreted more in the manner of John; and John has been argued to have more historical value than was once thought. The first development was exemplified by *The Riddle of the New Testament* in the early 1930s, and is represented now by the work of Harald Riesenfeld.[27] 'Did the life and death of Jesus of Nazareth control the life of the primitive Church? Or was his life and death submerged by a piety and faith wholly beyond his horizon?'[28] These authors conclude that there is a single basic Christology present as an organizing principle through all the material of the synoptic gospels as far back as it can be traced; Jesus is the promised Messiah who has inaugurated the Kingdom of God by his coming. They argue that there is no evidence that the material existed at some time apart from the Christology.[29]

The assumption that John is essentially pious fiction, for all that it is pertinaciously maintained in some circles,[30] has been impugned by a whole series of discoveries since the 1920s. A strong Aramaic tinge redolent of primitiveness has been detected in both narratives and discourses;[31] good reasons have been found for arguing John's complete literary independence from the synoptics, which does not consort well with its extreme lateness;[32] topographical details in John have been confirmed by archaeological finds; [33] form-critical analysis of parallel passages in the synoptics and John, when questions of relative priority are not begged, often indicate that John preserves the tradition in a more primitive form;[34] material closely related to the synoptic tradition is so firmly embedded in the discourses and dialogues of John as to be apparently inseparable from the argument of which it forms part, and in examining parallels to synoptic sayings, one is sometimes led into the heart of the Johannine theology.[35] Above all, the Dead Sea Scrolls discovered in 1949 provide a parallel contemporary with the life of Jesus for the vocabulary, mentality, and theological outlook of John.[36] Riesenfeld has pointed out that, in spite of the obvious and striking differences between the words of Jesus as reported by the synoptics and by John, there is an underlying unity of symbolism which it is more historically plausible to attribute to Jesus himself than to the fourth evangelist, however ingenious one supposes the latter to have been. The analogies of light, of shepherd and sheep, and of wheat and harvest, are applied in the gospels at large to the disciples, the kingdom of God, and Jesus himself; while the third application is most conspicuous in John, it is often strongly hinted at in the synoptics.[37]

All this tends to confirm the fifth of the positions which I outlined on the relation of the gospels to the historical Jesus. At this rate it looks as though a position which is compatible with traditional Christianity is after all supported by much of the most recent scholarship, even when the level of historical truth-conditions for Christianity is not set implausibly low.

Can we keep the traditional Catholic or Christian faith, whatever that was, in the light of modern biblical scholarship? If not, how much of it is to be abandoned, and what point remains, if any, in what is left? It is possible for decent people to ask such questions, in some agony of mind; and when they do they are worthy of something better than elegantly-expressed evasions, or being treated as ignorant fools.

One can stick to fundamentalism, in spite of everything; or one can abandon the faith, with regret or relief, on the grounds that its historical foundations have crumbled. I do not think, at all events, that it is proper to escape by the bolt-hole of denying any of the three propositions which I set down at the beginning. (Thank God at least for the general disappearance of the once-fashionable slogan that faith is not a matter of propositions.) Or one may take a view of Christianity as an elaborate story or symbol-picture, which expresses with great power what it is to live as a human being within the world, in the manner of the great myths. I think this last view is self-consistent; but it will not do to conceal the fact that it is radically discrepant with any traditional view of the faith, whether Catholic, Protestant or Eastern Orthodox. The Christian myth or symbol-picture is at this rate no more 'true' than any other; it is helpful to some and not to others; and one would suppose that its effectiveness, for any but the excessively sophisticated, is ineluctably wedded to the supposition that it is 'true' in a more literal and consequently more exclusive sense.

Is there any other self-consistent way out? It seems to me that there is, and I will sketch this as well as I can. 'It is impossible, if one is at once honest, intelligent, and informed, to maintain that every *prima facie* historical statement of the Bible, or even of the New Testament, is literally true; or even that so much of it is literally true as was insisted by the ordinary *magisterium* of the Catholic Church up to and beyond the beginning of the twentieth century. Yet, for the Christian and Catholic faith to be true, the gospels must be at least approximately historically true. Exactly *how* historically true they must be, is not possible to determine; but at least some historical beliefs about Jesus – that he was a practising homosexual, that he never performed any miracles, that the resurrection narratives are merely fictions put about by the apostolic community after Jesus' death – are incompatible with the traditional beliefs of the churches. The gospels present us – at least the consensus of Christian believers over two millennia, whether simple or sophisticated, shows us this much – with an almost uniquely[38] moving and inspiring picture of the man Jesus; suggestions as to how these narratives might have come into existence, which imply that the historical Jesus was radically different from the figure presented to us, have not on the whole stood the test of time. The gospels have the structure, and consequently the power over human imagination, of the great myths; where they are absolutely unique is in being both "myth" in this sense and, approximately at least, historically acccurate. Also, their basic metaphysical and eschatological presuppositions are true; the world is created and sustained by a benevolent God, and humankind has to hope or fear for an afterlife of weal or woe.' What would a Catholic add to this? 'The message which God has revealed through the words, deeds and fate of Jesus, about the new life which God has bestowed through him, has been entrusted to a community, in such a way that this community as a whole can never be in fundamental error about it. It is this community which under divine providence wrote and defined the New Testament in the first place, and which works out the implications of its teaching more and more fully over the course of time.'[39]

NOTES

1 See Karl Popper, *Objective Knowledge* (Oxford, 1972), pp. 52–60, 101–103, etc.
2 See Popper, *Unended Quest* (Glasgow, 1976), pp. 37–39, 41, 43.
3 *Objective Knowledge*, pp. 1, 4, 12, 29–30, 85; *Unended Quest*, pp. 41–44, 79–81, 171–173.
4 W. W. Bartley, *The Retreat to Commitment* (London, 1964).
5 See especially Bultmann's two contributions to the volume *Kerygma and Myth*, ed. H. W. Bartsch and R. H. Fuller (London, 1953).
6 I have argued this at greater length in 'A Christological Jeremiad', *The Month* (February 1983), pp. 51–58.
7 C. H. Dodd, *The Interpretation of the Fourth Gospel* (Cambridge, 1953), p. 446.
8 For a useful series of articles representing 'the new quest', see *The Historical Jesus and the Kerygmatic Christ*, ed. C. E. Braaten and R. S. Harrisville (New York and Nashville, 1964).
9 Morton Smith, *Jesus the Magician* (San Francisco, 1978).
10 Cf. the shrewd comment of Schubert Ogden and Van Harvey, that the exponents of the 'new quest' will not draw out the logical consequence of their own position, that Christian faith might conceivably be falsified as a result of historical inquiry: Braaten and Harrisville, p. 230.
11 I am afraid I cannot now find the source for this splendid remark.
12 Joseph Fitzmyer, *The Gospel According to Luke* (New York, 1979), p. 18.
13 Fitzmyer, *A Christological Catechism. New Testament Answers* (New York, 1982), p. 128.

14 *Ibid.*

15 Cornelius Van Til is perhaps the most distinguished contemporary representative of 'fundamentalism' in this sense. See *The Defense of the Faith* (Philadelphia, 1967).

16 For the best available account of the way in which the Bible as a whole 'works' in this respect, see Northrop Frye, *The Great Code* (Toronto, 1982).

17 I summarize here what I have tried to argue at greater length elsewhere; see 'The Mechanics of Atonement', *Theology* (January 1974), pp. 21–27.

18 See Konrad Lorenz, *On Aggression* (London, 1966), pp. 234f.

19 See R. C. Zaehner, *Concordant Discord* (Oxford, 1970), p. 443.

20 See M. Eliade, *Patterns in Comparative Religion* (London, 1963), p. 109 and *passim*.

21 See C. G. Jung, *Psychology and Religion* (London, 1958), pp. 154f.

22 R. L. Green and W. Hooper, *C. S. Lewis. A Biography* (London, 1974), pp. 117–118.

23 Cf. Bultmann, *Theology of the New Testament* (London, 1952), I, p. 300; II, p. 127; *Kerygma and Myth* (London, 1953), pp. 11, 44, 105, 107, 122; *Essays Philosophical and Theological* (London, 1955), p. 86; *Existence and Faith* (London, 1961), pp. 60, 253, 301. Karl Barth, *Church Dogmatics* III, 1 (Edinburgh, 1958), pp. 84–85. Karl Rahner, *Foundations of Christian Faith* (London, 1978), pp. 290–291. I have justified these contentions at greater length in 'Myth in Christian Religion' in *Theolinguistics*, ed. J. V. van Noppen (Brussels, 1981), pp. 133–141. Rahner's contention, that the Christian doctrine of the incarnation has nothing to do with the divine-man myths of antiquity, is diametrically wrong on the account I am giving.

24 *Nicomachean Ethics*, I, 3.

25 'John' seems a less cumbersome expression than 'the fourth gospel'; I do not wish by my use of the term to imply anything one way or the other about the authorship of the gospel.

26 For example, it seems to be accepted without question by the authors of *The Myth of God Incarnate*, ed. John Hick (London, 1977).

27 E. C. Hoskyns and N. Davey, *The Riddle of the New Testament* (London, 1931); H. Riesenfeld, *The Gospel Tradition* (Oxford, 1970). The fundamental unity of the gospel message, for all the fragmentation to which the gospels are subjected by critical analysis, is also stressed in the writings of Hans Urs von Balthasar.

28 *The Riddle of the New Testament*, p. 14.

29 *Ibid.*, pp. 162–163.

30 As Raymond Brown wittily remarks, 'We may still find writers stating that the Fourth Gospel cannot seriously be considered as a witness to the historical Jesus, but these represent a type of uncritical traditionalism which arises with age, even in heterodoxy': *New Testament Essays* (Milwaukee, 1965), p. 143.

31 The pioneer in this matter was C. F. Burney. There is a useful summary of recent evidence confirming the basic historicity of John

in S. Temple, *The Core of the Fourth Gospel* (London and Oxford, 1975), pp. 3–24.

32 See P. Gardner-Smith, *Saint John and the Synoptic Gospels* (Cambridge, 1938).

33 For example, the 'Pavement' mentioned in John 19: 13. More or less tentative identifications, which together have rather an impressive effect, have been made of other sites. Cf. Temple, *op. cit.*, pp. 15–16, 9.

34 Cf. C. H. Dodd, *Historical Tradition in the Fourth Gospel* (Cambridge, 1963), p. 427. Similar points are made in Brown, *op. cit.*

35 Dodd, *op. cit.*, pp. 115, 321, 419–420, 428.

36 Temple, *op. cit.*, pp. 22–24.

37 Riesenfeld, *op. cit.*, pp. 161–169.

38 It would not do to rule out *a priori* similar claims for stories, e.g., about the Buddha.

39 I think P. J. FitzPatrick goes a little too far in maintaining that the claim by Catholics to be in a specially fortunate position in this respect is 'specious': 'Once in Khartoum', *New Blackfriars* (March 1985), p. 113. But there is much to be learned from his thoughtful and disturbing article.

9

THE GENRE OF THE FIRST GOSPEL

Margaret Davies

'Imitation is the sincerest form of flattery' as the old adage goes. Although scholars sometimes suggest that the genre 'gospel' was something new, they also admit that literature always draws on what went before, combining, transforming, dividing motifs and genres already familiar to listeners, readers and writers. Otherwise literature would fail to communicate. Sense must be shared, and to share the sense, listeners and readers must be wooed by familiarity, at least to the extent that they are not completely baffled from beginning to end of a text.

Imitation can take effect in a number of different ways, however. Vocabulary, phraseology, motifs and story-line can be imitated from texts of a genre different from the imitation – a parody may use the same vocabulary, phraseology, motifs and story-line as a tragedy. Genre defines the whole, the organizing principle which gives individual elements their total significance. Nevertheless, genre cannot be discovered without careful attention to all the details, and rival definitions may be tested by examining which makes sense of most of the parts comprising the whole. Perhaps definition begins with an intuitive guess, but the guess must be informed by a knowledge of as much as possible of the literature available at the time and place of the text's production.[1]

—— I ——

The Gospel according to Matthew is written in Hellenistic Greek. It is therefore not surprising that scholars have discovered similarities to Greek literature roughly contemporary with the gospel, especially to biographies of religious leaders. G. A. Kennedy,[2] for example, argues that Matthew uses rhetorical devices common in religious rather than philosophical or legal Greek rhetoric. In philosophy, arguments are provided for the probability of premisses so that formally valid inferences may be drawn from them. In Matthew and in other Greek religious rhetoric, however, persuasion is not by reason but by authoritative proclamation. Assertions are absolute, and whatever does not fit with them is not refuted but treated as outrageous. In Matthew, as in its scripture,[3] theological beliefs are simply assumed: God is the creator and giver of life, the world is God's creation, and men are God's creatures, made in his image and likeness but without sharing his transcendent nature. This picture is neither analysed nor argued for. Its assumption means that scriptural quotations can be used as authoritative statements which support the gospel's contentions. The gospel would therefore be recognized by those familiar with Hellenistic Greek literature as a form of religious rhetoric, albeit an odd form to pagan sensibilities since these Matthaean presuppositions would have been shared by no one outside of Jewish and Christian communities in the first century C.E.

To suggest, moreover, that the first gospel is like a Hellenistic biography seems reasonable enough.[4] Like its pagan counterparts, it depicts the public life of the subject, either in chronological order, or thematically through a series of anecdotes (Matthew combines the two), in the third person but giving to characters within the story some direct speech. In form, Hellenistic biographies may be pedagogic (like Matthew), dramatic or entertaining, while in content they may be apologetic, exemplary, laudatory, philosophical or legitimizing, all features to some extent present in Matthew.[5] Indeed, even the individual motifs of some biographies from the period are found in Matthew too, as Downing demonstrates[6] – motifs like family background, concern for ancestral tradition, travels, deliberate risking of life, omens, prodigies, miracles, divine guidance, quality of thought, concern for law, for justice, for community, death and burial, influence after death. Downing rightly argues that common motifs do not define a common genre, but he goes on to suggest that, nevertheless, the synoptic gospels would have been comprehensible to audiences familiar with pagan biographies. This is true, however, only up to a point. Most pagan biographies depict the lives of military and political figures, and these have few motifs in common with Matthew, but even pagan biographies of religious leaders exhibit differences. The Hellenistic biography which seems closest to Matthew is Philostratus' *Life of Apollonius of Tyana*,[7] but it is unlike Matthew in a number of obvious respects. Philostratus' work is partly a travelogue describing the exotic in India and Egypt as Apollonius visits fellow-ascetics to improve his techniques of foretelling the future and performing wonders, and partly the portrait of an adviser to world rulers. The presuppositions of the text are Pythagorean, so that Apollonius is said to be divine in the sense that Pythagoreans believed all true ascetics to be divine. At the end of the story, Apollonius does not die but disappears from mundane sight into the eternal world of the immortals. Although, therefore, motifs appear to be shared by the two texts, especially if they are described in general terms, the different theological and anthropological assumptions determine the range and kind of motifs as well as their significance.

For example, neither Jesus nor Apollonius is married, and the Matthaean Jesus advocates celibacy for the sake of the kingdom of heaven (19:12), but, like Paul, because of belief in the imminent end of the world (16:28) and not from a desire to break free from physical fetters (contrast *Apollonius*, 8, 7). Hence Jesus is neither a vegetarian nor a teetotaller whereas Apollonius is both (1, 8).

Again, both Jesus and Apollonius foretell the future. Jesus predicts his own passion (16:21ff., 17:22f., 20:18f., 26:2) and the role his disciples will play (26:20ff., 30ff.), and he predicts God's imminent final judgement and the transformation of the world (13:36ff., 19:28, 24–25). Apollonius predicts the length of his stay with the king (Book 1, 22), pestilence at Ephesus (4, 4), who will initiate him into the Asclepian cult (4, 18), Nero's attempt to cut a canal through an isthmus (4, 24), that new land is produced by an earthquake (4, 34), a thunderbolt hitting Nero's cup (4, 43), Nero's downfall (5, 10–11), the fate of the three emperors who follow (5, 13), shipwreck (5, 18), his visit to Athens (5, 19), the burning of a temple to Zeus (5, 30), the manner of Titus' death (5, 32), the site of treasure to pay dowries (6, 39), Domitian's death (8, 23 and 26), his own disappearance and the death of Nerva (8, 27f.). Jesus' predictions serve to show that his own execution and his disciples' desertion were part of God's purpose which would be fully realized only at the final judgement. Apollonius' predictions prove that his ascetic practices have subordinated his senses to the divine ether in which the gods live (8, 7).

Again, both Jesus and Apollonius perform wonders. Jesus cleanses lepers, heals paralysis, lunacy, fever, blindness, dumbness, haemorrhage, exorcizes demons, raises the dead (e.g. 4:24; 8–9), miraculously feeds the hungry (14:15ff., 15:32ff.), stills a storm (8:23ff.), walks on the sea (14:22ff.) and destroys the fig tree with a curse (21:18ff.). Apollonius rids Ephesus of pestilence by persuading the population to stone a demon disguised as a beggar (4, 10), is master of the tempest (4, 13), exorcizes a demon from a raucous youth (4, 20; this example shares two features with the exorcism of the two demoniacs in Matthew 8:25ff.: the demons are rebuked and their exit is proved by the effect on something in the vicinity), saves his young pupil from being devoured by his vampire bride (4, 25), raises a young girl from the dead by touch and secret spell (4, 45), saves a village from the torments of a satyr's ghost by putting it to sleep on wine (6, 27), and tames a mad dog who had bitten a boy to effect the boy's cure with the lick of the dog (6, 43). However, Jesus' miracles are demonstrations of God's forgiveness of sin (9:2–8) or God's creative activity (14:22ff.) whereas Apollonius' display the divinity which Pythagorean asceticism releases from its corporeal fetters.[8]

Further, some motifs in the Matthaean text are never found in Hellenistic literature. Matthew looks beyond its subject's death in ways foreign to Hellenistic conceptions since it announces Jesus' resurrection and expects an imminent final judgement. The eschatological perspective of the first gospel places it in a genre distinct from that of Hellenistic Greek biography, since it not only creates new motifs but gives to common motifs a different significance.[9]

___ II ___

It has already been suggested that the Gospel according to Matthew is dependent on its scripture, most importantly for its assumed world-view. How far, then, has its scripture determined its vocabulary, motifs and genre?

Naturally, the process is dialectical. Scriptural quotations are said to be fulfilled in Jesus' life, but which quotations are used, and how they are modified and understood is partly determined by events in Jesus' life, like his crucifixion by the Romans. So also with the shared themes and motifs. For example, the genealogy in 1:1–17 imitates parts of that in I Chronicles 1 – 3. It depicts Jesus as son of David, as the Christ, albeit fulfilling only some of the possible Messianic visions of its scripture,[10] and as son of Abraham fulfilling Abraham's mission to the nations.[11] Joseph, Jesus' legal father, is like the patriarch Joseph, a dreamer who goes down to Egypt and who behaves justly towards a woman who he supposes has acted badly.[12] Like Moses, Jesus escaped the wrath of a ruler while his contemporaries were killed.[13] Like Israel, God's son, Jesus was called out of Egypt.[14] As Moses and Israel went through the water of the Red Sea to set out on a journey to the Promised Land, so Jesus went through the water of the Jordan to set out on a journey to the kingdom of Heaven.[15] Like and unlike Israel, God's disobedient son, Jesus, God's obedient son, is tested in the wilderness.[16] Like Elijah calling Elisha to follow him, Jesus called disciples.[17] As God gave Moses and Israel the law on the mountain, so Jesus gave the sermon on the mount.[18] As God performed ten wonders through Moses in Egypt, so God performed ten miracles through Jesus in Galilee.[19] Jesus fed the five thousand and the four thousand in the wilderness as God fed the Israelites in the wilderness.[20] Like Elijah, John the Baptist was persecuted for faithfulness to God,[21] and the parallels are developed further: like Moses, Elijah, Jeremiah and John the Baptist, Jesus is to be persecuted but vindicated by God, and Jesus' disciples are to be persecuted like Jesus and the prophets.[22] As Moses led the twelve tribes of Israel to victory against their enemies, Jesus, on a smaller scale, led his twelve disciples to victory in disputes with enemies.[23] Like the Spirit of God moving across the waters in the darkness in Genesis' prelude to creation, Jesus moved in the darkness across the waters in Matthew's prelude to the new birth.[24] Like the prophets of scripture, the Matthaean Jesus tells indicative parables, illustrating the way things are.[25] The prayer in Matthew 11:25–30 imitates Ecclesiasticus 51. The identification of the bread and wine with Jesus' body and blood to explain the significance of his death draws on imagery, ideas and vocabulary from various parts of scripture, about Passover, covenants, sin offerings and innocent martyrdom.[26] The details of Judas' suicide seem to combine II Samuel 17:23, Zechariah 11:12–13, Jeremiah 18:2–3 and 32:6–14. The Passion narrative not only quotes Psalm 21(22) but echoes other parts of that psalm and Psalm 68(69).[27] The resurrection appearances conform to scriptural theophanies,[28] and 28:18–20 may imitate II Chronicles 36:23.

Not only are parallel motifs to be found in Matthew and its scripture, but individual sentences are also similar in form.[29] For example, there are blessings in the Torah and in liturgical and wisdom sections of scripture,[30] woes in the prophets,[31] *amen* as a particle of solemn declaration in Jeremiah,[32] and collections of wisdom sayings.[33]

Moreover the juxtaposition of short sections of narrative and miracle with discourses and dialogues in Matthew is similar to that in the stories of the prophets Moses in Exodus and Numbers, and Elijah and Elisha in I and II Kings. However, a dominant element in most of these stories is almost missing in Matthew, where God rarely speaks directly as he does to Moses, the Israelites or Elijah. In Matthew, instructions from God are conveyed by angels, sometimes through dreams,[34] and only on two occasions does a voice from heaven testify to bystanders that

Jesus is the Son of God.[35] The form of the divine declaration is unlike both the usual prophetic 'thus says the Lord' and the stories of prophetic callings in Exodus 3 – 4, Isaiah 6, Jeremiah 1 or Ezekiel 1 – 3. It is slightly more like the proof that Elijah is the servant of God when on Mount Carmel he calls down fire on the sacrifice and God answers with fire, or like God's confirmation of Moses' leadership with thunderings from Mount Sinai in Exodus 19 – 20. The form seems to have been developed in the first century c.e. since Vermes is able to cite parallels from rabbinic stories about the first-century charismatic healer, Hanina ben Dosa.[36]

Motifs, sentences, phrases and vocabulary as well as arrangement, then, are shared by Matthew with its scripture, but sharing these details does not indicate a common genre. Although clear echoes of scripture can be heard in the Matthaean portrait of Jesus, it is not quite like those of the prophets, David, Israel or Yahweh.

First we should note that the theology of much of its scripture is modified in Matthew by a temporary dualism in which, although the world is God's creation, it has fallen foul of Satan's power which is evil. Matthew does occasionally see God as man's tempter, like its scripture,[37] but what seems to have happened is that scriptural references to beings in God's court or to angelic messengers have triggered developments.[38] Job's vision of the adversary Satan or the Devil is used by Matthew in the temptation story,[39] but elsewhere in the gospel, it is combined with a scriptural reference to a power opposed to God and represented by an idol, Baalzebub, the god of Ekron.[40] In Matthew, Satan and Beelzebul are identified as 'the prince of demons',[41] who tempts man to sin against God and possesses individuals, causing illness or madness.[42] A connexion between sin, especially the sin of idolatry, and various kinds of catastrophe – famine, war, illness – is frequently made in exhortatory sections of the Pentateuch, and the Gospel of Matthew links sin and illness mythologically as demon-possession.[43] The connexion was understood to raise questions about God's justice when it was applied to individuals (Job and Tobit).

The kinds of miracles which Matthew attributes to Jesus, therefore, not only mirror some of those performed by the prophet Elisha, but also include exorcisms.[44] In the Septuagint, only the book of Tobit, usually dated around 200 b.c.e., exhibits a belief in good and bad angels like that of Matthew. According to Tobit, the angel Raphael both accompanies Tobias on a journey, as the angel had accompanied the Israelites through the wilderness, and exorcizes Sarah's demon and cures Tobit's blindness.

Raphael therefore has something in common with the Matthaean Jesus, who also cures blindness by touch, though without the aid of an ointment made from a fish's gall, and exorcizes demons, though without the aid of smoke from a fish's heart or liver.[45] Matthew and Tobit, then, share a belief in angels as God's agents on earth, but one of the roles given to the angel in Tobit is given to Jesus in Matthew.

However, the extra-canonical book of Jubilees, usually dated in the second century B.C.E., has most in common with Matthaean mythological developments, in spite of the fact that its interests, in dating festivals according to the solar calendar and in justifying its new version of Genesis and Exodus as a revelation, are far from those of Matthew. Jubilees sees Satan as the prince of demons, whose minions take possession of men, corrupt them and make them ill (10:3ff.). In addition, and more optimistically, Jubilees, like Matthew, gives to individuals the protection of guardian angels.[46] It is the Matthaean belief in demon-possession, shared by Jews, Christians and pagans in the first century C.E., that determines its exorcisms, with motifs common to contemporary pagan biographies.[47]

Another development in Matthew is shared with only parts of its scripture. Statements about the kingdom of heaven, the new birth, the parousia of the Son of man and the final judgement, developed from Daniel 7 and 12 in particular, change the story of a prophetic martyr into a story about the complete transformation of creation. The Gospel of Matthew is not a human tragedy but a divine comedy which ends with the resurrection of Jesus and the hope of the future establishment of the kingdom of heaven.

Nevertheless, Matthew is not an apocalypse in the form of Daniel 7 – 12 or of most of those collected in the extra-canonical book I Enoch. It is not a revelation of a transcendent reality symbolically represented, and interpreted by an angel, whether through a dream or through a heavenly journey.[48] Even the 'Matthaean apocalypse' in chapters 24 and 25 is neither an account of a journey to heaven nor a dream, although it echoes the dream in Daniel 7 with its reference to the parousia of the Son of man and its final judgement scene. The Matthaean form is different, in spite of the fact that its content, concentration on the final establishment of God's kingdom and the reversals this will entail, is shared by most apocalyptic writings. Moreover, the angels who appear in Matthew 1 – 2 give their divine message to endangered individuals and are not concerned with the final judgement. Only in chapter 28 does the angel who announces Jesus' resurrection play the apocalyptic role of interpreter of an eschatological reality. If, then, parts of Matthew are 'apocalyptic' but the whole is not, how is it different?

The Matthaean Jesus is not taken on a heavenly journey, nor does he receive revelations in a dream, but he is inspired by the Spirit of God,[49] and as 'God with us' (1:23) reveals God in his earthly life and teaching. Not only are visions of a transcendent world related to men on earth in chapters 24–25 and 28, but Jesus' earthly life, enlivened by God's Spirit, is understood to provide knowledge of God, and his resurrection, a beginning of the new birth (19:28, 27:53), offers proof of the efficacy of his predictions about the imminent final judgement and the transformation of creation. The revelation is focused in Jesus and the story of his life, death and resurrection is not just a biography of an individual but a microcosm of God's macrocosmic judgement.

To sum up. More of the individual forms of sayings, the motifs and the arrangements of material are shared by Matthew and its scripture than by Matthew and pagan Hellenistic biographies. In many respects, the Matthaean Jesus is like an Old Testament prophet, especially Moses. Moreover, the scriptural world-view is presupposed by the first gospel, albeit with a dualistic colouring and an eschatological dimension. What is completely new, and what necessitates a development of the apocalyptic genre, is the belief that Jesus' earthly life exemplifies God's activity, and that his corpse disappeared because God raised him from the dead. Expectations about God's final vindication of the righteous are therefore justified by the story of Jesus' life, death and resurrection.

—— III ——

Well, after all that, what does it matter how the genre of Matthew is defined? Would we seriously misinterpret it if we took it to be a life of a prophet? In any case, definition of genre cannot restrict the questions that can be directed appropriately at a text. Because a particular poem is about love it does not follow that we cannot find in it answers to questions about food or fashion, matters which may be peripheral to the purpose of the poem but which may be touched upon nevertheless.[50] Of course, defining the genre of a text provides the emotional and intellectual satisfaction of putting things in perspective. It dispels the sense of vertigo experienced, for example, at a party when you are uncertain whether your hostess is trying to convince you that she is *au fait* with modern jazz or with computer programming.

To call the Gospel according to Matthew 'a divine comedy'

about creation and re-creation, attempts to give to its parts a satisfying coherence, but it does not imply that questions concerning, for example, the historical Jesus cannot be asked of it. What it does mean, however, is that answers about history cannot be gained in the way they would be if they were asked of a text like Martin Gilbert's biography of Sir Winston Churchill.[51] Moreover, Matthew, although it does not itself examine its theological presuppositions, invites questions about God as Gilbert's biography of Churchill does not. Gilbert's treatment is confined to history, Matthew's is both historical and philosophical.

NOTES

1 See the useful discussion of genre definition by E. D. Hirsch, *Validity in Interpretation* (Yale University Press, 1967), which may be separated from his unsuccessful attempt to rehabilitate 'author's intention', and by Alastair Fowler, *Kinds of Literature* (Clarendon Press, 1982).

On literature available in the first century C.E., see, for example, F. G. Kenyon, *Books and Readers in Ancient Greece and Rome* (Oxford, 1932).

We do not know exactly when or where the Gospel according to Matthew was written, but not long after 70 C.E., the destruction of Jerusalem, and in Syria are likely conjectures.

2 Of Kennedy's many studies of the history of rhetoric, *New Testament Interpretation through Rhetorical Criticism* (University of North Carolina Press, 1984), is the most relevant to the first gospel.

3 In the first century C.E., no canon of scripture had been defined by Jewish or Christian communities, but the Torah and most of the prophets were regarded as authoritative (see Matthew's 'the law and the prophets' e.g. 7:12), together with most of the Psalms (e.g. 22:44; 27:46). Daniel, which finally found a place among the Writings in Jewish scriptures, but among the prophets in the Christian canon, is quoted at crucial points in the first gospel (e.g. 13:32; 24:21, 30; 25:46; 26:64). Just which version or versions of scripture were known is uncertain, since some quotations in Matthew are near to the Greek Septuagint text, some to the Hebrew Masoretic text, some mixtures, and many are combinations of passages with necessary adaptations. Moreover, evidence suggests that quotations have been integrated into their context in the gospel: see R. H. Gundry, *The Use of the Old Testament in Matthew's Gospel* (Brill, 1967), p. 171. In any case, checking the exact wording of a quotation from a scroll written in continuous script, without divisions between chapters, paragraphs, sentences or words, and almost completely without punctuation, would have been a task irksome enough to have been neglected.

4 E.g. C. H. Talbert, *What is a Gospel?* (SPCK, 1978; Fortress, 1977), and
my review in *New Blackfriars* (April 1980), pp. 197–198; D. E. Aune,
'The Problem of the Genre of the Gospels: a critique of C. H. Talbert's
What is a Gospel?' in *Gospel Perspectives* II, ed. R. T. France and D.
Wenham (JSOT, 1981); or P. Shuler, *A Genre for the Gospels* (Fortress,
1982).
5 See D. L. Barr and J. L. Wentling, 'The Conventions of classical
biography and the genre of Luke-Acts' in *Luke-Acts*, ed. C. H. Talbert
(SBL Seminar Papers, New York, 1984).
6 See F. G. Downing, 'Contemporary Analogies to the Gospels and
Acts: "Genres" or "Motifs"?' in *Synoptic Studies*, ed. C. M. Tuckett
(JSNTS 7; Sheffield, 1984).
7 Published in Greek around 217 C.E., but supposedly based on the
memoirs of Damis, a companion and disciple, about Apollonius, who
lived during the first century C.E. and was active under emperors
from Nero to Nerva. See the edition in Loeb Classical Library.
8 Lucian's *Alexander the False Prophet*, written in Greek about 180 C.E.
against Alexander, a priest of Asclepius in the second century C.E.
who gained a large following and whose cult flourished for about a
century afterwards, depicts Alexander as a charlatan who claimed to
be a divine teacher. Again, insofar as the story portrays Alexander as
a healer, the biography has something in common with the Gospel
according to Matthew but neither Alexander's frenzied behaviour
(12), nor his medical remedies given in writing and based especially
on diet and the use of bear's grease (19), has parallels in Matthew.
Lucian's work is polemical, seeking to exemplify the sanity of Epicu-
rean philosophy to a fellow-Epicurean in contrast to the chicanery of
Alexander. Both the cult and Lucian's philosophy held beliefs very
different from the first gospel, which have led to a work whose
contrasts are greater than its similarities with the gospel.
   Pace Morton Smith, *Jesus the Magician* (London, 1978), Jesus' miracles do not prove his divinity, since Jesus shares this activity not only
with his disciples (10:8) but also with the disciples of the Pharisees
(12:27), and in the first gospel, human beings do not attain divinity
through ascetic or healing practices since human creatures do not
share divine transcendence.
   Again, H. C. Kee's suggestion that literature developing the beliefs
of the Isis cult may throw light on the miracle stories of the synoptic
gospels is useful only in relation to motifs. Indeed, Apuleius' *The
Golden Ass*, written in Latin about 180 C.E., which transforms a traditional story about the adventures of a young man too curious about
magic for his own good – compare Lucian's shorter Greek version,
Metamorphoses, written about the same time – into an apology for the
Isis cult, since the hero is saved from the consequences of his stupid-
ity by the goddess Isis and enabled by her to live a life of serenity,
honour and usefulness, is quite unlike the Gospel of Matthew both
because it depicts the religious quest of a disciple and because it is a
Platonic allegorization advocating Platonic beliefs which are not

171

shared by Matthew. Nor is Kee's further suggestion, that material found only in Matthew is akin to contemporary histories by Suetonius, Tacitus and Josephus, with their interest in portents, omens and oracles, any more helpful in defining the genre of Matthew. Kee's argument appears more plausible than it is because he treats this Matthaean material out of context and so can give to the individual motifs a significance they do not have in the context in which they are placed. If Matthaean dependence on scripture is recognized, earthquakes in Matthew are seen to echo the language of its scriptural theophanies (Exodus 19:18, I Kings 19:11–12, Psalm 113[114]: 7), just as dreams giving divine guidance, especially to Joseph, are reminiscent of the scriptural patriarch Joseph, the dreamer of dreams. See H. C. Kee, *Miracles in the Early Christian World* (Yale University Press, 1983), and below.

9 Even contemporary Jewish Hellenistic biographies do not share this eschatological perspective with Matthew. Josephus eschews eschatological beliefs altogether, interpreting Messianic prophecies to refer to the Flavian house. The portraits of scriptural characters in *Jewish Antiquities*, published under Domitian, are 'biblically based but hellenistically conceived': H. W. Attridge on Josephus in *Jewish Writings of the Second Temple Period*, ed. M. E. Stone (Fortress, 1984), p. 255, by which Attridge means that they are unified by themes like *pronoia*, borrowed from Greek philosophy, and that they are made more dramatic by focusing explicitly on psychology (unlike Matthew), by heightening the emotional impact of important scenes (like Luke but unlike Matthew) and by developing the erotic possibilities of some episodes (unlike the gospels): pp. 212f.

Philo's *Life of Moses*, Book I, has more in common with Matthew since Matthew presents Jesus in some sense as a second Moses (see below), but Philo's portrait is influenced by Platonism. Moses is an ideal philosopher-king displaying the virtues of justice, courage and temperance. The text describes him existing within a theological framework which sometimes equates God and fortune, and sometimes, conforming the vocabulary more closely to that of the Pentateuch, sees God as the saviour of those who suffer. But true to his Platonic beliefs, Philo, unlike the Pentateuch, portrays the Hebrews as free men of high lineage, virtuous and pious, deserving God's graciousness. Philo's anthropology exhibits a Platonic dualism of immortal mind and corruptible body. So the Hebrews are said to have discovered that their souls are sprung from divine seeds and that their stock is akin to God, and Moses at the end of his life is said to leave his mortal life for immortality, summoned by a God who transformed his two-fold nature into a single unity, his whole being into pure mind.

One of the themes of Philo's *Life of Moses* and of his *On Rewards and Punishments* is the blessings of a virtuous life and the curses of a vicious life. The rewards are those we would expect a Platonist to desire, a serene life of virtue in contemplation of God leading to a life of prosperity and health. Beyond death lies immortality for the good man or perpetual grief for the bad man (*On Rewards and Punishments*, 69–70 and 100). Although *On Rewards and Punishments* looks forward to the future triumph of the virtuous with an accompanying transformation of political and natural existence in this world, it does not envisage a final eschatological judgement or resurrection into a new creation. Philo's writings do not, then, share Matthew's eschatological perspective.

See also D. L. Tiede, *The Charismatic Figure as Miracle-worker* (SBL Dissertation Series 1; 1972). Unfortunately, in discussing the use of the term 'divine man' in Hellenistic literature, Tiede does not examine what 'divine' means in each context. Also, P. Cox, *Biography in Late Antiquity* (University of California Press, 1983), esp. pp. 30ff.

10 See, for example, 2:1–12, 20:29–34, 21:5–11, and the implied inadequacy of the title in 16:13–28 and 22:41–46. The prediction of the king's vengeance against enemies in Psalm 17(18):46–50 finds no fulfilment in the Matthaean portrait.

11 Genesis 12:3, Matthew 2:1–12, 4:14–16, 8:5–13, 28–34, 15:21–28, 28:16–20.

12 Genesis 37 – 48, especially 39, Matthew 1 – 2.

13 Exodus 1:22 – 2:10, Matthew 2:13–18.

14 Hosea 11:1, Exodus 4:22, Matthew 2:15.

15 Exodus 14 – 15, Matthew 3:13–17.

16 Exodus 14 – 17, 32 – 34, Numbers 11ff., and notice too the connection with Moses fasting forty days, Exodus 34:28, Matthew 4:1–11.

17 I Kings 19:19ff., Matthew 4:18ff., 8:18–22, 9:9, 28:16–20.

18 Exodus 20:1ff., Matthew 5 – 7.

19 Exodus 7 – 12, Matthew 8 – 9, although Jesus' wonders and those of Moses individually have nothing in common.

20 Exodus 16, Numbers 11, Matthew 14:13–21, 15:32–38.

21 I Kings 19:1ff., Matthew 11:14 and 14:1–12.

22 Exodus 2:11ff., 17:2ff., 32:30ff., Jeremiah 20, 26, 38, 43, Matthew 16:13–26, 17:3–5, 5:11–12. Traditions about the martyrdom of the prophets seem to have developed after the persecution of Antiochus Epiphanes, 167–164 B.C.E. For example, *The Martyrdom of Isaiah*, a Jewish work now incorporated into the Christian *Ascension of Isaiah*, depicts Isaiah's arrest and execution under Manasseh – he was sawn in two. The legend probably developed from the general reference to Manasseh shedding innocent blood in II Kings 21:16. See M. A. Knibb in *The Old Testament Pseudepigrapha*, vol. 2, ed. J. H. Charlesworth (Doubleday, New York, 1985).

23 Exodus 17:8ff., Numbers 16, 21:21ff., 31, Matthew 12:1ff., 15:1ff., 19:3ff., 21:23ff.

24 Genesis 1:1ff., Matthew 14:22–27. For *palingenesia*, see Matthew 19:28.

25 Isaiah 5, II Samuel 12, Matthew 13:1ff., and the discussion by M. D. Goulder, *Midrash and Lection in Matthew* (SPCK, 1974), chapter 3, in which he points out that Matthaean parables are indicative, Lucan

173

imperative, and that Matthaean parables are not fables from nature but are interested in human experiences (of farming or fishing, for example), which makes them closer to Isaiah 5 and II Samuel 12 than to the fables of Ezekiel.

26 Exodus 12, 24, Leviticus 4ff., II Maccabees 7, Matthew 26:26ff. See R. J. Daly, *Christian Sacrifice: the Judeo-Christian background before Origen* (Studies in Christian Antiquity 18: Catholic University of America Press, Washington, 1978).

27 Matthew 26:36f., Psalm 21(22):20; Matthew 27:35, Psalm 21(22):18; Matthew 27:39, Psalm 21(22):7; Matthew 27:42, Psalm 68(69):9; Matthew 27:46, Psalm 21(22):1; Matthew 27:48, Psalm 68(69):21; Matthew 27:34, Psalm 68(69):21.

28 J. E. Alsup, *The Post-Resurrection Appearance Stories of the Gospel Tradition* (SPCK, 1976).

29 See especially R. Bultmann, *The History of the Synoptic tradition*, Eng. trans. (Oxford, 1968).

30 Deuteronomy 33:29, Psalm 1:1, 2:12, 33(34):8, Ecclesiasticus 28:19, 48:11, Tobit 13:14, Matthew 5:3–10, 11–12.

31 Isaiah 5:8ff., 33:1, Jeremiah 13:27, and a collection of seven in Matthew 23:13ff.

32 Jeremiah 28:6, Matthew 6:5, 16, etc.

33 See Bultmann, *op. cit.*, pp. 69f. It is difficult to gauge the significance of wisdom parallels because proverbial forms are common to all cultural traditions, as common as basic forms of rhetoric like those instanced by G. A. Kennedy.

   Further parallels between Matthew and its scripture could be drawn on the level of individual words; for example, *dikaiosunē*, *eleēmosunē* and *dikaios* are key terms in Matthew and in the Septuagint: see B. Przybylski, *Righteousness in Matthew and his world of thought* (SNTS Monograph 41; C.U.P., 1980), p. 77.

34 Matthew 1 – 2, 28.

35 At Jesus' baptism in 3:17 and at his transfiguration, 17:5. Surprisingly few of the details of Jesus' transfiguration conform to that of Moses in Exodus 34:29ff. In each, the face is transfigured, but the vocabulary depicting it differs.

36 G. Vermes, *Jesus the Jew* (Collins, 1973), pp. 206ff. Another detail in Matthew, the authority conferred on Peter and the disciples 'to bind and loose' in Matthew 16:19 and 18:18 appears to reflect rabbinic usage – whatever a rabbinic legal decision 'binds' is forbidden, and whatever it 'loosens' is allowed.

37 Matthew 6:13, 4:1, Genesis 22:1, Exodus 16:4, Amos 3:6.

38 E.g. Psalms 77(78):25, 49, 137(138):1, Genesis 16:7ff., 19:1ff., Exodus 3:2, 4:24, 14:19, I Kings 19:5.

39 Job 1:6ff., Matthew 4:1–11.

40 II Kings 1:2, 6. The Hebrew means 'Lord of the flies' and the Septuagint translates it *Baal muian*, although Symmachus' version simply transliterates *Beelzeboub*. The corruption *Beezeboul*, which could mean either 'Lord of the lofty place' or 'Lord of filth', may have been

deliberate or accidental. Notice also Deuteronomy 32:17, Isaiah 65:11, where idol worship is characterized as sacrificing to demons.

41 Matthew 9:34, 10:25, 12:24ff. In 12:26 and 27, Satan and Beelzebul are used in parallel.
42 E.g. Matthew 8:16, 28ff., 9:32ff.
43 E.g. Exodus 23:23–33, Leviticus 26:3–33, Deuteronomy 28:1–68, and note the association of the woman's sin and her son's death in I Kings 17:18, cf. Matthew 9:1–8.
44 II Kings 4:8ff. and Matthew 9:18ff.; II Kings 4:42ff. and Matthew 14:13ff., 15:32ff.; II Kings 5:1ff. and Matthew 8:1ff.
45 Tobit 11:5ff. and Matthew 9:27ff., 20:29ff.; Tobit 8:2ff. and Matthew 8:28ff., 9:32ff.
46 Matthew 18:10, Jubilees 35:17, and cf. Psalm 90(91):11.
47 See especially *Apollonius of Tyana*, 4, 20 and Matthew 8:28ff., mentioned earlier; J. M. Hull, *Hellenistic Magic and the Synoptic Tradition* (SBT 28; SCM, 1974); and M. Smith, *Jesus the Magician* (London, 1978).
48 See E. P. Sanders, 'The genre of Palestinian Jewish Apocalypses' in *Apocalypticism in the Mediterranean World and the Near East*, ed. D. Hellholm (Tübingen, 1983).
49 Matthew 3:16 and 4:1. E. P. Sanders, *op. cit.*, suggests that this mode of revelation should also be treated as a feature of some apocalyptic literature, for example, I Enoch 91–104.
50 E.g. Lord Byron's *Don Juan* (1818). Or we may learn about English burial customs at the beginning of the twentieth century from Thomas Hardy's 'To Meet, or Otherwise' from *Satires of Circumstance* (1914).
51 Martin Gilbert, *Winston S. Churchill* (Houghton-Mifflin, Boston, 1971).

10

'THE COMING OF THE SON OF MAN'

Mark's gospel and the subversion of 'the apocalyptic imagination'

Timothy Radcliffe OP

In the sixtieth year of our era Paul appealed to the emperor and sailed to Rome. And the gospel he preached there, in and out of prison, was shaped by what Collins has called 'the apocalyptic imagination'.[1] Apocalyptic was simply the unquestioned matrix of all early Christian thought, 'the mother of Christian theology'.[2] According to tradition Paul died four years later in the great Neronian persecution, and this was the beginning of a crisis which forced the church to free itself of the limitations of an apocalyptic view of reality. It is the thesis of this article that Mark's gospel was written because of the failure of the 'apocalyptic imagination' to make sense of the persecution of the church by Nero in A.D. 64 and the destruction of the Temple in A.D. 70. It was not the experience of suffering as such that apocalyptic could not cope with. Indeed the genre probably evolved to make sense of Israel's repeated experiences of humiliation and persecution. It is the literature *par excellence* of the oppressed, but the crises of the sixties and seventies subverted apocalyptic's usual strategies in the interpretation of suffering.

Meeks has claimed that the apocalyptic universe was characterized by three fundamental dualities: 'a) the cosmic duality heaven/earth, b) the temporal duality this age/the age to come, and c) a social duality: the sons of light/the sons of darkness, the righteous/the unrighteous, the elect/the world'.[3] Apocalyptic was such a successful way of dealing with suffering because it apparently confirmed the validity of these dualities. The cosmic duality of heaven and earth was evident if the earth turned out to be a place of pain and persecution. The apocalypticists must surely be right. One could endure the suffering because this age would soon be over, and so the worse the suffering the more one must hang on for the imminent redemption. And Meeks has shown in a brilliant article[4] how Paul, especially in I Thessalonians, is able to use their experience of persecution to confirm the truth of his teaching and to buttress the solidarity of the community. Paul had told them from the beginning that they were to suffer and so when they do they have further grounds for believing his every word: 'You yourselves know that this is to be our lot. For when we were with you, we told you beforehand that we were to suffer affliction just as it has come to pass, and as you know' (3:3–4). But their foreknowledge of this suffering and their expectation of the Day of the Lord confirms that they are set apart, the children of the light: 'But you are not in darkness, brethren, for that day to surprise you like a thief. For you are all sons of light and sons of the day; we are not of the night or darkness' (5:4f.). So, the worse things get, the clearer it is that salvation is to be found only within the community. Meeks puts it well: 'When they in fact experience hostility, Paul uses that fact as a means for interpreting their identity as Christians. Their separation from their neighbours has had its predicted outcome, so the complex of teaching that accompanied and effected that separation is confirmed. In that sense, then, the experience of hostility itself is employed to reduce dissonance: the experience helps to make sense of the separation and thus to reinforce the boundaries between the group and the larger society. Moreover, the language of destiny sets the identity of the Thessalonian Christians into a cosmic, theological context. Visibly they are a tiny club gathered cautiously in someone's house in Thessalonica. But Paul is teaching them that "really" their troubles are part of a comprehensive pattern of God's activity in and for the world.'[5] And one could show that in all his letters Paul is always able to give suffering a positive interpretation. In Romans he is even able to claim that it is a cause for hope: 'More than that, we rejoice in our sufferings, knowing that suffering produces endurance, and endurance produces character, and character produces hope, and hope does not disappoint us, because God's love has been poured into our hearts through the Holy Spirit which has been given to us' (5:3ff.). But if this is so, if the 'apocalyptic imagination' thrives on crisis and affliction, then why was it that the persecution of the church by Nero and the destruction of the Temple should lead to its collapse? Why was it necessary to invent a new genre to make sense of the experience, the gospel? I believe that it was because apocalyptic was unable to give sense to the collapse of the Christian community in Rome. In this case suffering did not lead to a confirmation of the duality of inside/ outside, the sons of light/the sons of darkness.

The first letter of Peter addresses its recipients as *paroikoi* (e.g.

2:11), and J. H. Elliott has shown that this is a legal term in the first place.[6] To be a *paroikos* was to lack full citizenship, to be a resident alien, a stranger and a foreigner. And this was clearly the status not only of most of the recipients of the letter but of the church from which it came, the church of Rome. Rome is given the name Babylon (5:13), the place of exile. Most Roman Christians seem to have been *paroikoi*, resident aliens, immigrants, or, to give them their proper Roman designation, *peregrini*. And this is not surprising, for the simple reason that most of the people who lived in Rome then were *peregrini*. As Juvenal wrote, 'The Syrian Orontes has long since poured into the Tiber, bringing with it its lingo and its manners, its flutes and its slanting harp strings'.[7] It was of course on the Syrian Orontes, at Antioch, that the followers of The Way were first called Christians! And these rightless, stateless immigrants were forbidden to participate in popular assemblies, excluded from military service, unable without permission to contract a valid marriage, could not be the heir of a Roman citizen and so on.[8] To these *paroikoi*, the church offered itself as an *oikos*, a household, in Elliott's phrase, 'a home for the homeless': 'In contrast to the individualism of the cults, on the other hand, the Christian household offered incorporation into a family, a place of permanent belonging, a supportive circle of brothers and sisters'.[9] The apocalypticism of the early church found in the experience of alienation and persecution confirmation of the boundaries between the inside and the outside, until A.D. 64.

On 19 July a fire destroyed most of Rome and Nero decided to blame the disaster on the Christians once the people started to point the finger at him. Tacitus describes what happened: 'Therefore, to scotch the rumour, Nero substituted as culprits, and punished with the utmost refinements of cruelty, a class of men, loathed for their vices, whom the crowd styled Christians. Christus, the founder of the name, had undergone the death penalty in the reign of Tiberius, by sentence of the procurator Pontius Pilate, and the pernicious superstition was checked for a moment, only to break out once more, not merely in Judea, the home of the disease, but in the capital itself, where all things horrible or shameful in the world collect and find a vogue. First, then, the confessed members of the sect were arrested; next, on their disclosures, vast numbers were convicted, not so much on account of arson as for hatred of the human race. And derision accompanied their end; they were covered with wild beasts' skins and torn to death by dogs; or they were fastened on crosses, and when daylight failed were burned to serve as lamps by night' (*The Annals*, Book XV, xliv). This confirms that Christianity was seen as a foreign religion, the sort of thing that resident aliens would accept. Their reputation for *odium humani generis*, a traditional accusation against the Jews, suggests that they were seen as a tightly knit sect with clear boundaries between insiders and outsiders, but most significantly the household seems to have broken up under the pressure of persecution. Most of the martyrs were convicted on the evidence of other Christians; Christians named each other to the authorities. We know from Pliny's letters[10] that this was how Christians were often to be exposed in the future, but a house divided against itself cannot stand. It was this experience, the failure of suffering to confirm the boundaries, that led the church beyond apocalyptic.

The evidence suggests that it was not just the degree of suffering but division within the church that led to the collapse. If Paul's letter to the Philippians was indeed written during his Roman captivity, then this would suggest that some Christians were envious of others, and actually delighted in Paul's captivity: 'Some indeed preach Christ from envy (*phthonos*) and rivalry, but others from good will. The latter do it out of love, knowing that I am put here for the defence of the gospel; the former proclaim Christ out of partisanship, not sincerely but thinking to afflict me in my imprisonment' (1:15–17). So even before the great persecution the seeds of the breakdown of the household of God were sown. And when *I Clement* was written towards the end of the first century, the deaths of Peter and Paul were attributed to the presence of envy in the church: 'Through envy and jealousy, the greatest and most righteous pillars have been persecuted and put to death. Let us set before our eyes the illustrious apostles. Peter, through unrighteous envy, endured not one or two, but numerous labours; and when he had at length suffered martyrdom, departed to the place of glory due to him. Owing to envy, Paul also obtained the reward of patient endurance, after being seven times thrown into captivity, compelled to flee, and stoned'.[11] So immediately before and after the persecution we have evidence of a collapse of community, the breakup of the household, that it was beyond the powers of the 'apocalyptic imagination' to redeem. The challenge which brought into existence the first gospel was to find a form of narrative, a way of telling the story, that would make sense of that time when 'brother will deliver up brother to death, and the father his child, and children will rise against parents and have them put to death; and you will be hated by all for my name's sake' (Mk 13:12f.).

So the crisis of A.D. 64 saw the collapse of one of the three fundamental dualities that, according to Meeks, structured the apocalyptic perception of reality, the duality of insider/outsider. It is just conceivable that this way of thinking might have remained plausible, by, for example, redefining the boundaries, if the failure of the Jewish war and the destruction of the Temple in A.D. 70 had not led to a failure of faith in another duality, that of this age and the age to come. Any suffering was bearable if one could believe that the end was nigh, but the rebellion collapsed, the place of God's dwelling on earth was desecrated and still the Kingdom of God did not come. It is true that some people went on writing apocalypses and longing for the end. Within Judaism we have IV Ezra and II and III Baruch and within Christianity there is the book of Revelation. But both religions had to evolve new literary and theological forms to cope with the failure of the Kingdom of God to appear, the collection of the oral traditions or the evolution of the gospels. One could no longer make sense of suffering by appealing to an imminent end: 'And then if anyone says to you, "Look, here is the Christ!" or "Look, there he is!" do not believe it. False Christs and false prophets will arise and show signs and wonders, to lead astray, if possible, the elect' (Mk 13:21f.). So the gospel form had to evolve to make sense of the collapse of the second of the fundamental dualities of apocalyptic.

One objection to this thesis might be that many scholars have argued that the gospel was written in the late sixties before the Temple was ever destroyed. But it is hard to imagine why Mark would have written a gospel which is so dominated by references to the fate of the Temple if it was still standing. From the moment that Jesus arrives in Jerusalem one might almost say that it provides the unifying theme of the narrative. He goes immediately to it and overturns the money changers' tables; he curses the fig tree, which clearly symbolizes the Temple; it is in the Temple that he tells the parable against the tenants of the vineyard. In chapter 13 he foretells its destruction: 'Do you not see these great buildings? There will not be left here one stone upon another, that will not be thrown down' (verse 2). When he is arrested and brought before the high priest, he is accused of saying that he will destroy the Temple and build another; when he is crucified, he is mocked, 'Ah, you who would destroy the Temple and build it in three days, save yourself and come down from the cross' (15:29f.), and when he dies the veil of the Temple is torn in two. This obsession with the doomed sanctuary would have no sense if it was still standing when Mark wrote, especially as Josephus tells us that the Romans had never intended to destroy it when they captured Jerusalem. Titus was horrified when a soldier tossed in the burning firebrand that started the conflagration.[12]

It may seem curious to us that the destruction of a building in a minor province several hundred miles away should have been a traumatic event for Christians living in the capital of the empire forty years after the foundation of the church. We must remember that for first-century Jews Jerusalem did not seem far away from Rome. Raymond Brown has written that 'a particular aspect of Roman Judaism deserves special attention, namely, its close political and intellectual affiliation with Jerusalem and Palestine. . . . Intellectually, even after the destruction of Jerusalem by the Romans, there was a constant interchange between Palestinian Judaism and Roman Judaism'.[13] And the faith probably came to Rome as a result of this interchange. 'The dominant Christianity at Rome had been shaped by the Jerusalem Christianity associated with James and Peter, and hence was a Christianity appreciative of Judaism and loyal to its customs.'[14] So it is plausible to imagine that the Jewish rebellion was the focus of intense eschatological expectations for the Christians of the Roman church and the destruction of the Temple a devastating event. And the war was not seen at the time as a minor fracas in a provincial backwater. Josephus was not altogether exaggerating when he prefaces the *Bellum Judaicum* by saying 'The war of the Jews against the Romans was the greatest of our time; greater too, perhaps, than any recorded struggle whether between cities or nations'.[15] Frend asserts that contemporary public opinion would have agreed with Josephus: 'The capture of Jerusalem was regarded as a great feat of arms, legitimizing the title of Vespasian to be celebrated and remembered throughout the Empire. The coinage of the time provides the proof. As Hart points out,[16] it is "in all metals – not only gold and silver, it is on the poor man's brass, the money of the people, even to the little *quadrans* with its emblematic palm tree". The whole Empire must concentrate on the one theme "JUDAEA CAPTA"'.[17]

The destruction of Jerusalem and the Temple was not something that the Roman Christians would just have heard or read about. They saw it. It was re-enacted in their streets in the Triumph of Vespasian and his son Titus. Just as in Spain the passion of Christ is dramatically replayed in enormous tableaux in the streets, so the Roman Christians had to witness a sort of passion play of the end of the holy city and the place where God had put his name. Enormous tableaux, three or four stories high, illustrated every stage of the campaign:

> Here was to be seen a smiling countryside laid waste,
> there whole formations of the enemy put to the sword;
> men in flight and men led off to captivity; walls of
> enormous size thrown down by engines, great strong-
> holds stormed, cities whose battlements were lined
> with defendants utterly overwhelmed, an army
> streaming inside the ramparts, the whole place reek-
> ing with slaughter. . . . Such were the agonies to which
> the Jews condemned themselves when they embarked
> on this war; and the art and marvellous craftsmanship
> of these constructions now revealed these incidents to
> those who had not seen them as clearly as if they had
> been there.[18]

And the Temple was virtually dismembered before their eyes.
The altar of shewbread, the Menora, the ritual trumpets, even
the Scroll of the Law, were all carried in public through the
streets. And finally this passion play ends with a real death, the
execution of the rebel leader Simon, son of Gioras. The emperor
and Titus went to the Temple of Jupiter and waited while Simon
was dragged through the street, mocked and beaten and finally
executed. When it was heard that he had died the sacrifices were
offered to the victorious gods. Mark's gospel has often been
described as a passion narrative with a long introduction, and it
was partially provoked by witnessing an enacted passion before
the eyes of the Roman Christians. And when Mark links the
death of Christ to the tearing of the Temple veil he was referring
to something that was probably well known to most of his congregation, for when Vespasian dedicated the Temple of Peace in
A.D. 75, about the time that the gospel was probably written, he
put in it the Scroll of the Law, the Temple vessels and 'the
crimson curtains of the Inner Sanctuary'.[19]

So then, the community in Rome were faced with a twofold
crisis, the failure of the sufferings of the Neronian persecution to
be redeemed by the strengthening of the community, and of the
destruction of the Temple by the coming of the new age. Two of
the fundamental dualities of the 'apocalyptic imagination' were
rendered questionable, the boundary between the insider and
the outsider, and between this age and the age to come. I believe
that Mark's gospel was written in Rome[20] to offer a new genre, a
new theological perspective that could cope with this crisis, and
in the limited space of this short article I can only outline his
strategy. The obvious starting point is chapter 13, the so-called
'Little Apocalypse'. At first sight it looks like a typical example of

apocalyptic, with its predictions of disaster and cosmic collapse, but a closer reading would suggest that it is actually a subversion of apocalyptic. It overthrows the duality of this age and the age to come. This is suggested by the final verses of the chapter:

> But of that day or hour no one knows, not even the angels in heaven, nor the Son, but only the Father. Take heed, watch; for you do not know when the time will come. It is like a man going on a journey, when he leaves home and puts his servants in charge, each with his work, and commands the doorkeeper to be on the watch. Watch therefore – for you do not know when the master of the house will come, in the evening, or at midnight, or at cockcrow, or in the morning – lest he come suddenly and find you asleep. And what I say to you I say to all: Watch (13:32–37).

R. H. Lightfoot was probably the first scholar to explore in depth the relationship between these words and the events of chapters 14 and 15.[21] The apocalyptic theology of the early church had hinged on the coming of the hour, but even after the blasphemy of the burning of God's dwelling place, still the hour did not come. But within the Marcan narrative the coming of the hour is relocated. It is in the garden of Gethsemane that the disciples should have watched for the hour: 'And he came the third time, and said to them, "Are you still sleeping and taking your rest? It is enough; the hour has come; the Son of man is betrayed into the hands of sinners. Rise, let us be going; see, my betrayer is at hand"' (14:41–42). The Son's ignorance of the moment of the hour turns out not to be about the end of history, the second Coming, but as to whether the Father would let the cup pass. And Lightfoot also points to the close relationship between the possible times for the coming of the hour which Mark gives us at the end of chapter 13 and the chronology of chapters 14 and 15. It is in the evening that Jesus celebrates the Passover with his disciples; the hour comes in Gethsemane with Judas' betrayal, presumably at midnight; at cockcrow Peter denies Jesus, and in the morning the Sanhedrin holds a consultation and hands Jesus over to Pilate. In fact one might note that each of these moments is a moment of 'handing over' in a slightly different sense; of Jesus handing over his body to the disciples, of Judas and then Peter 'handing him over' into the hands of his enemies, and of the Sanhedrin handing him over to Pilate. All these contribute to the coming of the hour. And this interpretation is confirmed by 13:30, 'Truly, I say to you, this generation will not pass away before all these things

take place'. By any reckoning a generation had passed away since
Jesus was supposed to have spoken these words, some forty
years previously, but there is no difficulty if Mark is in fact
thinking of that coming of the hour which occurs in Gethsemane.
Likewise it helps us to understand the glorious irony of Jesus'
reply to the high priest during his trial, when he asks him if he is
the Christ, the Son of the Blessed.

> And Jesus said, 'I am; and you will see the Son of man
> seated at the right hand of Power, and coming with the
> clouds of heaven.' And the high priest tore his gar-
> ments, and said, 'Why do we still need witnesses? You
> have heard his blasphemy. What is your decision?'
> And some began to spit on him, and to cover his face,
> and to strike him, saying to him, 'Prophesy!' And the
> guards received him with blows (14:62–65).

If Jesus was referring to the parousia then he would simply have
been wrong; the high priest was dead by the time the gospel was
written and still the end had not come. Clearly it must refer to that
coming in power which was his enthronement on the cross,
ironically recognized as 'King of the Jews', when, as prophesied,
the sun was darkened between the sixth and the ninth hour. And
it is typical of Mark to have the irony of the high priest asking why
they need witnesses. They do not; they will see Jesus in glory
very shortly and not recognize him. The guards ask him to prophesy and that is exactly what he has just done.

Scholars have tended to miss these allusions because we have
been caught in the nineteenth-century prejudice that Mark is a
naïve historian who just wants to tell us what really happened.
But he is not that at all. He is telling a complex parable within
which we can find ourselves. He is not pointing us outside the
text to some redemptive event which is yet to come. His references are nearly always intratextual. One very neat example is
Jesus' dialogue with James and John over the places to his left and
right in glory. Jesus replies by telling them, 'You do not know
what you are asking' (10:38). And that is literally true, since his
moment of glory is that of his crucifixion. Instead he tells them,
'To sit on my right hand or my left is not mine to grant, but it is for
those for whom it is prepared' (10:40). And these turn out to be
rather unexpected candidates: 'And the inscription of the charge
against him read, "The King of the Jews." And with him they
crucified two robbers, one on his right and one on his left'
(15:26f.).

Mark does not bring our attention back to the Christ enthroned on his cross because he wants to tell us that suffering is not so bad after all, it can even be a moment of glory. That would not have helped the Christians of Rome; for most of them the time of persecution had not been a period of glory but of failure, envy and betrayal. In the first place he is deconstructing the apocalyptic universe. The dualities of this age and the age to come and of heaven and earth are subverted in the image of the King sitting in glory on this gibbet. But more profoundly, Mark is offering us a new sort of narrative structure, an extended parable within which we belong. However mythological much of the language of apocalyptic looks, it is fundamentally historical in the sense that it places one firmly at a particular place in the story of God's plan for the world. For Paul we live after the death and resurrection of Christ and before the parousia, in the time of the outpouring of the Holy Spirit. We may suffer but these are the sufferings that give us hope for the coming of the Lord. But Mark's congregation found that they no longer knew where they were in the history of salvation. He offered them not so much a location in that history as a place within a narrative. We read the gospel to discover ourselves as the disciples who are called, who go to Jerusalem not knowing what is going to happen, who betray Jesus and flee, and who find ourselves at the empty tomb. It does not offer an account of the past but a narrative of the present. It functions like a parable, for parables work by having one identify with the participants. And so it is ironical that this gospel, which looks like the first 'history' of Jesus, is in fact fundamentally unhistorical in its intention. We do not find ourselves at the end of the story, but inside it, which explains why it has such a curious non-ending.

The gospel ends in apparent failure, with the women saying nothing: 'And they went out and fled from the tomb; for trembling and astonishment had come upon them; and they said nothing to anyone, for they were afraid' (16:8). The reason why Mark does not mention any resurrection appearances is not because he did not know of them; we know from I Cor 15 that the tradition of Jesus' appearances to his disciples was very ancient and would certainly have been known in Rome. But Mark did not intend to give us an historical account of what happened on Easter morning but a narrative that could interpret his listeners' experience. The problem in Rome in the mid-seventies was the absence of the body of Jesus. In the 'Little Apocalypse' we have already heard that people were claiming to have found the Christ returned to earth; there were sightings, but we must not believe them: 'And then if anyone says to you, "Look, here is the Christ!"

or "Look, there he is!" do not believe it' (13:21). It is the experience of the absence of the body that Mark in his resurrection account claims as a sign of victory: 'he is risen, he is not here; see the place where they laid him' (16:6). The silence of the women at the tomb expresses that of the Roman Christians, and leads them beyond it. They know that the women had no need to be afraid and that their silence was not ultimate, and so discover that their own need not be either.[22]

The end of the gospel is not where Mark wishes to leave us. The final scene propels us forward to Galilee, where they will see him as he said, but it also draws the reader back into the narrative where we belong as disciples. We must remember what had gone before, what he said while he was still with us. Even the failed attempt to anoint the body of Jesus draws us back into the story, to the successful anointing prior to his death by the anonymous woman in the house of Simon the leper. And there is a typical Marcan irony in Jesus' words to the disciples: 'Let her alone; why do you trouble her? She has done a beautiful thing to me. For you always have the poor with you, and whenever you will, you can do good to them; but you will not always have me. She has done what she could; she has anointed my body beforehand for burying. And truly, I say to you, wherever the gospel is preached in the whole world, what she has done will be told in memory of her' (14:6–9). As always in Mark, the references are intratextual. The women will discover very soon that they cannot anoint Jesus because 'you will not always have me', and whereas the named women who go to the empty tomb fail to pass on the good news, it is the anonymous woman's deed which will be remembered and preached throughout the world.

We started from Meek's observation that the apocalyptic universe was characterized by three dualities, between heaven and earth, between this age and the age to come, and between insiders and outsiders. We have tried to show how Mark subverts this apocalyptic perception of reality by overthrowing the first two dualities, most obviously in Jesus as the King enthroned in glory on the cross. This only leaves the third duality to consider and we have already seen that the beginning of the crisis for Mark's church was the collapse of clear boundaries during the Neronian persecution. We will conclude this article with a brief suggestion as to how Mark makes sense of that moment of failure.

Paul offered his hearers participation through baptism in the death of Christ, in the hope that we would share in his resurrection. Mark's gospel offers a participation in a different story, the constitution and collapse of the community, and the promise of its restoration. We read of the calling of the disciples, the appointment of the twelve; we hear of their failure at the death of Christ, but we are promised that this is not the end of the story: 'You will all fall away; for it is written, "I will strike the shepherd, and the sheep will be scattered." But after I am raised up, I will go before you to Galilee' (14:27f.). So the narrative embraces the collapse of the church in the sixties but leads us beyond that. More subtly it shows the disciples as being from the beginning ambiguous characters, neither simply insiders nor outsiders. This is not because, as many scholars have argued, Mark wished to attack Jerusalem Christianity or the early church leaders, but because he wished to explore and articulate his experience of the collapse of the clear boundary between insiders and outsiders that characterized the 'apocalyptic imagination'. For example, it belongs to being 'inside' to understand, and yet the disciples are shown from the beginning to be both those who do and who do not understand. For example, after the parable of the sower Jesus talks to the inner group:

> And when he was alone, those who were about him with the twelve asked him concerning the parables. And he said to them, 'To you has been given the secret of the kingdom of God, but for those outside everything is in parables; so that they may indeed see but not perceive, and may indeed hear but not understand; lest they should turn again, and be forgiven'. And he said to them, 'Do you not understand this parable? How then will you understand all the parables?' (4:10–13).

There is the same conjunction of understanding and incomprehension in Peter's confession in chapter 8. He is on the side of God, for he recognizes that Jesus is the Christ, yet he is on the side of Satan since he cannot accept that it is necessary[23] for the Christ to suffer and die. And just as it is those to whom the secret of the kingdom is given who fail to see, so also it is the outsiders who succeed, like the Syrophoenician woman and Bartimaeus the blind beggar. The boundaries are blurred. And, as one would expect, this happens most acutely at the moment of crucifixion, when all the disciples have fled and the community has collapsed, and when the centurion sees the dead Christ and makes his confession, 'Truly this was the Son of God'. The moment of enthronement is when all the three fundamental dualities of the 'apocalyptic imagination' are subverted.

To the *paroikoi*, the resident aliens, the immigrants who seem to have constituted the bulk of the population of Rome, the church offered an *oikos*, a home for the homeless. And Samuel Dill, the social historian, has written that 'probably no age, not even our own, ever felt a greater craving for some form of social life wider than the family and narrower than the State'.[24] But the home collapsed, for a house divided against itself cannot stand. And so it was appropriate that to these *peregrini*, to give them their proper legal status, Mark offered a narrative that took the form of a 'way'. It starts with John the Baptist, a *paroikos par excellence*, going into the wilderness to prepare a way for the Lord; it has as its centre Jesus making his way to Jerusalem to suffer and die, followed by the disciples who do not understand what was happening. It closes with the angel inviting the disciples to take to the road again and go to Galilee, where they will see him as he told them. To the *peregrini* it offered a *peregrinatio*; for us all it was the birth of something quite new, a 'gospel'.

NOTES

1 John J. Collins, *The Apocalyptic Imagination* (New York, 1984).

2 E. Käsemann, 'On the Subject of Primitive Christian Apocalyptic' in *New Testament Questions of Today* (Philadelphia, 1969), pp. 108–137.

3 W. Meeks, 'Social Functions of Apocalyptic Language in Pauline Christianity' in *Apocalypticism in the Mediterranean World and the Near East*, ed. D. Hellholm (Tübingen, 1983), p. 689.

4 *Ibid.*

5 *Ibid.*, p. 692.

6 John H. Elliott, *A Home for the Homeless* (Philadelphia, 1981).

7 *Satires* 3, line 62.

8 Adolf Berger, *Encyclopedic Dictionary of Roman Law* (Philadelphia, 1953), cited by Elliott, *op. cit.*, pp. 36f.

9 Elliott, *op. cit.*, p. 199.

10 Book 10, letter 96.

11 *The First Epistle of Clement*, chapter v; trans. in *The Ante-Nicene Fathers*, vol. 1, ed. A. Roberts and J. Donaldson (Michigan, 1969), p. 6.

12 *Bellum Judaicum*, VI, 254.

13 R. E. Brown and J. P. Meier, *Antioch and Rome* (New York, 1982; London, 1983), p. 96.

14 *Ibid.*, p. 110.

15 *The Jewish War*, trans. G. A. Williamson (London, 1959), p. 27.

16 H. St J. Hart, 'Judea and Rome, The Official Commentary', *Journal of Theological Studies*, N.S. iii (1952), p. 184.

17 W. H. C. Frend, *Martyrdom and Persecution in the Early Church* (Oxford, 1965), pp. 180f.

18 Josephus, *op. cit.* [note 15], p. 385.

19 *Ibid.*, p. 386.
20 See, for example, the exploration of the evidence in Brown and Meier, *op. cit.*, pp. 194ff.
21 In 'The Connexion of Chapter Thirteen with the Passion Narrative' in *The Gospel Message of St Mark* (Oxford, 1950).
22 Cf. N. Petersen, *Interpretation* 34 (1980), p. 153.
23 Though there is, of course, a sense in which such things are 'unnecessary'; cf. de Selby, *Layman's Atlas* Cop. 3. 93, referred to by H. McCabe, *Law, Love and Language* (London, 1968), p. 131, note 1.
24 *Roman Society from Nero to Marcus Aurelius* (New York, 1964/1911), p. 267, quoted by Elliott, *op. cit.*, p. 180.

11

TAKING AWAY THE SIN OF THE WORLD

Brian Wicker

— I —

A Any act of war aimed indiscriminately at the destruction of entire cities or of extensive areas along with their population is a crime against God and man himself. It merits unequivocal and unhesitating condemnation (*Gaudium et Spes*, Second Vatican Council 1965, para. 80).

B In current conditions 'deterrence' based on balance not as an end in itself but as a step on the way towards a progressive disarmament, may still be judged morally acceptable. Nonetheless, in order to ensure peace, it is indispensable not to be satisfied with this minimum, which is always susceptible to the real danger of explosion (Pope John Paul II to the Second UN Special Session on disarmament, June 1982).

Of course, each of these statements is only the tip of a much larger iceberg. To take A first: the Second Vatican Council in 1965 was condemning, without further ado, not only counter-city 'massive retaliation' (which had been the orthodoxy of deterrence during the 1950s) but also by implication the willingness to commit counter-city hostage-killing, entailed by the strategy of mutual assured destruction prevalent at the very time the Council was sitting. Since 1965, of course, the notion of limited nuclear war, on which the escalatory 'ladder' of flexible-response doctrine rests, has become increasingly implausible to politicians and military alike. Consequently, the American bishops, in their pastoral letter *The Challenge of Peace*, saw the Vatican Council statement as institutionalizing the operational unusability of nuclear weapons in any circumstances. Since then the possibility of a nuclear winter has only added even more validity to their judgement. Indeed, more recently still, Cardinal Casaroli, in a speech to a UN Day of Peace in Vienna, has gone even further in saying that:

> the consensus which exists on the unacceptable character of the actual use of nuclear weapons ought logically to be extended to the threat to have recourse to them.[1]

However, position B also has its 'iceberg' of implications. The most obvious is that there is some kind of sense to the notion that, in so far as nuclear deterrence helps to keep an admittedly fragile peace, it ought to be tolerated unless and until something better is put in its place. This seems to be only commonsense. It probably expresses something like the view of things taken by the man in the street, as well as the not very different view of very many people in politics and the military who cannot see any immediate way out of the dilemma presented by nuclear weapons. (In fact, of course, Pope John Paul's position is far more *restrictive* in its concession to nuclear deterrence than that of most of these 'commonsense' people.) To the extent that position B marks a clearly recognizable expression of a widely accepted point of view, it cannot easily be dismissed despite its obvious shortcomings.

So there is something that is right about each of these positions. Position A effectively rules out any operational use of nuclear weapons, since (taken together with a sober assessment of the risks of escalation and of the consequences for humanity if the risk fails), as the American bishops have said, it means that there is no way the initiation of nuclear war could be justified. As moralists and military are increasingly inclined to admit, nuclear weapons have no military use. But position B is right on another point. A mutually assured nuclear deterrence, as part of the very structure of international relations, especially between superpowers, *can* make those nations unthreatenable, and to that extent secure. Given the history of the twentieth century this is surely a major gain. A nation that is not threatened is less likely to feel the need to threaten others. While such security is extremely unstable and unsatisfactory, it is something to go forward from rather than to throw away.

In this paper I want to dwell on the theological implications of these two apparently opposed positions and their interaction. I shall begin by conducting a kind of dialogue between some of the themes which Herbert McCabe has pursued consistently over the years about the primacy of language and meanings, and some of the ideas put forward by Stan Windass for a 'Common Security Programme'.[2]

_____ II _____

> Jesus died of being human. His very humanity meant
> that he put up no barriers, no defence against those
> he loved who hated him. He refused to evade the
> consequences of being human in our inhuman world.
> So the cross shows up our world for what it really is,
> what we have made it. It is a world in which it is
> dangerous, even fatal, to be human: a world
> structured by violence and fear.... (Being human
> means being one) for whom to live is simply to love –
> for this is what human beings are for. The aim of
> human life is to live in friendship – a friendship
> amongst ourselves which in fact depends on a
> friendship, or covenant, that God has established
> between ourselves and him.[3]

Does this then mean that being fully human includes simply letting man's inhumanity to man take its course? Is this what Christianity is about? What about justice? Human rights? The poor and the oppressed? The paradox seems to be insoluble. But only if what is said about defencelessness here is misinterpreted as an *ethical principle*. Jesus's defencelessness must not be written off, as pacifism can all too easily be written off, as an option to which some are called, but to which most of us (luckily?) are not. On the contrary, Herbert McCabe's claim is a sober statement of an historical and theological fact: a truth about humanity which applies to everybody. (Of course it is easy to see how it may be misinterpreted as a statement of pacifist principle: that is, a moral/political programme which, if accepted by enough people, would bring peace. For any kind of ethical and political programme has to be largely utilitarian in character. It says that if you follow this line, and behave in this way, certain desirable consequences will follow: for example, justice and peace. One of the results of sin is that sacramental truths get systematically misunderstood as programmes of action, moral platforms, models to be imitated. We find ourselves then having to weigh consequences, assess probabilities, assign priorities. Moral philosophy takes over, helping us to 'evade the consequences of being human in our inhuman world', not only by justifying violence to defend ourselves but sometimes even by using non-violence for the same purpose.) Jesus was not a pacifist because he was not trying to promote justice and peace by espousing an ethical principle. That is to say, what drove him was not a hypothetical imperative ('If you love people enough they will respond by loving you and thus create a society of peace and justice'), nor even any categorical imperative ('Love and do what you will'). He was not driven by anything: he was his own man: just *being* what we are all called to be. To put the point in another way, Jesus's refusal to invoke the right of self-defence ('Do you think that I cannot appeal to my Father who would promptly send more than twelve legions of angels to my defence?'; Matt 26) was not an appeal to pacifist principle any more than his cleansing of the Temple rested on a rule about the just use of force. For us to follow him is not a matter of following some principles, but of being incorporated into him, becoming part of his body. Then we too become signs showing what our world is really like. His life is a statement of what it is to be fully a human being: that is, a sacrament of the life to come. Because it is not a piece of moral philosophy, it is not in competition with moral philosophies, whether pacifist or otherwise. That is why it does not cancel philosophical discussion of the nature and limits of 'just defence'.

Statements A and B are both about friendship and justice and their conditions in the nuclear age. Yet they seem to point in opposite directions. This is certainly how many people have interpreted them. Those who feel themselves to be drawn to A have welcomed the condemnation of the actual use of nuclear weapons in *Gaudium et Spes* and correctly concluded that if the use is illegitimate, so too is the willingness to use them which is inherent in nuclear deterrence. They have rightly recognized that one part of being human in an inhuman world consists in rejecting all the empty pomps and promises of nuclear weapons. They see that nuclear deterrence is a *diabolical* invention: and that we ought to have nothing to do with it. Those on the B side, however, have welcomed what they see as the 'realism' of the Pope's position. He sees that, despite the instability and obscene excess of current nuclear arsenals, the reality of international relations, as governed by the facts of nuclear possession, includes a measure of superpower unthreatenability. They claim that this fact needs to be recognized as a basis upon which to build a more secure world. International relations are real at their own level and cannot be reduced to relations of some different sort. We have to deal with states as they are, not as we would like them to be. Whether we like it or not, history has brought us to the point at which nuclear deterrence is an inextricable element in the fabric of life. The question then becomes not how to abolish nuclear weapons, but how to avoid using them.

Thus described, neither position is free from incoherence. The A position is *logically* consistent all right: the trouble is that it fails to address the obvious fact that nuclear deterrence, at present, is a fundamental part of the only structure of international relations that actually exists. Hence it is literally impossible to have nothing to do with it. Of course, gestures of rejection and refusal, both individual and collective, are wholly appropriate and necessary: this follows from the diabolical nature of the structure. The demonstrations and agitation of the peace movement are not merely in order: they are essential ingredients of the attempt to become human in a nuclearized world. But they do not extricate a single person from the spider's web. We cannot escape from the sin of the world, the original sin, by any kind of conscientious refusal to take part. Nuclear deterrence, a sin of the world, is part of us. It is the unacceptable face of our own security. To look upon it is to understand the violence, cruelty and illegality which shore up our comforts, our 'peace', our 'rule of law'. This is why the only way to change the nuclear deterrence world is from within, by belonging to it, because there is no other world to belong to. Nobody is in a position of superiority from which to condemn those who are most obviously part of that world – the military, the negotiators, the technologists. (Of course, disagreeing, confronting, putting forward alternatives are all part of working together.)

So much for the difficulties of A's position. But B's position is no better. There is no way of avoiding the paradox that any declared policy of nuclear deterrence, for whatever purpose it is adopted, involves the willingness to commit unspeakable crimes against God and man: and that even if limited nuclear war were possible, it is too dangerous for human beings to risk. To justify this willingness on 'the threat is not the use' lines involves an illicit use of moral argument:[4] while to do so on consequentialist lines, however 'principled', involves other equally intractable contradictions. Avoiding the difficulty by claiming that by itself the very possession, without the willingness to use, deters (so that you can have deterrence without a declared policy for use at all) does not describe the situation that has actually to be faced, nor is there any likelihood of its becoming so.[5] Yet, self-contradictory or no, position B is probably accepted by the majority of thinking people, because they can see no alternative. It expresses the 'realism' of *l'homme moyen sensuel*: making yourself unthreatenable by evil means seems to be better than being unjustly dominated by foreigners. That, or something like it, is where most people are, and it has to be where change starts from.

—— III ——

None of this helps, however, to show what a strategy for making the transition would look like. Can we say, even in outline, anything about this? Well, we can begin by noting that one of the most obvious features of major technical advances tends to be that they look like reversions. The formal elements fail to match up with the material possibilities. The first iron bridge was put together with carpenter's gadgets: wedges, dovetails, dowels. In the same sort of sense, when nuclear deterrence was invented, it was supposed that it had to work as if it were a piece of old-fashioned military machinery. The concepts it used were essentially mechanical: the 'ladder' of escalation, the 'trip wire' of battlefield weapons, the 'umbrella' of the ICBMs. (Even 'Star Wars' is only a Heath Robinson contraption, albeit the bits of string have turned into lasers, the pulleys and levers into computers and pop-up weapons of stupefying complexity.) In the old days of the US nuclear monopoly, the mechanical concept was, I suppose, quite appropriate, since the point of the nuclear machines was that they were designed to be used. It was expected that they had to 'work' in the same sort of sense that guns or aeroplanes had to work. But once rough parity between the superpowers was achieved, and mutually assured destruction ('based on balance') became the governing doctrine, a quite different conception took over. Now the machines were designed never to have to 'work': they were thought of as essentially separate from the ordinary business of operational defence, and their 'working' took on a quite new significance, at a different level from that of ordinary weaponry. So their meaning became radically ambiguous: they were machines designed simultaneously to be used and never to be used. Both meanings were equally necessary. Thus the concept of defence by mutual deterrence became inherently paradoxical. It still is.

Although the nuclear weapons in modern deterrence theory are thought of as existing at a different level of meaning from the weapons which exist to be used for actual defence, they cast their shadow over the whole field of defence thinking. They exist at a different level of meaning, but this meaning infects the ordinary meaning of defence itself. Defence cannot be the same kind of enterprise as it was before nuclear weapons and it cannot ignore their existence. How then are we to describe this relation between the different levels of meaning, when we bear in mind the drastic breach that has been created between one category of weapons which exist to be used in military operations, and a quite different set of weapons which exist, not only to be *not* used in military operations, but also to inhibit to some degree all military operations whatever? Can there be a coherent relationship between the commonsense of defence and the paradox of deterrence? Or are these simply incompatible conceptions which cannot add up to a coherent scheme?

Logically I think the answer to this question has to be, Yes: we *are* at present caught in a logically incoherent system of thought about defence. But history does not bother too much with logical contradictions. It is littered with them. And sometimes history solves them in its own inimitable way: namely by moving on to something else. Perhaps a parallel (which is more than a parallel) may be helpful here to illustrate what I mean. I take it from the stories (which are also histories) of war in our own Western culture. To begin near the beginning: in the *Iliad* there are two distinct but interacting levels of conflict: I mean the actions of the men and the actions of the gods. These are distinct levels of *meaning* in the first place. For example, a victory by one side against the other in a battle *means* that Zeus has decided that the scale of 'justice' shall fall downwards on the side of the vanquished. Conversely, an adverse decision by Zeus *means* that one side or another in battle is already doomed. A battle which seems undecided often signifies conflict among the gods. A verdict by the gods is what a battle outcome signifies: but what the gods decide also determines what will happen. (There is this double meaning in the very word 'means', of course.) There is thus a reciprocal relation of meaning between the two levels of conflict: an action at either level signifies some equivalent event at the other. But there is also a reciprocal *causal* connection between the two levels. What the gods decide determines what will happen to the men: but what the men do, for example by going through the right observances, can equally determine how the gods decide. For example, in Book 12 of the *Iliad* we are told that the reason why the wall built by the Achaeans to protect their ships only lasted a few years was that they failed to make the ritual offerings to the gods. But conversely the reason why the wall collapsed was that Apollo and Poseidon had decided on its demolition by turning against it all the waters of the rivers that run down from Ida.

These reciprocal relations, which are simultaneously relations of meaning and relations of causality, together constitute *belief* in the gods. The complete scheme adds up to a coherent system only because of these belief-relations. But these relations are only embodied in a genuine belief system in those epic poems called 'primary' epics: poems, that is, which belonged more or less anonymously and wholly to the community in which they were preserved and transmitted from generation to generation. With the arrival on the scene of the 'secondary' epic, that is a poem more or less consciously contrived to *imitate* the heroic world, for a society which, having become detached from it, was looking for some means of glorifying itself by creating an artificial attachment to a mythic past, the belief-system begins to decay. One can, I think, see the beginnings of this process in the *Aeneid*. When the very notion of the heroic poem itself is put in doubt by contact with the new belief structure of the Enlightenment, authentic belief in two equal levels of conflict becomes almost impossible. *Paradise Lost* is the critical case here.

In his classic treatment of seventeenth-century poetry, Basil Willey showed that the reason for Milton's choice of a Biblical theme for his epic (instead of the Arthurian subject with which he had once toyed) was that for Milton and his contemporaries fact and fiction had begun falling apart. But the Bible was still different. 'All proper contact with biblical material (constituted) in quite a special sense contact with Truth.'[6] Puritans, scientists, Platonists had together contrived to rob all other source-material of its claim to the 'true', but Milton could still expect his readers, as himself, to regard any poem based on a Biblical topic to be founded on the truth about their own past. Now this material seemed to suggest a 'two-level' conception of conflict: parallel to the struggle between human beings and the 'serpent' of sin, there was an upper-level conflict between the angels. As long as this two-tiered concept could be plausibly believed in, as in *Paradise Lost*, the two levels of action, human and divine, could still add up to a more or less coherent scheme, with a system of reciprocal belief-relations comparable to those of the primary epic.

Nevertheless a price had to be paid for preserving this coherence in a time when conditions were becoming increasingly hostile to it. Milton was able to create a coherent system of belief-relations to connect his two levels of action in the poem only because he 'lived in a moral rather than a physical world' and more or less consciously excluded from his view those scientific and allegorizing developments all around him which were undermining the general belief in the literal truth of the Bible itself. According to Willey, Milton's solution was characteristic: 'The biblical events, if allegorical at all, were the deliberate allegories of God himself: and when God allegorises he does not merely write or inspire parables, He also *causes to happen the events which can be allegorically interpreted*'.[7]

This is the awkward compromise which saves Milton's poem from disbelief in the reciprocal relations of both meaning and causality – except of course, that in the Christian epic the causality is only one way. God can determine what happens on the human level, but men cannot (as in Homer) determine what will happen on the divine level. This erosion of reciprocal causality is the beginning of a new way of understanding the whole 'machinery' of heroic conflict.

I use the word 'machinery' advisedly here, for with its introduction (by Dryden) into the discussion of heroic story-telling, a new twist in the history begins. The use of the word 'machines' to refer to the divine level of conflict in heroic stories originates, as the *Oxford English Dictionary* indicates, from the use of stage machinery in the late seventeenth-century theatre. The *deus ex machina* regularly descends from the skies to sort out the conflicts of men. He does so from a contraption of ropes and pulleys. This inevitably encourages us to regard the god himself as simply a piece of machinery. So it is with Dryden's treatment of Milton's epic vision.

> His subject is not that of an Heroic Poem, properly so called. His design is the losing of our happiness; his event is not prosperous, like that of all other epic works; his heavenly machines are many, and his human persons are but two.[8]

The 'heavenly machines', for Dryden, are of course the angels and archangels, who together correspond to the pagan deities of Homer and Virgil. The upper level of action in the heroic poem has been reduced to that of 'machinery', essentially detached from the lower world, which is now the human world on its own ground alone. From Dryden onwards, the gods of heroic poetry become no more than the outward visible signs of what is going on below. They are not felt as real causes of events in the human world, but (except in a fanciful sense) only as 'decoration'. It is no surprise to find Alexander Pope, early in the following century, writing a very serious – I mean *morally* serious – poem (designed for purposes of serious conflict-resolution) and finding it perfectly possible to do this at first without the introduction of any 'heavenly machinery' at all. Only later did he find it useful to introduce 'machines' into the poem (*The Rape of the Lock*): I mean the sylphs. But these 'machines' are essentially redundant to the real action: they merely decorate it, and shed a certain glow upon it. Nobody believes seriously that they have any power to influence it. Their presence merely makes

> every trivial incident in his poem 'appear of the utmost importance'. The sylphs are mirrors to his scene. By them the central action is reflected and multiplied a hundredfold, gaining in subtlety and mystery as well as in ironical importance.[9]

It is not surprising to find that when he is writing philosophy, as distinct from telling a heroic story, Pope finds it possible to dispense altogether with any heavenly 'machinery', or apparatus of 'mythology' to explain how things are with the human condition: The *Essay On Man* contains no 'machines' – for, once the divine world has been reduced to 'machinery', it soon becomes redundant altogether. We are not surprised to find, at the next twist of the historical/literary spiral, the poet has to face the world unaided, on his own:

> The new poet must therefore either make poetry out of the direct dealings of his mind and heart with the visible universe, or he must fabricate a genuine new mythology of his own. . . . Keats and Shelley often follow the second of these methods; Wordsworth typically follows the first.[10]

—— IV ——

In the ancient world, and indeed in the mediaeval world too, war was not a secular business but a sacred one: the participation of the gods or of God was an intrinsic part of the action. War existed on two levels at once: the human and divine. Actions at one level became statements at the other level: that is, signs giving meaning to the actions themselves. What functioned as a sign at one level became an action at the other. Today, too, war exists as a phenomenon on *two levels at once*: the 'conventional' and the 'nuclear'. The relation between these levels is the modern equivalent of the interaction between the men and the gods. For the effect of nuclear weapons is to introduce a kind of omnipotence into our world. Nuclear weapons are 'absolute': they are the thunderbolts of Zeus. Their use decides what happens, there is no gainsaying them. To justify their use men have to claim to have superhuman powers of foreknowledge of consequences and supernatural exemption from the rules of human morality. Nuclear weapons make us gods.

In the early days of nuclear weapons, their 'absolute' character was not fully appreciated. They were regarded as TNT writ large. They were usable, as blockbuster bombs were usable: and it was presumed that they were controllable too, at least to some degree. Provided one took the necessary routine precautions, there was no reason why they should not fit into the ordinary armoury of a nation. There was a reasonable comparison between (say) Hiroshima and Dresden in terms of destruction, and also of control. As long as men made the necessary obeisance to the new weapon, the weapon could be relied on, from its technological Olympus, to do what was expected of it. It could be propitiated. But the development of the hydrogen bomb, the ballistic missile and all the rest of the apparatus of nuclear deterrence, on both sides, has made all that thinking obsolete. We are no longer in the position of being able to believe in the bomb in the old way: we have had to *allegorize* it, as Milton had to allegorize the archangels. Our present problem is exactly parallel to his, caught between believing in the bomb as an effective weapon, like Zeus's thunderbolt or God's decree, and seeing it as just a piece of the 'machinery' of our human story, which enormously enlarges the meaning of what we do but is unable to intervene in our ordinary actions. Just as Milton was caught between the old belief system and the new, only able to believe fully in the old system because he managed to insulate himself from the full effects of what was going on around him, and could 'allegorize' these elements in the old system which he could not literally believe in, so we too are caught between two worlds. Nuclear deterrence is a paradox because it entails, at one and the same time, believing in the usability, as a weapon in the old sense, of the nuclear device, *and* recognizing that only by 'allegorizing' it can we expect to survive intact into the new world which we are entering.

The 'allegorizing' of nuclear weapons is manifested in various ways. The most obvious is the *unreality* of nuclear discourse: its remoteness from the flesh and blood of human action. It exists in an elegant, sanitized world set apart. In an important sense, nobody believes in the nuclear myths, or scenarios, as literal truths. They are unimaginable. Just as Milton found God unimaginable, and could not make Him convincing even to himself, so we cannot make nuclear war convincing to ourselves, except as an intellectual abstraction. Yet with another part of our mind, we know it may happen: the myth may be literally true after all. We may 'cause to happen the events which can be allegorically interpreted'. Yet there is a positive side to this allegorizing of nuclear deterrence: it represents a refusal of the mind to believe, to go in for the propitiatory offerings that would be needed to take it literally. Here is a progressive side to our 'enlightenment': we can see a future possibility of being free from the bondage to the old god, the old concept of a weapon. The next stage we need to reach in order to get to a world without nuclear weapons, is one in which nuclear weapons become simply the 'machinery' of conflict – merely enlarging its meaning by acting as 'mirrors to the scene through which the central action is reflected and multiplied a hundredfold' – but only *because* they do not actually take part in it, or even have the power to do so. If we can get to that stage (the equivalent of Pope's position), perhaps eventually we can arrive at the next stage further on: in which we can look at our world as it is without the need of any nuclear 'mythology' at all (Wordsworth's stage).

––– V –––

Meanwhile however we have to consider the process of transition. While it is unrealistic to envisage a permanent future with nuclear weapons, it is equally unrealistic to imagine one without just defence. Without defences human societies cease to exist. The business of defending a particular group is not an inhuman or subhuman activity, although it is certainly a concession to 'sin'. A just defence makes for friendship, in this less-than-fully-human world. It is not provocative: it does not invite attack, or threaten the innocent, or prepare for retaliation, let alone pre-emptive strikes. A genuinely defensive defence stems from a kind of virtue, for only when we are secure from unjust attack can we begin to build justice and peace. So part of the transition to a post-nuclear world has to be the development of really defensive defence. It is one argument of this paper that modern technology, vigorously and humanely pursued, can help a society to acquire an effective and just defence. The problem, however, is the transition, and especially the moral question of how to relate nuclear to conventional weapons during that process.

The message that nuclear weapons convey is that the nation which possesses them is unthreatenable. A nuclear power is one which is making this claim both for the present and the foreseeable future. But the trouble is that the intentions involved in making this claim seem inescapably to include a willingness to commit mass murder, if need be, in pursuit of it. Any system which incorporates nuclear weapons seems to be caught in this paradox: in order to succeed in the wholly desirable objective of deterring nuclear war and reducing its likelihood, a nation has to be willing to commit acts of criminality that beggar the imagination.

Much ink has been spilled in trying to resolve this paradox. I have analysed some of these attempts elsewhere. However, two recent books have raised points which are worth discussing in more detail here, since they make certain points which may take us in the right direction. These are David Fisher's *Morality and the Bomb* and Anthony Kenny's *The Logic of Deterrence*.[11]

Both authors ask themselves the question: What exactly is it that deters? In the past, various answers have been given to this question. Thus, in the early 1950s, the answer would have been: a massive American monopoly of nuclear weaponry. Later the mutual threat of unacceptable damage through second-strike capability provided an obvious reply. Today, however, the answers are less obvious. Second-strike capabilities are put in doubt, both by new offensive and by defensive technologies: that is, by the capacity of one side or the other either to prevent the second strike from reaching the target (e.g. by anti-ballistic missile defences) or by preventing it from ever being launched (e.g. by super-accurate counterforce weapons available for a first strike). A combination of these two developments constitutes the 'first strike drift' which is widely perceived as a danger at the present time. In such a situation the question arises: What is it (if anything) that deters?

One answer commonly given at present is: *uncertainty*. Instead of being deterred by the certainty of unacceptable destruction, as in 'old-style' nuclear deterrence, the nuclear powers are now deterred, we are told, precisely by not being able to tell what would happen if a nuclear war began. Not only are they unsure about the *consequences* of such a war: i.e. could it remain limited? is controlled nuclear war feasible? would it lead to the nuclear winter? They are also unsure about the intentions of their enemies. When, where, how would the threshold to nuclear war be crossed? What exactly is the strategic calculation on which the other side is working? How far can either side rely on the declared intentions of the other to go, if necessary, the whole way from an initial step across a frontier to a major strategic exchange? Would one side 'back off' before it was too late? If it is the uncertainty which deters, the argument presumably runs, the more uncertainty the better. Hence the case for a British 'independent' deterrent involving as it does the extra uncertainties associated with a 'third centre of decision' in a crisis.

This is the tenor of David Fisher's argument (chapter 6) that for effective deterrence we do not need to harbour a conditional intention to use the weapons. We simply need to have not publicly ruled out their use. It is then for the other side to make up its mind about what 'we' really intend to do. Indeed, it may be theoretically possible for the heads of Government and the military to have secretly ruled out *any* possible use, and still have effective deterrence because the other side does not know this. The argument is not quite as cynical as it sounds. It does not necessarily involve intending to avoid doing X while intending the other side to think the reverse. The point is that our 'primary' intention is to *dissuade* the other side from attacking. But for this intention to be effective, a secondary intention (dependent on the first) has also to be operative, namely to encourage the other side to think that the nuclear option *might*, in certain circumstances, be used.

To his credit, Fisher admits that this argument only works as long as there is some possibility of a legitimate *use* of nuclear weapons. This is the only honest basis for what is, in effect, a purely 'political' refusal to rule out the option of use. For if there can be no legitimate use, then the refusal to rule out that option is either fundamentally dishonest or the deterrence amounts to no more than bluff. It follows from this that there has to be *some* conceivable situation in which we might use the weapon. And since Fisher, again to his credit, openly admits that this cannot avoid some direct killing of innocent non-combatants, it follows that a certain amount of limited direct killing of the innocent must be licit. Hence the argument ends with something called 'principled consequentialism'. The point of this is that a *little* direct killing of the innocent is all right, provided it does not necessarily lead to the wholesale genocide that many opponents of deterrence envisage, once this particular dam is breached. Limited threats short of genocide may be enough to deter, especially if they are 'countercombatant' only. Fisher goes on to argue that it is conceivable we might be able, on this basis, to devise a targeting policy which respected the just war criteria of proportionality and discrimination sufficiently to be morally tolerable.

Two points stand out from my summary of a complex piece of argument. One is that the whole thesis is based on the idea that deterrence is a form of 'dissuasion'. That is to say, it is not primarily a policy of deterrence by the threat of war-fighting: it is a policy designed to *say* something, namely that 'we' are not threatenable. In other words, it marks a move towards turning nuclear weapons into high-level symbolic weapons, rather than low-level real ones. It makes them part of a new international language for the nuclear age, designed to communicate a message, not to destroy anybody. To this extent, the argument constitutes a certain 'humanization' of a sub-human (i.e. sublinguistic) world of 'brute force'. But at the same time, the weapons themselves are still much more than mere 'signs' within a language. They are not yet mere 'machines' in a mock-heroic story. They are still weapons of 'brute force' and this brutishness is still a necessary part of their meaning. This is why a little dose of murder is still, at the back of it all, a vital ingredient of the argument. Fisher has not disposed of this problem by his adoption of 'principled consequentialism'. The question is whether a little bit of direct killing of the innocent, committed for the sake of hugely beneficial consequences, is ever permissible? If so, then refusing to rule out the option simply as a means of keeping the other side guessing and hence deterred, will be justified. If not, then Fisher's argument fails to do what it is designed to do.

At this point, Anthony Kenny's argument may take us one step further. He fastens on the fact that, even if the *government* may have secretly abjured any intention of ever using the nuclear weapon, this does not apply to those in the military who have to be willing to carry out the still-not-ruled-out option embodied in the declaratory policy. True, such willingness may not amount to a conditional *intention* to commit mass-murder: but even so, it is still morally illegitimate, for it is not permissible to be willing to do something which it could never be permissible to carry out. Such willingness is undoubtedly required of e.g. the submarine commander. He must be prepared to obey the order to put into effect the option which has not yet (to his knowledge) been ruled out. Is not such readiness to obey immoral orders essential to deterrence? Well, Kenny thinks not. All that is needed for deterrence is the *power* to inflict unacceptable damage. This by itself is enough to instil the necessary fear. And simply having a power in itself cannot be illicit. It is the willingness to use the power for illicit – albeit 'beneficial' – ends that is the unacceptable thing about deterrence policy at present. So deterrence might be licit after all if it were publicly made quite clear in advance, that no orders of a murderous nature were to be obeyed by anyone who might be in a position to carry them out. 'Suppose that the Western Powers announced a decision of policy that nuclear weapons were never to be used on cities or military targets near centres of population.

Suppose that this decision was a serious, carefully thought out one, prepared for and announced in such a way as to be credible. Suppose that all who were trained in the operation of nuclear weapons systems were given standard orders never to accept commands from anyone to employ them on unacceptable or unknown targets. Might it not then be possible, without incurring the guilt of our present unacceptable policies, to retain sufficient nuclear hardware to enforce the best disarmament bargain we can with the Warsaw pact powers?'[12]

This suggestion of Kenny's takes Fisher's argument one step further, by attempting to combine the argument for deterrence by 'uncertainty' with an explicit and sincere rejection of even a little murderousness. The difficulty is whether or not the proposed standing orders remove just that element of uncertainty from the deterrence equation which is needed. The more credible the renunciation of murderous use (a renunciation which, Kenny holds, is necessary not only for moral purposes but also in order to begin the winding-down of the arms race spiral) the less uncertain the other side is going to be about our likely behaviour in a crisis.

Clearly there are very serious difficulties with each of the arguments which I have just summarized. Fisher, for all his moral rigour, leans in the end towards permitting the impermissible in order to ensure that the deterrent effect of uncertainty works; while Kenny tends to repudiate the morally impermissible to a point where the deterrent effect of uncertainty is seriously jeopardized. What is significant about the debate between them, however, is the degree to which both have passed beyond the old-style confrontations of war-fighting threats and brute force to a new concept, which is better described (in the French jargon) as 'dissuasion', not deterrence. In both arguments the destructive potential of the weapons themselves seems to fall into relative insignificance: their *meaning* in a system of international signals begins to take the prominent role. Yet both are still caught in the apparently insoluble paradox of deterrence itself. Is there any way out? Well, perhaps we should look once again at the literary analogy. As long as there was genuine belief in the interaction between two worlds (human and divine) the war epic could be seen as a coherent and relevant form of story-telling. But from Milton onwards, the collapse of that belief led to the progressive decline of the heroic epic itself. Yet, long after the heroic poet had lost all his credibility, critics and scholars were still hankering after his ideal. For example Dryden, who had understood how the angels and other supernatural beings of *Paradise Lost* had become 'machines' (despite all of Milton's poetic power), still claimed as late as 1697 that the heroic poem was 'undoubtedly the greatest work which the soul of man is capable to perform'. Pope's devotion to the cause was evident, not only through the sincere flattery of the War Poet implicit in *The Rape of the Lock*, but also in his translations of Homer (which became best-sellers). Only with Wordsworth do we find, in England, a poet of sublime cast who was free from all propensity to attempt writing heroic poetry of war. (*Lyrical Ballads* is, among other things, almost the first collection of stories about anti-heroes.) Dryden's is here the pivotal case, as the *Discourse Concerning the Original and Progress of Satire* shows. Boileau had argued that a Christian heroic poem was hardly possible, since – given an omnipotent Creator – there could be no real conflict on the upper level of the poetic story (that of the supernatural 'machines'). There could therefore be no true parallel between the human and the superhuman actions. Dryden answers him by suggesting that stories from the Old Testament, using for example the angelology of apocalyptic books such as Daniel, could still fill the bill. The interesting thing in this debate is the evident need to find, perhaps even invent, a 'machinery' to fill an otherwise unfillable gap. The absence of any *real* belief in the role of the 'machines' in human conflict is plain enough. What is being sought is a purely *literary* device: and the resulting literary work itself would exist, if it could be written at all, primarily for *moral* purposes: for neo-classical purposes of 'instruction and delight'. Dryden's problem is that he genuinely values the heroic poetry of the past for what it tells us about human nature (he realizes that narrative has cognitive, not only a moral power). But at the same time he is convinced that the 'machinery' on which it rests is false, and indeed absurd; 'grounded as it was on ridiculous fables'.

In terms of the modern problem, we too are in the position of Dryden: we know our nuclear scenarios are myths and allegories 'grounded on ridiculous fables', but at the same time we cannot see our way out of the maze. So we misinterpret the problem in *moral* terms only, as if it were simply a difficulty in moral philosophy. We fail to see the historical significance of where we are: that nuclear weapons have an obsolete meaning – geared to the old system of beliefs about the winnability of war – but also an emergent meaning, which is sacramental rather than moral: they 'show up our world for what it really is' – a world 'structured by violence and fear' in such a way that it is *radically* unstable, because it is founded on a self-contradiction.

So first, we have to get ourselves into something like the state of mind of a writer of *mock-heroic*, who completely controls but in no sense feels himself controlled by his superhuman 'machines'. (A comprehensive test ban treaty would, I suppose, signal just such a move: it would be an act of conscious *disbelief* in the power of the 'god' of the nuclear weapon; an acknowledgement that nuclear weapons are obsolete, like Dryden's 'ridiculous fables' of the ancient Greeks.) Of course for a time there would still be talk of the old gods, and a certain hankering after their myths: but once a fundamental belief has gone, it cannot be put back into place. The fact that people still had the power to make nuclear weapons would be as irrelevant as the fact that, even now, we have the power to write heroic poetry. Nobody dreams of trying to do it, there is no point any more. We would eventually have to face the world without our absolute weapons, just as we have had to do without Zeus's thunderbolts.

—— VI ——

It is worth noting finally that the age of Wordsworth was also the age of Von Clausewitz. 'Nature' without the gods is not only the Lake District or the Alps: it is also Waterloo and Austerlitz. The problem of war, and defence – at this, secular, level – really *is* a moral problem (the just war problem). Clausewitz's study showed what happens when the moral problem of war is shelved: total war is the contrary of morality. So we cannot cope properly with real problems of justice in war, or defence, until the nuclear weapon, the absolute weapon, has been removed from the scene: for it has led to an insoluble set of contradictions – and from these, of course, as every logician knows, anything whatever can be deduced. There can be no rationality in defence so long as this obsolete 'god' stands in the way. Only when nuclear weapons are seen, on all sides, to be on the way out, becoming merely the decorative machinery of mock-heroic strategies, will we be able to think straight about the real problems of how to defend ourselves intelligently.

NOTES

1 Address in Vienna, 6 March 1986. A recent statement signed by five French bishops is relevant here: 'A nation does not have the right to threaten to do something which it never has the right to do': *La Paix Autrement*, report in *The Tablet* (15 March 1986), p. 295.
2 See especially Herbert McCabe, *Law, Love and Language* (Sheed and

Brian Wicker

Ward, London 1968); Stan Windass, *Avoiding Nuclear War* (Brassey's, London, 1985).

3 McCabe, 'A Long Sermon for Holy Week', *New Blackfriars* vol. 69, no. 789 (March 1986), pp. 111, 107; repr. in *God Matters* (Geoffrey Chapman, London, 1987), chapter 8, pp. 97, 93.

4 See my *Nuclear Deterrence: What Does the Church Teach?* (CTS, London, 1985), pp. 19ff.

5 On the last two points, see Part V of the present article.

6 Basil Willey, *The Seventeenth Century Background* (Chatto & Windus, London, 1946), p. 228.

7 *Ibid.*, p. 239 (the author's own italics).

8 Dryden, *Discourse Concerning the Original and Progress of Satire*: in *Essays of J. Dryden*, ed. W. P. Ker (1900), vol. ii, pp. 31ff.

9 Ian Jack, 'A Complex Mock Heroic' in *Augustan Satire: Intention and Idiom in English Poetry 1660–1750* (Oxford, 1952); repr. in *Twentieth-Century Interpretations of the Rape of the Lock*, ed. G. S. Rousseau (Prentice-Hall, Englewood Cliffs, NJ, 1969), p. 4.

10 Willey, *op. cit.*, p. 297.

11 David Fisher, *Morality and the Bomb* (Croom Helm, London, 1985); Anthony Kenny, *The Logic of Deterrence* (Firethorn Press, London, 1985).

12 Kenny, *op. cit.*, p. 79.

208

12

THE THEORY AND PRACTICE OF
AUTOBIOGRAPHY

J. M. Cameron

For more than a week my pen has lain untouched. I
have written nothing for seven whole days, not even a
letter. Except during one or two bouts of illness, such a
thing never happened in my life before. In my life; the
life, that is, which had to be supported by anxious toil;
the life which was not lived for living's sake, as all life
should be, but under the goad of fear. The earning of
money should be a means to an end; for more than
thirty years – I began to support myself at sixteen – I
had to regard it as the end itself.

I could imagine that my old penholder feels reproachfully towards me. Has it not served me well?
Why do I, in my happiness, let it lie there neglected,
gathering dust? The same penholder that has lain
against my forefinger day after day for – how many
years? Twenty, at least; I remember buying it at a shop
in Tottenham Court Road. By the same token I bought
that day a paper-weight, which cost me a whole shill-
ing – an extravagance which made me tremble. The
penholder shone with its new varnish, now it is plain
brown wood from end to end. On my forefinger it has
made a callosity.

Thus the opening paragraphs of Gissing's *The Private Papers of
Henry Ryecroft*.[1] I choose it as a starting-point as giving us a first
sharp taste of autobiographical writing as it has developed since
the great age of sensibility represented by such writers as Rousseau and Sterne. There is the note of self-pity, something the
writer sees no need to apologize for. His life has been that of an
anxious and fearful drudge. His pity is projected into his inanimate world. His penholder *feels reproachfully*. They have grown
old together – a frugal family indeed, the writer, his pen, and a

paper-weight, but they have a common history of anxious toil and the passage of time is marked by a physical decay, the wearing away of the original varnish, and the writer is physically marked by the common history: the callosity on his finger, as eloquent as the hands of the ploughman or the cobbler or the bandy legs of the jockey. This picking out of a concrete, particular characteristic belongs to an established literary technique. We remember Poll Sweedlepipe in *Martin Chuzzlewit* with his right hand cold and smelling of shaving-soap, another badge of another profession. It doesn't, again, surprise us that Gissing should go on, immediately after the passage quoted, to speak of 'the scent of the flowering earth . . . the green of hillside larches . . . the singing of the skylark above the downs'. For nature as mother, nurturer, source of moral wisdom, best anodyne for pain, is a part of the tradition out of which this piece of writing comes.

There has been much discussion of what modernity consists in, that is, what is the constellation of feelings and attitudes and ideas that marks off modern European culture from other cultures in the past or present; and much discussion of how this change came about. That such deep changes do occur in the history of culture seems evident. One example, a famous one, is that picked out by Auerbach in *Mimesis*,[2] the change wrought in the consciousness of classical culture by the reception of the Bible, and especially of the gospels, in the ancient world. He remarks how a literary convention, that of the separation of styles, is destroyed when the story of the Passion of Christ, as depicted in the gospels, grips the consciousness of many: 'it engenders a new elevated style, which does not scorn everyday life and which is ready to absorb the sensorily realistic, even the ugly, the undignified, the physically base' (Anchor ed., p. 63). This is a much bigger change than that marked by the rise of autobiography – indeed, *this* rise is only a moment perhaps in the big and not as yet ended change Auerbach is talking about. That one of the few instances of autobiography of the modern sort in the ancient world is Augustine's *Confessions* is of course a piece of evidence for Auerbach's thesis. At any rate, I propose to assume that the rise of autobiography and its peculiar consciousness is a principal sign of modernity, of that which marks out our culture from that of the Middle Ages. Behind Henry Ryecroft stand Rousseau and Sterne, and behind Rousseau and Sterne, Montaigne and Descartes. These are only luminous points in a movement of thought that is broader and deeper than just the thought of these individuals.

What in Descartes I have in mind is how, for example, in the *Meditations* and the *Discourse* he uses autobiography as a component of the philosophical approach he wants to commend. In the first Meditation he gives us the unforgettable picture – unforgettable because he is here inserting at the beginning of his philosophical epic a piece of humble domestic detail that would once have been thought irrelevant to lofty concerns: 'I am here, sitting by the fire, wearing a winter dressing-gown, holding this piece of paper in my hands'.[3] This detail, in all its humbleness, is a starting-point for his argument that it follows from his sometimes dreaming that there is no criterion for picking out dreaming from non-dreaming experience – not even the fact that 'I am here, sitting by the fire . . . et cetera', for I can dream this, and so far as the content of the experience is concerned there is no distinguishing the dream from waking life; not even coherence will do, for I may have very extravagant waking experiences and very well-ordered dreams. The humblest facts, attentively perused, will explode into philosophical paradox. For a fragment of autobiography in a straight sense, we have to go to the *Discourse on Method*. As a preparation for deploying the argument for the doubtability of everything we ordinarily take for granted, he tells us that he intends to show us 'what paths I have followed, and to represent my life in it as if in a picture'. He wants us to live again with him his own experience, in order that we may be converted to his new standpoint. He tells us how he was educated and how confused he was by everything but mathematics; and how poetry pleased him and how eloquence and the rules of rhetoric fascinated him. And then we are plunged into the actuality of the author's own time and space.

> At that time I was in Germany, where I had been called by the wars that are not yet ended there. While I was returning to the army from the coronation of the Emperor, the onset of winter detained me in quarters where, finding no conversation to divert me and fortunately having no cares or passions to trouble me, I stayed all day shut up alone in a stove-heated room, where I was completely free to converse with myself about my own thoughts.[4]

It is as though in the midst of a tranquil but solitary existence a moment of illumination is awaited. It does not really matter if 'all day shut up alone in a stove-heated room' is a literary device, or a conflation of several occasions. The point is that this kind of specification, this touch of actuality, is not simply to move or to amuse, but to bring out the philosophic task as the author sees it. That the season is winter, the war quiet, that the imperial throne has an occupant (in Chinese terms, the link between heaven and earth is re-established), the author untroubled by particular passions or anxieties, alone, *dans un poêle*, as the French text rather curiously has it – all these things are as it were novelistic devices to give the moment weight. Specifying the moment in this way makes us more likely to accept all that is to come – the suggestion that bodily existence may be an illusion, that the whole spectacle of human existence may be a delusory appearance arranged by a malicious demon. This rhetorical device, this use of the humdrum detail as a foil to the fantastic, is employed in the best science fiction, as in the early H. G. Wells. Here is the scene just before the arrival of the first Martians (in *The War of the Worlds*) who are to stalk the land bringing death, suffering and social chaos.

> It was a warm night. Coming home, a party of excursionists from Chertsey or Isleworth passed us singing and playing music. There were lights in the upper windows of the houses as the people went to bed. From the railway station in the distance came the sound of shunting trains, ringing and rumbling, softened almost into melody by the distance. My wife pointed out to me the brightness of the red, green and yellow signal lights, hanging in a framework against the sky.[5]

In the same way the hero of *The First Men in the Moon* on his way back from the moon, in the blackness of space, comes across a fragment torn from a London evening paper, and this reinforces and makes more acceptable the extravagance of the rest of the narrative.

If we compare this starting-point for philosophy, this placing of the personal life in all its concrete particularity as the beginning and foundation of the philosophical argument, with earlier models of philosophizing, the differences are very striking. In Plato, in Aristotle, in the medievals, we begin with a society and a culture and an intellectual history that are all of them the data for the active philosopher. In the first book of the *Metaphysics* we begin with man as an animal species, then we go on to experience – *human* experience, not *my* experience – and its relation to science and art; and then by way of a discussion about what men call wisdom we go on to a discussion of the Milesian philosophers, of the Pythagoreans, and of Aristotle's immediate predecessor, Plato. We are firmly set in the human world and an intellectual tradition. There is no suggestion that getting things right philosophically involves striving to become a naked individual who sets aside what has come to him through his particular historical existence, so that an absolutely fresh start can be made. Of course, this is not what Descartes in fact does; he carries with him, as all commentators since Gilson have shown, a vast amount of impedimenta from his philosophical predecessors; but it is what he affects to do: to begin with a *tabula rasa*. And he recognizes that in the field of morals – that is, in all that touches on questions of how to live in the world – it is necessary 'to obey the laws and customs of my country; faithfully keeping to the religion in which . . . I was brought up from childhood' and accepting as rules for the conduct of life those opinions 'accepted in practice by the most judicious men'. It is as though he wants to argue that his revolutionary epistemology does not threaten the social order. We know that he was well aware of the fate of Galileo and was anxious to avoid it. But there is more to his anxiety than that. We may suppose that he is aware that there is in Europe a profound change in the way in which the individual is looked upon; that man is beginning to be seen as having an existence that is not constituted by his social role but by his original existence apart from and independent of all social relations.

In this period the idea of the uniqueness of the self, the 'I', is intellectually and morally troublesome. Montaigne, a mirror and maker of the new consciousness, wrote (*Les Essais*, I, xxvii): 'Si on me presse de dire pourquoy je l'aymois, je sens que cela ne se peut exprimer, qu'en respondant: Parce que c'estoit luy; parce que c'estoit moy'. This comes close to 'Richard loves Richard, that is, I am I' (*Richard III*, V, iii, 183), and this was preceded by, in *Henry VI Part 3*, V, vi, 80–83:

> I have no brother, I am like no brother;
> And this word 'love', which greybeards call divine,
> Be resident in men like one another,
> And not in me: I am myself alone.

What is here seen as a falling away from humanity is elsewhere thought to be a common aspiration, as it were, a mood of the age, a universal malady. In the *First Anniversary* Donne associates it with changes in natural science and especially changes in astronomy; but he also stresses its social revolutionary significance.

> Prince, Subject, Father, Sonne, are things forgot,
> For every man alone thinkes he hath got
> To be a Phoenix, and that then can bee
> None of that kinde, of which he is, but hee.[6]

The subversion of the prince–subject and father–son relation is not peculiar to Donne. We find it in the famous speech about 'degree' – the principle of hierarchy – in *Troilus and Cressida*, I, iii:

> How could communities,
> Degrees in schools, and brotherhoods in cities,
> Peaceful commerce from dividable shores,
> The primogenity and due of birth,
> Prerogative of age, crowns, sceptres, laurels,
> But by degree stand in authentic place?
> Take but degree away, untune that string
> And mark what discord follows . . .
> ....
> Strength should be lord of imbecility
> And the rude son should strike his father dead. . . .

And the speech continues to prophesy universal chaos under the striking image of self-cannibalism:

> And appetite, an universal wolf
> ....
> Must make perforce an universal prey,
> And last eat up himself.

The new man, who stands outside the social hierarchies and the constraints of the family, is Edmund, the Bastard, in *Lear*. He asserts a direct relation to 'Nature' and on that ground repudiates the claims of custom, attacks the notion of legitimacy, and characteristically attacks astrology, that contemporary representation of earthly order in the heavens, and the assertion of the intertwining of human fates with the order of the Cosmos.

> My father compounded with my mother under the Dragon's tail, and my nativity was under Ursa Major, so that it follows, I am rough and lecherous. Fut, I should have been that I am, had the maidenliest star twinkled on my bastardizing.

What is it, though, to be a phoenix, one who in his uniqueness, his illimitable individuality, is uncopiable, so that there can be 'None of that kinde, of which he is, but hee'?

214

What it is to be a phoenix is in fact a compressing of different questions. The principal meaning in the passages we have been looking at is that of one whose role is not defined by his place in a hierarchical society – prince, knight, cleric, merchant, peasant, et cetera – but one who may choose what he is to be and establish himself by calling upon his own inner resources, his intelligence and his psychic energies. In a society in which the cake of custom is being broken, in which traditional groupings are changing their character, in which received patterns of behaviour are challenged, there is a general anxiety. And the one who provokes it – e.g. Edmund – also shares it; for the world no longer sustains him; he must sustain himself. And to declare that one stands outside the hierarchies is just that, a declaration, and no more than that. Edmund does not abolish his bastardy by claiming that it does not matter or is even a piece of good fortune, as enduing him with more powerful energies than those possessed by the offspring of the conventional marriage bed – he is, so to speak, a child of nature and not of convention. The general anxiety provoked by the phoenix, the individual upstart man, is then a phenomenon of transition from, as Sir Henry Maine put it, status to contract, from a society ordered by inheritance – at its most extreme it would be a caste society – to a society ordered by the much weaker instrument of voluntary agreement between individuals. (I am speaking all the time about how society is conceived, not about how in fact it is.) But the phoenix idea is not simply an idea, delusory and dangerous in the eyes of those who would defend traditional society, liberating and healing in the eyes of those each one of whom deems himself to be a phoenix. It demands analysis and justification; it directs attention to phenomena that have not been fully adverted to, or have not been thought dignified enough to be talked about except in low comedy. (This is why Montaigne is so important a figure in this transition. There is a straightforward link between Montaigne on bodily functions and the reflections of Leopold Bloom at stool in the early pages of *Ulysses*.) The phoenix theme finally issues in the claim made by Rousseau at the beginning of the *Confessions*.

> I have resolved on an enterprise which has no precedent, and which, once complete, will have no imitator. My purpose is to display to my kind a portrait in every way true to nature, and the man I shall portray will be myself.
> Simply myself. I know my own heart and understand my fellow man. But I am made unlike anyone I

have ever met; I will even venture to say that I am like
no one in the whole world. I may be no better, but at
least I am different. . . .

Once men had read these words, each 'knew' he was unlike
every other. But if this is a common achievement, or state, then in
this respect each man is just like all the others. In all the combinations of factors, complex beyond tracing, that constitute a human
life in all its density, each man is unique, but rather in the way any
set of fingerprints is unique. I do not think this kind of uniqueness is adequate to the passion that throbs in Rousseau but it
would be one of the ways in which we might understand him.
Another sense, one Rousseau, as a former citizen of Geneva and
thus a child of Calvin, may have been sensitive to, is that of the
uniqueness of each man's calling, vocation. But neither of these
seems adequate to the text. The great revelation Rousseau com-
municates to us, his peculiar sexuality (his masochism, his relations with *Maman*), is by no means unique; still less are the
snobbery and paranoia he manifests.

For all the doubts we may have over Rousseau's claims – I mean
over the question whether they have sense or not – we cannot
doubt their monumental importance. They represent a point in
the development of the phoenix concept, a point at which this
kind of consciousness becomes general and even a source of
commonplaces among members of the educated middle class. It
seems in a vague way to operate in the popular psychology and
even the social policy of the 'western' societies. I do not think that
strictly it can entail anything, for it cannot be reduced to a coherent proposition that could serve as a premiss of any kind of
argument; but it seems nevertheless constitutive of thought and
sensibility. All the great received ideas about personal development, self-development, self-realization, making up one's own
values, finding out what is right (true) for *me*, no doubt have
many sources; but one certainly is the ontological megalomania
expressed by Rousseau. It is as though there is at the centre of the
individual's social role an unfractured, many-faceted crystal, unique in its configuration; and the great social task is to uncover this
innermost crystal, wipe it clean and then enjoy its splendour. If
we build into this picture the difficult notion that the 'I' is like 'no
one else in the whole world', it remains nevertheless true that it is
a condition of our talking about men, individually or in groups,
that we should have at our disposal a set of descriptions that are
applicable to the generality of men. No doubt we have to start
with one man who is this man and no other, and this man it is to

whom we ascribe predicates. But when we are in love we are in love as others are in love; our pangs of jealousy, our irascibility, our hilarity, are predicable of others; but because each of us is himself and not another we are strongly tempted to assert our uniqueness in Rousseau's terms. Of course, our being characterized by predicates drawn from the common stock leaves us with a sense of injustice. Even one's name is only a name in virtue of its being able to function indifferently as a marker for any man upon whom it may be conferred. Each man yearns for a logically proper name, but the yearning is senseless, for it belongs to the idea of a name that it can be conferred and thus cannot stand in a unique relation to what it names. What is perhaps unique is the act of speech that at one particular moment may pick out *this* man, as in 'Saul, Saul, why persecutest thou me?' Here again uniqueness belongs to the idea of vocation, of my being singled out for a task no one else can perform.

Once we are encouraged to turn within, to examine ourselves, to find answers to our most fundamental questions, we seem embarked upon a task that can only be done over a lifetime, for what I find within here and now, at any given moment, is – if I find anything at all – too slight to serve as a foundation for any kind of enterprise. It is only through recollection and conjecture, through my becoming my own historian, that what I am can be established. The question then arises as to what, out of an indefinite number of memories, perceptions, and what have you, out of an indefinite number of particulars, I am to pick out as constituting the skeleton and flesh of my account of myself. Much work in the autobiographical mode (and by the way I shall not distinguish here between fictional and non-fictional pieces of autobiography), begins with or inserts quite early apposite dates and surrounding persons and events to provide the beginning of the skeleton.

> I was born in the Year 1632, in the city of *York*, of a good Family, though not of that Country, my Father being a Foreigner of Bremen, who settled first at Hull. . . .

Sterne, in *Tristram Shandy*, both exemplifies and parodies the mode by beginning before the hero's conception:

> I wish either my father or my mother, or indeed both of them, as they were in duty both equally bound to it, had minded what they were about when they begot me. . . .

217

Sometimes the author begins with childhood, before he fills in – if he does – the framework of dates, parentage and so on. Newman begins the *Apologia* with:

> I was brought up from a child to take great delight in reading the Bible; but I had formed no religious convictions till I was fifteen. Of course I had a perfect knowledge of my catechism.

Dostoevsky's *Notes from Underground* begins:

> I am a sick man.... I am an angry man. I am an unattractive man. I think there is something wrong with my liver. But I don't understand the least thing about my illness, and I don't know for certain what part of me is affected.

Stendhal's *The Life of Henri Brulard* begins:

> I was standing this morning, 16 October 1832, by San Pietro in Montorio, on the Janiculum Hill in Rome, in magnificent sunshine. A few small white clouds, borne on a barely perceptible sirocco wind, were floating above Monte Albano, a delicious warmth filled the air and I was happy to be alive.

John Stuart Mill:

> It seems proper that I should prefix to the following biographical sketch some mention of the reasons which have made me think it desirable that I should leave behind me such a memorial of so uneventful a life as mine. . . . It has seemed to me that in an age of transition in opinions, there may be somewhat both of interest and of benefit in noting the successive phases of any mind which was always pressing forward, equally ready to learn and to unlearn either from its own thoughts or from those of others.

If we did not already know it, we should be pretty certain that the writer of this had spent a lot of his time drafting memoranda in a public office.

This is a random selection – perhaps there couldn't be a representative one. But certain things seem evident. Given it is incontestable that in one obvious sense the task of the autobiographer is that of the historian, differing from other historical tasks only in the fact that the author is his own subject, the impulse to write one's own history and the casting about for material are occasioned by different attitudes. Of the fragments I have just quoted that by Mill is the closest to ancient pre-Cartesian and pre-Romantic models. It reminds us of the resolution expressed at the beginning of Herbert of Cherbury's *Life* (by himself):

> ... as my age is now past threescore, it will be fit to recollect my former actions, and examine what I have done well or ill, to the intent I may both reform that which was amiss, and so make my peace with God, as also comfort myself in those things which, through God's great grace and favour, have been done according to the rules of conscience, virtue, and honour.

That is, the life being described is to be seen and judged by public criteria applicable to other men. This is not altogether true of Mill, for he inserts into his story accounts of his 'breakdown' and of his relations with Harriet Taylor; but these are not candid, or candid-seeming, accounts, but heavily censored by Mill, and especially by Harriet, who revised the manuscript with great care. It is a contribution to public discourse about human life in general, just as Plutarch's *Lives* is – or Morley's *Life of Gladstone*. Even such a life, one in which public categories predominate, will betray things that, we may suspect, the author does not intend to communicate. An obvious example in Mill is his failure to mention his mother, an eloquent 'silence' indeed. 'I was born in London, on the 20th of May 1806, and was the eldest son of James Mill, the author of *The History of British India*.' And in chapter two there is a sustained study of his father's character, in which it seems to be suggested that his chief fault was to have married early and improvidently and to have begotten many children. But what is novel in modern autobiography is that the materials and the intentions seem not to have, necessarily, a dignified character or to aim directly at edification. In short, a modern autobiography of the kind that interests us here is not so much autobiography as autopsychography, the story of the soul. Elements of autobiography may enter into the story – dates, places, parentage, and so on; but the staple will be that of which the author has, he supposes, privileged knowledge, inner events which may or may not be connected with actions that have effects in the public sphere.

Here again, I think the rationale of this practice is Cartesian, both as in Descartes and his followers and in the empiricists, especially Hume. Descartes is often taken to be almost excessively rationalist, the great patron of the virtue of *clarté*; but in fact the tendency of his philosophical strategy is away from the old notion of man as rational animal, with *its* tendency to emphasize ratiocination as the primary *human* activity, to the notion that *cogitationes*, *pensées*, are not merely thoughts of a mathematico-logical character but, equally, sensations of heat and cold, bitter-ness and sweetness, and, by an inevitable extension, harder to define feelings and moods. The inner life of the soul then is shot through with feeling and sensation, a rich phantasmagoria that seems almost to be a world existing alongside the physical and social worlds or, as with Hume, that of which the physical world is a hypothetical explanation. There occurs a strange inversion of the traditional account of things, which is also the account of Johnsonian commonsense: certainty attaches to the inner world; the 'outer' world is a matter of conjecture. The soul is better known to us than the body. About the contents of his soul each man is able to make incorrigible judgements, whereas judge-ments about the physical (or the historical) world are matters of probability. That I feel a short stabbing pain is a matter about which I cannot be mistaken; that this pain is causally related to a given state of my nervous system is a judgement that could be mistaken.

Now this whole thesis is commonly thought today to be a mess; and I think it is indeed a mess. But I do not propose to challenge it. All I am concerned to do is to point out its historical role as determining the transition to a kind of autobiographical writing that I have called autopsychography. We can easily fail to see, so much are we the children of the Cartesian and empiricist tradi-tions, how extraordinary much earlier periods would have found Ruskin's *Praeterita*, for example, his recollections of raisins and custard.[7]

> . . . I recollect my mother giving me three raisins, in the forenoon, out of the store cabinet; and I remember perfectly the first time I tasted custard, in our lodgings in Norfolk Street. . . . My father was dining in the front room, and did not finish his custard; and my mother brought me the bottom of it into the back room.

One assumes that men have always had such moments, bright in the having, irresistible in their charm when we look back. But the passionate noting of them comes from their being considered constituents of an inner psychic drama. It seems also to be con-nected with the decline in a sense of decorum which excluded what was thought to be too trivial, too humble, sometimes too physically repellent, from what is thought to be in principle a piece of edifying discourse. This sense of decorum was re-established by neo-classicism against all the great tendencies of the modern period; but the success was limited and temporary. The best illustration of what is at stake seem to me Johnson's discussion in an essay in *The Rambler* of a famous passage from *Macbeth*.

> Come, thick night!
> And pall thee in the dunnest smoke of hell,
> That my keen knife see not the wound it makes;
> Nor heav'n peep through the blanket of the dark,
> To cry, Hold, hold!

Johnson criticizes the passage on the ground that 'dun', 'knife', and 'peep through the blanket' are *low* expressions, that is, they are usages that belong to an undignified way of life, and a servile one, for they come from the kitchen, the bedroom, and the stable. Such scenes, such ways of life, such expressions are to be excluded from dignified discourse. This meant that Shakespeare was a great problem for neo-classicism, as indeed was everything comprised under the title of the 'Gothick'.

I propose to say that autobiography as autopsychography is a special kind of historical writing which differs from other kinds of historical writing in that the writer is or appears to be a privileged observer and also that the writer has a direct access to a world of thought and feeling that is his or her world, not the public world, but existing within the public world and connected with it in a myriad of ways – e.g. I dream about the public world, my feelings of guilt and shame commonly arise out of my actions in the public world and involve references to others. It is clear there is no merit in the claim that my recollection of a past event in which I was involved is more accurate than that of another, an observer, or an inquirer into records – this is plainly false. After all, if I remember my early summers as continuously fine and hot, I should be ill advised to assert this without consulting the meteorological records. But let us suppose that such criticism is often carping and assume that in the autobiographical mode things can be said that are true in the commonplace sense and that the accounts of those things which happened to, or were performed by, or were suffered by or were entertained by . . . the autobiographer have a claim to authenticity that the narratives of others cannot have. And let us add further that the recollections of feeling – perhaps above all in the Proustian sense – are the substance of a certain kind of autobiography and are wonderfully fascinating and a pleasure to read about and additions to knowledge about human nature.

What is peculiar to autobiography as autopsychography is that in this mode *everything* that can be done or suffered by individual human beings can be brought in, so that many things that in earlier periods have been ignored or relegated to the mode of low comedy are included: a taste in food or drink, particular occasions – especially first occasions – of sensory experience, the felt signs of age in the body, impulses of lust and fear, how the sunset moved on on a particular occasion, olfactory, tactual, and other sensations had on the occasion of a visit to a foreign country, moments of shame, the pangs of guilt, acts of meanness, the scent of the hawthorn, the smell of death – the catalogue need not be prolonged: such things are almost required by the mode.

What is strange is that in the midst of what it would not be extravagant to call an autopsychographical culture the rather strange question 'Who am I?' begins to be asked in a peculiarly agonized tone of voice. This is not the same question as 'What is man?' though the two questions must be connected. This is not like the question 'Who was the man in the Iron Mask?' This may be an historical mystery but it could in principle be cleared up. No doubt one can say: Only God knows who I am, but this is to say that the question is permanently baffling, or baffling under the conditions of human life. We are inclined to think that the question 'Who am I?' only has sense in the mouth of one who suffers from amnesia, for he does not remember his name, where he lives, if he has begotten any children, et cetera. Ordinarily, if we are asked who we are, we give our names, proffer our driving licences, and say where we live. Why should we begin to ask, not 'What am I?' as a member of the human race, but 'Who am I?' in cases in which we know our names and addresses? Why should talk about *identity* reverberate in the classroom and the cocktail-party at a time in which we seem to have a superabundance of information about ourselves and others?

A short way of dealing with the question about who I am would be to say that it is a confused form of a different question: *What* am I? I think this is very often what such writers as Erikson are talking about. But not entirely. It is not an accident that the Erikson style of question about identity should be raised by one who thought within the categories of psychoanalysis; for psychoanalysis, with Marxism, puts forward the idea that no 'straight' account of how it is with us as moral and social beings can be taken at its surface value; for it is written in a code that needs to be deciphered. 'Who am I?' is a desperate call for one to come to my aid, to decipher my story, to solve the riddles that refer to the crucial episodes of my life only obliquely, to tell me what lies behind the mask of appearance I customarily present to the world, *and* to myself. It is not that the task of autopsychography is to unmask or decipher. By no means. Autopsychography as discourse is itself the mask, the narrative in cipher, the riddle. Even if (I here take the Freudian position for granted) I were to engage in the fearful and scarcely possible labour of self-analysis, an account of my self-analysis would not be the story of my life, but the explanation of how and why my life was lived in just these ways, at least, in certain crucial episodes.

On this view, even the most strenuously thought-out story of my life, of my inner life as well as of those external happenings that could be known about by others, would be, by itself, a misleading story, lacking its proper interpretation, for the interpretation woven into the autobiography would itself be a part of the phenomena that constitute the task for the analyst. 'The division of the psychical into what is conscious and what is unconscious is the fundamental premiss of psycho-analysis.'[8] It is the dynamism of the unconscious, with its forces intensified by the repression by the super-ego, an act of repression which is itself unconscious, that lies behind all that activity of living which, prior to analysis, seems the substance of our lives. Our earliest life, our life as children, is of course enigmatic anyway, and is peculiarly resistant to autobiographical research. We have to be *taught* that our fully recollected adult life is enigmatic; but we *find* the life of our childhood enigmatic. It is the great merit of Freud – setting aside all questions about the scientific status of his theory – to have seen behind the tantrums of the nursery the terrible and august figures of Oedipus and Electra. If we understand *Othello* and *Lear*, *Macbeth* and *Antony and Cleopatra*, and are moved intensely by them in later life, it is through recognition, because we have already lived through the frenzies of jealousy, the desolation of betrayal, the torments of ambition, the pangs of despised love, in our earliest childhood. We forget how our lives as small children are ravaged by lust and rage; for we are powerfully impelled to trivialize what is frightening, even awe-inspiring, and this is simply self-protection. I do not want to tie all this too closely to the Freudian hypothesis. The weight, so to speak, of our lives as children is evident enough. For instance, the anxieties and terrors of childhood necessarily surpass those of adult life, for they seem to occur in the mode of infinity; they have no foreseen end. We are not then aware that the powers of nature and of adults are limited, that everything passes and comes to an end. Again, the pleasures of childhood, especially those of sensation, are intense, not dulled by habit and familiarity or by the ingestion of nicotine and alcohol and other drugs or by the distraction of worldly cares. We conjecture – this insight comes from Romanticism – that what sudden perception, sight, or scent that in middle or old age floods us with an inexplicable pleasure is linked with an earlier intense pleasure of our days as children. This gives Proust one of his central tasks as a novelist in the mode of autobiography.

Another major influence in our world questions the possibility of a true autobiography: I mean all the current thoughts that come from Marxian theory. The theory of ideology – and its derivative theory of 'false consciousness' – poses the following question. What are we to say about, for example, the truth of religious beliefs and the validity or legitimacy of moral beliefs? The Marxist theory in these matters was an immense break with the theory of the Enlightenment. Where the thinkers of the Enlightenment saw simply deception and error, the Marxists saw a false consciousness that sprang from factors beyond the control – and the knowledge – of the individual and the group. The old picture of the kings, nobles and priests cunningly deceiving the masses implied that they were not themselves deceived; this is why it could be said that all would be well when the last king had been strangled with the bowel of the last priest. This was never very plausible and perhaps could only captivate men who were historically very ignorant. How absurd it would be to maintain that, for example, totemism was a fudged-up theory imposed upon ignorant people by those who knew better! The ruling classes, then, are as much under the enchantment of the ideology they are said (obscurely) to impose in their own interests as are those whose *real* interests are betrayed by the ideology. Both are victims of false consciousness; *all* are unaware, except perhaps at certain climactic moments in human history, of the social forces that shape their conduct, their judgements, and their aspirations.

These two major influences, then, seem to suggest that it is virtually impossible for the individual person to give a correct, complete, soundly interpreted account of his or her own life. We are faced with the conclusion that, in that very period which has seen the rise of autobiography in the form of autopsychography, that has stressed the phoenix character of the individual – that is, the uniqueness and value of the individual – is also the period that seems to have established that we are necessarily strangers even to ourselves. It is the one who stands apart, the analyst, or the sociologist equipped with the hypotheses of historical materialism, who seems capable of telling the truth about this or that soul, though not of course about his own. Of course, if there is any truth in this it makes nonsense of much contemporary education and social policy, which seems to rest on the prejudices of the Enlightenment: in particular it is taken for granted – despite repeated disappointments – that description and rational argument, *direct* communication, is the right course to follow in the sexual education of children and adolescents.

I do not in fact believe that either the theory of psychoanalysis or the theory of Marxism has the logical status claimed by its proponents, but I think it is also true that they give the world a new look and that this new look really discloses puzzles, enigmas, mysteries, connexions between how men think and feel and what they do in that systematically patterned way we call the life of institutions. We really are strangers to ourselves and to each other. The act of telling our stories, both as public autobiography and as communication of the self to the self – autopsychography – is immensely difficult. For most of us the truth about ourselves, a deeper understanding of our experiences, comes from what at first does not look as though it is about ourselves at all: in poetry, in the drama, in the novel.

Men in all societies seem to have known, down to the nineteenth century, that if we wish to speak about morality, or about man's place in human society and history, or about man in the cosmos, the most effective means of communication is always indirect. It is the story, the parable, the anecdote, descriptions that are analogous and not direct, that really communicate truths. These truths are not in a form that can be explained in other and more direct terms. It is true, we can often give allegorical explanations, and these have their value; but after the explanation has been given we still return to the dark wood within which we find ourselves, as in Dante, or to the picture of the wounded man by the roadside, shunned by the respectable citizens and succoured by the raffish Samaritan (how close Schindler is to that figure!), or to the tower and the deep valley and the fair field full of folk that Langland presents to us at the beginning of *Piers the Plowman*; for the allegorical does not exhaust these figures; they retain that which is known to us in the sense that we are acquainted with it, but which surpasses us, for it contains the inexpressible.

If all this is anywhere near the truth, it seems to follow that the making of autobiography as autopsychography is, insofar as it *can* be, concerned with the truth about the individual human life, a critical as well as imaginative activity. The autopsychographical component in autobiography – all that goes beyond the bare external framework – uses in the telling literary structures that are enigmatic in the way in which all imaginative writing is enigmatic. If we ask a critical question about the treatment of event or character in autobiography, in general we handle the problem in just the way we should if we were appraising a novel. Does he get it right? Is it convincing? These are questions we raise about James in his autobiographical writings as in his novels.

We may even find ourselves wanting to say, against Rousseau, that the more penetrating the autobiography, the more it is about mankind in general. This is certainly true of Rousseau's *Confessions*, as it is of Augustine's; the ambiguity of sexual feeling as Rousseau depicts it enlightens us about ourselves, just as we may learn from Augustine as well as from Freud that each man is an abyss. The subjectivity of the autobiographer and the subjectivity of the reader are linked in what is like a teaching that leaves us more knowledgeable about ourselves. Here is the great triumph of indirect communication. The strength of autobiography is the strength of all imaginative writing. Autobiography is a formal mode, and it does not matter in its supreme instances whether or not the historical claim implicit in the mode is fictive or not. Newman even argued that the literatures of mankind, especially its myths and fictions, are as a whole and at what we should today call the level of 'deep grammar', in the autobiographical mode. 'Literature stands related to man as Science stands to Nature; it is his history.' And: 'Literature is to man in some sort what autobiography is to the individual; it is his Life and Remains.' If *this* is true, it is a powerful argument for the traditional curricula of liberal education in grammar schools and universities. For if the old culture which put the Greek and Roman classics, the Bible, and the canon of vernacular literature – Dante, Shakespeare, Cervantes, Milton, Molière . . . down to Henry James and Joyce – at the centre of attention in the schools and in the family, were to vanish, it would produce the symptoms of collective amnesia. 'Who am I?' turns out to be the desperate cry of one whose memory has been blotted out.

NOTES

1 George Gissing, *The Private Papers Of Henry Ryecroft*, ed. John Collis (Harvester Press, Brighton, 1982).
2 Erich Auerbach, *Mimesis; The Representation of Reality in Western Literature* (Princeton, 1953).
3 *The Philosophical Writings of Descartes*, trans. J. Cottingham, R. Stoothoff and D. Murdoch (Cambridge, 1985), vol. II, 13.
4 *Ibid.*, vol. I, 116.
5 H. G. Wells, *The War of the Worlds* (Pan Books, 1975).

6 John Donne, *The Complete English Poems,* ed. A. J. Smith (Penguin, 1971), p. 269.
7 John Ruskin, *Praeterita* (Oxford, 1978).
8 Sigmund Freud, *The Ego and the Id,* Standard ed., vol. xix (London, 1961), p. 13.

13

PRAYER, POETRY AND POLITICS

Enda McDonagh

THEOLOGIA PRIMARIA AND THEOLOGIA SECUNDARIA

Theologians, like so many others engaged in intellectual enterprises, have always been exposed to the temptation of operating at a series of removes from the reality of proper concern to them – God. Not that one may aspire to 'a direct investigation of the deity', as Frederick Coplestone once remarked. Only in an indirect, mediating way can the ultimate and absolute reality become the subject of human analysis and reflection. Yet so much theology is talk about talk about talk about God. It is mainly investigation of the work of other theologians, working perhaps at their own several removes. Even the periodic renewals calling for *ressourcement* or return to sources easily slip into identifying the sources as theological texts of another epoch, the patristic or medieval or whatever.

All this is essential theological work. The classical thinkers of the Christian tradition have a great deal to offer subsequent generations as they wrestle with the meaning, expression and practice of Christian faith in a new context. Without Augustine and Aquinas, Basil and Bonaventure, Luther and Calvin, contemporary theologians would be greatly impoverished. The best theological work in the present is usually done by those who have taken seriously in dialogue these great thinkers of the past.

And yet. One of the lessons taught by these thinkers is how they wrestled with their own situation and their own faith. This may be more obvious in personal terms in Augustine and Luther, more obvious in terms of intellectual context in Aquinas and Calvin. But for all it was a faith seeking understanding which was personal and communal, expressed in word and deed. Prior to the critical, analytical theology, there was an understanding, expressive and active faith with its own immediate awareness of God, its struggles to express that in words and symbol, its commitment to realize that in life and love. What this essay proposes is that theologians, particularly systematic and philosophical theologians to whose company Herbert McCabe properly belongs, would attend to the *theologia primaria* in their own lives as basic to their further critical theological endeavours, their *theologia secundaria*. Their *theologia primaria* becomes, in turn, fruit of that endeavour in a dynamic spiral.

In organizing *theologia primaria* under the headings of prayer, poetry and politics, I have not been simply arbitrary or seduced by the attractions of alliteration as I hope the body of the essay will show. Undoubtedly I have been influenced by my own experience and the power exercised by the three *p*s within the Irish tradition and Irish history, a love for which I share with Father McCabe. They presumably bear some relation to the wider intellectual tradition which reaches back to the classical triad of the true, the good and the beautiful. They carry echoes of Kierkegaard's aesthetic, ethical and religious. And the prayer–poetry relation was certainly influenced by Hans Urs von Balthasar's *Herrlichkeit, The Glory of the Lord*, III. More significantly here the three may be seen to have connexions with the Johannine phrase: 'the way, the truth and the life' (Jn 14:6). This essay will not pursue these possibilities. The validity of the choice must be established independently of these potential and powerful forerunners.

While the choice is not arbitrary neither does it enjoy some kind of sacred, absolute character. Others will want to organize their *theologia primaria* quite differently or make quite different distinction and connection between *theologia primaria* and *theologia secundaria*. Or it may be that they will consider the original concerns of this essay in a totally different way. The more modest ambition of this essay is to explore how a theologian may be helped by this particular approach.

FIRST SUMMARY: THE P-CIRCLE AND CHRISTIAN INTEGRITY

In the main body of the essay the interaction between each pair of this triad will be explored more fully, leading to an attempt at a more complete understanding of their overall interaction as a triad. For now it is worth recognizing briefly the distinctions and unity which operate between them. Prayer is taken to be the hard core of faith, the heart of human response to God's self-communication in creation, in the people of Israel and their history, in Jesus and his history. It is a human response motivated, inspired and empowered by a divine initiative. It seeks expression which can only be in human words and symbols and actions which, as human, are inadequate to the divine mystery they seek to express and mediate. This expression remains symbolic, sacramental. The traditional understanding of faith seeking understanding might be along this line interpreted as prayer seeking expression seeking understanding.

Poetry is a human phenomenon which may be inspired by the ultimate mystery of humanity and cosmos. Some of the greatest poets, e.g. Dante, were. In our more secular world poetry is predominantly in content and concern a secular activity and achievement. Yet the concern and content clearly reflect the mysterious in humanity and cosmos, the joys and sorrows which often lie too deep for words but in their power issue in creative expressions of great beauty. The poet like the person of prayer is a respondent to mystery and a creative expresser of it. The possibilities of interaction between prayer and poetry lie there.

The politician seems a quite different animal. At his best he is the servant of human existence in community, at his worst the exploiter of community and individual for personal power and profit. The poet can provide the symbols of unity in community and unity is an urgent concern of the politician. Where that unity becomes oppression the poet, if true to his vocation, may become the symbol of protest and prophet of freedom.

Politics and prayer interact in mutual support where the political commitment to serving the community in justice, freedom and peace clearly echoes the basic Christian prayer, 'Thy kingdom come'. In practice, the temptations to sacred and secular power may prove too much for either side and protest and correction may be the way of fidelity for one or both.

The Christian, however, has to be a person of prayer, sensitive to the mysteries of the human and the cosmic as well as the divine. She/he must express those sensitivities as best she can in words and symbols, in truth and beauty. Poetry becomes a symbol for human creativity and its beauty as prayer is a symbol for all human faith in the Creator-Redeemer God. Finally, the Christian must follow through or start from the service of humanity in community as recognition and response to the human mystery which by Incarnation makes the divine mystery flesh, visible, tangible and in need.

THE PARTNERS IN PAIRS

Further exploration of the triad requires examining more fully how the partners relate in pairs.

(a) *PRAYER AND POETRY*

For many critics St John of the Cross, master of mystical prayer, is one of the finest poets in the Spanish language. He himself insisted that it was the poetry and not the commentaries which mattered in seeking to understand and follow his way of prayer. Hans Urs von Balthasar puts it succinctly: 'It is as a poet rather than a prose writer that he (John) is a Doctor of the Church'. Of course the most notable expression of prayer in poetry is the Hebrew Book of Psalms. (It is a pity that contemporary translations in English often obscure that poetic quality.)

Poetry which trembles on the edge of prayer may be found in all languages and religious traditions. This occurs most obviously but not necessarily or exclusively in poems dealing directly with religious themes and in modern poets of such powerful religious sensibility as Hopkins, Eliot and R. S. Thomas.

> Thou mastering me
> God! giver of breath and bread;
> World's strand, sway of the sea;
>   Lord of living and dead;
> Thou hast bound bones and veins in me, fastened me flesh,
> And after it almost unmade, what with dread,
>   Thy doing: and dost thou touch me afresh?
> Over again I feel thy finger and find thee.

This opening stanza of Hopkins' *The Wreck of the Deutschland* suggests so much of the power and intimacy of a Hebrew psalm. The whole poem, and it is primarily a poem accessible in its power and beauty to non-religious readers, exercises a profound at least pre-prayer influence on the willing reader. So much of his other poetry is such a direct celebration of the presence of God in Christ and cosmos that it can scarcely be distinguished from prayer and yet 'the achieve of, the mastery of the thing' ensures it an exalted place in the secular canon of modern poetry in English.

Eliot is not usually so direct although *Ash Wednesday*, *The Four Quartets*, *Journey of the Magi* and so much else are poised to raise the mind and heart to the God of Jesus Christ we call Our Father:

> Were we led all that way for
> Birth or Death? There was a Birth, certainly,
> We had evidence and no doubt. I had seen birth and death,
> But had thought they were different; this Birth was
> Hard and bitter agony for us, like Death, our death.

231

We returned to our places, these Kingdoms,
But no longer at ease here, in the old dispensations,
With an alien people clutching their gods.
I should be glad of another death.

Final stanza: *Journey of the Magi*

My concern is not so much with prayer that assumes clearly poetic form or with poetry that moves close to prayer because of its religious content, although these are important in themselves and to the completeness of my argument. I want to argue a deeper relationship of unity and distinction, challenge and convergence between prayer taken more generously as awareness of and response to the ultimate reality we call God, and poetry more generally as the formal and concentrated and above all beautiful human expression of the reality, including the tragic reality of this world. I will be speaking mainly from within the Christian tradition and its Jewish foundations, but some of the argument will be clearly of wider relevance.

The prayer and the poetry are both responses to reality, acknowledging that reality in its richness, even its mystery. Mystery is an element always associated with the ultimate reality, God, not as an excuse for ignorance or a cover for fraud, but as a signal to the unfathomable richness of the ultimate source and destiny of all being. Approaches to the ultimate are always inadequate and indirect. Acknowledgement of the ultimate is equally inadequate and indirect. The language of the relative, limited and created can only stumble over the reality of the absolute, unlimited and uncreated. What humanity says of God and to God is born of the relative and finite and stretched to reach the absolute. Human words and concepts in this context are true and not true. God is personal and loving but not just as humans are personal and loving. The words are used analogously, as the technical term beloved of Thomas and Thomists has it. The stretch in the words reaches back to our own activities in prayer as we praise God and thank God for his love, as we address God as 'Our Father', as we consider how 'The world is charged with the grandeur of God'. Human language in response to divine reality is charged with meaning it cannot quite contain or fully express. The 'instress' of God in humanity and cosmos has no adequate human 'inscape'. The mystery breaks through language and escapes our confining, dominating, domesticating pretensions. But it is the mystery, the reality which seeks expression, moves and inspires human response in mind and heart and language. 'When we cry "Abba! Father!" it is the Spirit himself bearing witness' (Rom 8:16). Prayer is divine gift before it is human achievement. We can only speak of that which we have received, but that which we have received (the Spirit), to him who has entrusted himself to us (God). Prayer is the halting human response to the divine initiative which seeks expression in the characteristic human gift of language. Such expression will always be inadequate but will at least seek to be less inadequate through the authenticity of the respondent and the beauty of its form. The psalmist was always conscious of this double responsibility.

The poet (and the musical composer or painter or sculptor) may seem (to the religious person) to be dealing with much less exalted reality and so have much less problem with adequacy of expression or form. At his best, in Shakespeare or Bach or Michelangelo, the artist is struggling with mysteries of humanity and cosmos, which are not readily accessible, comprehensible or expressible. Depth of experienced reality combines with beauty of expressed forms to mediate in artistic masterpiece the mysterious dimensions of the human and the cosmic. The interaction of reality as given, perhaps given within the self, and artist as creative recipient, is frequently described as inspiration. So the artist is spoken of as inspired or possessed or driven to write or to paint.

There are clear parallels between prayer as understood and practised in the Christian tradition and poetry or other artistic activity. These may be summarized under the rubrics of mystery, inspiration and the search for adequate (beautiful) form. Yet all three may be no more than parallels moving in quite different planes of reality, divine and human mystery, divine and human inspiration, total inadequacy of human language in prayer, and beauty, even perfection of form, in poetry.

Granted these are very different levels of divine and human reality, it is still worth exploring how far prayer and poetry may illuminate or challenge one another. The third rubric of expression stresses the inadequacy of prayer-language and the beauty of poetry. This contrast might be sharpened by reference to poet and prayer-master St John of the Cross. The high regard in which his poetry is held, and he himself did recognize its value, differs sharply from his necessarily more modest view of his composition as prayer. Hopkins was very confident that his poetry would survive but he refused to seek publication lest it interfere with his dedication to the religious life and its primary characteristic, prayer. Yet both these were creative artists whose own poetry expressed their deepest responses to the mystery of God and humanity. For those responses only the most beautiful form believable would be tolerated, even if nothing would ever be adequate. The poet, the seeker after beauty of language and form, which is native to all but ignored or undeveloped in most, must be encouraged to provide the most adequate response to the divine mystery possible to each.

In prayer as in poetry such development requires application and practice. W. B. Yeats, who called on Irish poets to learn their trade, had a strong sense of the difficulty and labour of expressing mystery and attaining beauty. He develops this in his poem, *Adam's Curse*:

> We sat together at one summer's end,
> That beautiful mild woman, your close friend,
> And you and I, and talked of poetry.
> I said, 'A line will take us hours maybe;
> Yet if it does not seem a moment's thought,
> Our stitching and unstitching has been nought.
> Better go down upon your marrow-bones
> And scrub a kitchen pavement, or break stones
> Like an old pauper, in all kind of weather;
> For to articulate sweet sounds together
> Is to work harder than all these, and yet
> Be thought an idler by the noisy set
> Of bankers, schoolmasters and clergymen
> The martyrs call the world.'
> And thereupon
> That beautiful mild woman for whose sake
> There's many a one shall find out all heartache
> On finding that her voice is sweet and low
> Replied, 'To be born a woman is to know –
> Although they do not talk of it at school –
> That we must labour to be beautiful.'

> I said, 'It's certain there is no fine thing,
> Since Adam's fall, but needs much labouring . . .' .

Prayer is undoubtedly one of the fine things which 'since Adam's fall needs much labouring'. The inadequacy of expression can never be removed but for the true lover of God it should and can be reduced. But Yeats bears continual witness to the labour required for response to human mystery and the final inadequacy of poetic achievement, including his own. In *The Circus Animals' Desertion*, both in its stripping away previous illusions (false gods) and in its recognizing the need to start from the humblest beginnings again, he offers saving light to the 'successful' man of prayer.

These masterful images because complete
Grew in pure mind but out of what began?
A mound of refuse or the sweepings of a street,
Old nettles, old bottles, and a broken can,
Old iron, old bones, old rags, that raving slut
Who keeps the till. Now that my ladder's gone,
I must lie down where all the ladders start,
In the foul rag and bone shop of the heart.

The humble, even useless and ugly material, 'a mound of refuse or the sweepings of a street', out of which Yeats fashioned his 'masterful images' reveals the transforming, creative power of poetry and of the poet. In Christian and Jewish tradition prayer exercises a transforming, creative influence on the person at prayer. The publican who sits at the back of the Temple and simply asks for pardon goes down to his house 'justified', transformed, re-created (Lk 18:9ff.).

The pattern of the psalter and of some individual psalms relates experience of a saving Yahweh to experience of a needy Israel in continuous interaction. In the liturgy and history of Israel they played a saving, liberating, re-creating role. Psalm 126 recalls past achievements of the Lord as prelude to Israel's cry for help to conclude with a confident declaration of re-creation.

When the Lord restored the fortunes of Zion
We were like those who dream.

The climactic experience of liberating and re-creating prayer occurs in Jesus' own prayer in Gethsemane. In Matthew's account (26:38ff.) we read: 'Then he said to them "My soul is very sorrowful, even to death; remain here, and watch with me". And going a little farther he fell on his face and prayed, "My Father, if it be possible, let this cup pass from me; nevertheless, not as I will but as thou wilt".'

This liberation of Christ was rehearsed and completed on Calvary in the same movement from the Eloi of 'My God, my God, why have you forsaken me?' (Mt 27:46, Mk 15:34) to the Abba of 'Father, into thy hands I commend my spirit' before 'he breathed his last' (Lk 23:46). On Golgotha, in the garden of Gethsemane as in the garden of Genesis, the creative, transforming, liberating 'artist' is God, the Spirit of God. Human prayer is the immediate field of the divine artist as poet who enables us 'in the ground of our beseeching' (Eliot) to say with Jesus, 'Abba, Father' (Romans). The suffering of the human artist in his work of transformation (Yeats' 'much labouring' after Adam's fall) connects

235

with that of our redemption/transformation by the divine artist.
R. S. Thomas expresses this magnificently in his poem *The Musician* where he recalls watching Kreisler at close quarters on stage:

> I could see, too, the twitching of the fingers,
> Caught temporarily in art's neurosis
> As we sat there or warmly applauded,
> This player who so beautifully suffered
> For each of us upon his instrument.
> So it must have been on Calvary
> In the fiercer light of the thorns' halo;
> The men standing by and that one figure,
> The hands bleeding, the mind bruised but calm,
> Making such music as lives still
> And no one daring to interrupt
> Because it was himself that he played
> And closer than all of them the God listened.

Divine and human creativity in prayer and poetry share also a
sense of celebration. The human and cosmic wonders which
poetry celebrates must be recognized in their unique selfhood,
'All things counter, original, spare, strange' (Hopkins). Yet their
'enselving' reality and mystery cannot, except at the cost of final
meaninglesssness, be closed off from the ultimate reality and
mystery who 'fathers forth whose beauty is past change. Praise
him'. As Hopkins above all recognized, the very stuff of poetry
and poetic celebration must self-transcend to the ultimate, or
self-destruct. Poetry as celebration of the beauty and mystery of
humanity and cosmos has this inbuilt final reference to prayer.
But prayer in turn needs this attention to the human and cosmic
to 'original, spare, strange' creatures and to the words which
worthily mediate their mystery, if it is to be a worthy response to
the true, ultimate mystery, the creator and redeemer God.

(b) POETRY AND POLITICS

Dante more than any other great poet had an explicit political
philosophy, developed for example in his *De Monarchia* and influential at least in the seating arrangements of his great poetic
vision in *The Divine Comedy*. And the interactions between poetry
and politics have been frequent and profound, nowhere more so
than in Ireland. Yeats, so long preoccupied with Irish resurgence
and its symbols, subsequently agonized

> I lie awake night after night
> And never get the answers right,

Did that play of mine send out
Certain men the English shot?

(*The Man and the Echo*)

In a very recent work *Station Island* Seamus Heaney, in conversation with one of his ghosts, a friend murdered during the current 'troubles' in Northern Ireland, remains ambivalent about his ambivalence:

'Forgive the way I have lived indifferent –
Forgive my timid circumspect involvement',
I surprised myself by saying. 'Forgive
my eye', he said, 'all that's above my head.'
And then a stun of pain seemed to go through him
And he trembled like a heatwave and faded.

Poetry, ballad and song have played and continue to play a role in Irish political life as they do in so many other countries. The institution of the national anthem, with its predecessors in tribal songs and battle hymns, testifies to the recognition by political leaders everywhere of the political value of music and verse. Other symbols like national flags, memorial parks and anniversary celebrations of former heroes and famous victories play a similar role in inspiring and uniting a people politically. So much of the Northern Ireland 'troubles' is a battle of symbols, no less bitter or significant for that.

Yet politics in its daily round of organizing, developing and servicing a people, in its concern for social structures, individual rights and economic viability seems to need more of the virtues of prose than of poetry. The political reason in this context would appear to be more calculating and instrumental than imaginative and creative. The politics of symbols and images too often fails to deliver the basic necessities to the multitude it inspires. And yet – social engineering in a politics not just of prose but nowadays of computer prose may be no more successful on bread-and-butter issues, as so many authoritarian, bureaucratic states illustrate, while the mystery and the freedom of the individual are dissolved.

In defence of that individual freedom and with the promethean ambition of forging the conscience of his race, James Joyce sought to escape the net of nationalism, of Irish politics, as well as the nets of religion and language. His artist-hero, Stephen, has at least the merit of symbolizing that individual freedom of which literature and the arts are often the best witnesses in face of political, cultural or religious tyranny. A host of writers from

Eastern Europe or South Africa or Latin America become, in André Brink's phrase, 'a chain of voices' protesting individual freedom in face of social tyranny. The more subtle political, economic manipulation and social engineering of the west with its trivializing, consumerist values require and to some extent receive the probing eye, sensitive ear and prophetic voice of the poet and artist. There is, or ought to be, a natural tension between the prose and the power of politics with its thrust to control and the creativity and freedom of poetry and art. The artist in celebrating the mystery of humanity and cosmos reminds the politician that there are needs and gifts other than guns or even butter. He must often be the voice of those harassed by the guns and deprived of the butter because in them the human mystery, vulnerable and tragic, may be most radically exposed.

Healthy politics needs not just the protest of art but also its celebration. The mastering power which attracts people in state politics or economics or industry or even religion, lacks a sense of reverence and celebration, a sense of the beauty and integrity of people, of nature, of things 'counter, original, spare, strange'. The consequences of this are seen in the destruction of the environment and disruption of the eco-system so characteristic of our time. Beyond the protest, poetry in its celebration offers politics a way of redemption from destructive, dominating power. In its turn, politics, plain and prosaic or coloured and poetic, offers the artist the possibility of a social context without which individuals could not enjoy freedom or selfhood. Mutual challenge, mutual correction and at the limit mutual confirmation connect poetry and politics. Despite Plato's fears the Republic will degenerate without the prophecy and celebration of its artists. Without the community service of politicians, there will be no republic for artists to criticize and no social context in which to survive and celebrate.

(c) *POLITICS AND PRAYER*

Central to Christianity's prayer is the petition 'Thy Kingdom come' which to many modern ears has a political ring, as it must have had to Jesus' own contemporaries. Various recent political and liberation theologians speak of the need to unite the mystical and the political. Their critics voice the reasonable fear that prayer may be reduced to politics, secular, this-worldly politics and politics given a mystical significance so that Christian prayer becomes unnecessary and impossible. Seek first the political Kingdom! The critics themselves are often unaware of the political implications of their own forms of prayer, of how far such forms and the attitudes they express, endorse and promote particular political structures with associated oppression and injustice.

A recent *New Yorker* cartoon has a very modern Ms addressing an equally modern Mr with the words, 'OK, so you say you love me, but what's the subtext?' A hermeneutic of suspicion is essential but, in the claim and counter-claim of theological as of other debate, it can lead to the paralysing division of conservatives and liberals or, as in this context, of 'political' and 'a-political' theologians.

The Jewish and Christian traditions combine clearly and consistently worship of God and service of neighbour, love of God and love of neighbour, prayer and, at least in a general, but not individual or unstructured, sense, politics. Yet in the Jesus version certainly there is an equally clear distinction and disjunction between response to God and to Caesar; between a kingdom already at hand in this world and a kingdom of this world; between restoring Israel and inaugurating a new Israel; between the objective of the Zealots or of those who would make him king and the objective of Jesus himself; between the prayer of Jesus and his disciples and the conventional politics of his contemporaries, Jewish and Roman.

In maintaining both the conjunction and the disjunction the community of disciples, the Church, has not always been successful. Sometimes their apparently most successful conjunctions, such as the 'Christianized' empire of the late fourth century or that uncomfortable residue of medieval Christendom, the nineteenth-century Papal States, proved as much obstacle as support to the prayerful mission of the Church. At other times apparently disastrous disjunction, as with the Penal Laws against Catholics in Ireland, created a depth of prayer commitment to which Irish Mass rocks and subsequent Irish devotion to the Mass give powerful testimony. The search for an effective balance in conjunction and disjunction between prayer and politics must be renewed in new contexts with fresh generations of Christians and politicians.

The community task of politics, directed to enabling people to live together in a particular place and time, has its own inner tensions. Combining solidarity or cohesion of the group with the freedom of the individual has assumed peculiar forms and distortions in the modern world. Christian prayer demands an authentic personal response to God as Father. That is only possible in and through Christ, as member of the Body of Christ, as brother or sister of Christ and of all the daughters and sons of God. *Per Christum*, essential to all Christian prayer and forming the shape of Christian liturgy, underlines their inescapable community dimension. At that ultimate level the tension between individual personal authenticity (and freedom) and community solidarity becomes entirely creative and fulfilling. The summons to that level and the reach for it in prayer provides challenge and support for political efforts at maintaining cohesion/solidarity and respecting freedom. Yet the very ultimacy of prayer may lead Christians to ignore the importance of historical expressions of solidarity or freedom or both. The transcendence of God embodied in prayer liberates the human being from the cosmic and political enclosure. Biological unit of the eco-system or citizen of the political system do not express exhaustively the range and reality of the human person. Prayerful openness relativizes cosmos and state. The basic dignity, freedom and transcendence of the person require space and respect for that space, a space for personal freedom including freedom to pray, to seek and relate to the ultimate truth, beyond any political pretensions of princes or governments or state structures. Prayer and the freedom to pray, personally and communally as Christian prayer requires, necessarily includes the ideas of limited government and personal freedom, basic to modern recognition of human rights. Individuals or communities engaged in prayer without attention and commitment to its implications for human rights are rehearsing once again those liturgical 'feasts' and 'solemn assemblies' condemned so sharply by Amos, because of neglect and exploitation of the poor, the refusal of the work of justice. Present Christian concern for human rights connects intrinsically with the renewal of liturgy and prayer, although both the concern and renewal may for many be more verbal than real, 'worshipping with their lips while their hearts are far from me' (Is 29:13). Political engagement in pursuit of human rights tests the authenticity of prayer without providing a substitute for it. Authentic prayer stimulates and supports such engagement, while offering a prophetic critique of its neglect or distortion.

For Israel and for Jesus, the concern of God, the divine bias focused on the neglected and deprived. Salvation was to be primarily for them as 'the mighty were put down from their seats and the humble exalted'. The non-privileged, the excluded, victims were to be given priority by a God of love and justice. Victimization was finally confronted and in principle overcome on Calvary. The call and the power of the Cross is for an end to victimization. 'No more victims.' *Nie wieder*. The hollowness of human and Christian response to that call and power does not remove their continuing validity. It does require continuous conversion by Christians to removal of victimization, political, racial, economic and sexist. The re-enactment of Calvary in the Eucharist, the central prayer of Christians, challenges and empowers them to oppose and overcome their own practices of victimization, the practices and structures of the societies in which they live and which they endorse.

The terms 'victimizers' and 'victims' provide one way of examining the structure of any society, and in global village terms, of world-society, with a view to transforming it, although many people and groups may be both victims and victimizers. In a political context the transformation to end victimization must be structural. It will also be historical with the limitations and ambiguities of history. A prayer-view of victimization, accepting the in-breaking kingdom, calls for continuing transformation in face of historical ambiguity and in the name of eschatological fulfilment. Such a vision includes forgiveness and reconciliation. 'Father, forgive them'; 'Forgive us . . . as we forgive them'; 'Go first and be reconciled with your brother'; 'God, through Christ, reconciled us to himself and gave us the ministry of reconciliation' (II Cor 5:18). The temptation of politics to destroy or exclude the former victimizers/oppressors has to be balanced by the reconciling, forgiving inclusiveness of prayer. The Christian temptation to suppress conflict and keep the oppressed resigned in the name of reconciliation must be corrected by the political demands of justice and freedom in society. Prayer and politics interact in mutual confirmation, challenge, correction and transformation.

FINAL SUMMARY – FROM CIRCLE TO SPIRAL

The interactions of prayer, poetry and politics are not those of a static circle. Development or decline in mutual promotion or corruption are the options, with the inevitable historical mixture of both. It is the predominance of development and mutual promotion or decline and mutual corruption which determines at any stage the direction of a circle which can go spiralling up or spiralling down and at varying speeds. And it is partly the task of the theologian to examine the connections between these three *loci* of creative-redemptive activity and the directions of their spiralling movement.

To do that he must have access to the *loci*, to the worlds of prayer, poetry and politics. This does not mean that he must be a mystic in the sense that St John of the Cross was, a poet like

Hopkins or Heaney, or be actively engaged in parliamentary politics. He must share these activities in sympathy and imagination by being open, effectively, to the achievements of mystic, poet and politician. The imagination and the skill must be developed through education and dedication. Submitting himself to the biblical awareness and response to God, to writings of the mystics and of other authorities on prayer, will be part of his brief. Entering into the world of the artist, allowing it to re-create him in some fashion, will be a further stage in his attempt to understand the symbolic expression of the mystery of humanity and so of divinity. Making his own the ambitions, frustrations and achievements of politicians in pursuit of justice and peace, liberation and reconciliation will ground the engagement with kingdom and neighbour which is essential to Christian faith in search of understanding.

Will all this be only at second hand? Is the theologian condemned forever to examining at a remove, however sympathetically and imaginatively, the attitudes and achievements of others? Obviously not in the case of prayer. Prayer is the concentrate of faith which is basic to theology. Without prayer he may do interesting scholarly work but not theology. Prayer is not a substitute for critical and creative intellectual reflection but it is basic to the intellectual reflection called theology. A person of prayer the theologian must be but scarcely a person of poetry, that is, a poet or artist himself!

Without a sense of symbol and symbolic expression, faith-expression and theology become impossible. What the poet or artist accomplishes in concentrated beauty, every person can manage in some lumbering and loose way. To have no sense of the language of poetry or music or painting, primitive and undeveloped as it may be, is to lack a sense of mystery and of its proper, limited, human expression. Some criticism of the recent liturgical renewal and scriptural translation is pertinent here. A biblical scholar remarked of a colleague once, 'He is a scholar, but he has a tin ear for the English language!' It seems, if true, a serious handicap in attempting to understand the word of God as expressed in human words. I think it was Irishman Desmond Fennell who remarked, à propos some recent liturgical hymns and homilies: 'And the Word became banal and dwelt among us'. Without sensitivity and attention to symbol, image and word, in theological creation and criticism, the Word of God in both first- and second-order *theologia* will be reduced to banality. Creative as well as critical skills are demanded of the theologian.

Traditionally at least the theologian has worked with words. So perhaps he ought to pay more attention to them in their aptness, accuracy and beauty. But politics? What has the theologian to do with that secular pursuit? And how can she or he combine intellectual commitment with such practical distractions? The argument returns to the intrinsic connexion of the three *ps*. But what of first-hand experience? Must he join some political movement or party? Address public meetings? Go out canvassing? Stand for election? Any or all of these might be appropriate in particular circumstances and are increasingly likely to happen with the increasing number of theologians who are lay people. But such specifics are not primary. A Christian theologian as member of society is engaged in politics, for good or ill, as supporter or opponent of systems and activities which serve or disserve fellow-citizens and neighbours. Becoming conscious of this, he will be forced to take a stand for or against certain structures and practices as he explores the love of neighbour which expresses love of God, as he examines the historical and social dimensions of the prayer of faith. It is not possible to continue in society without an attitude, a stand and so an engagement. Disengagement is also an engagement. In accepting the political engagement he sees it in close interaction with the rest of his faith-commitment as challenge and critique. And so he is led to further theologizing and from that to fuller and fuller engagement. This is the dynamic of the creative, developing spiral. The engagement of disengagement can only lead to the spiral of decline.

The balance of forces in the spiral, possible and necessary for Christians and theologians, will vary with place and time and with particular individuals. But the dimensions of life signalled in a general way by these three are integral to both faith and theology.